SCOTT TUROW

**Critical Companions in Popular Contemporary Writers
Second Series**

Isabel Allende *by Karen Castellucci Cox*

Julia Alvarez *by Silvio Sirias*

Rudolfo A. Anaya *by Margarite Fernandez Olmos*

Maya Angelou *by Mary Jane Lupton*

Margaret Atwood *by Nathalie Cooke*

Ray Bradbury *by Robin Anne Reid*

Revisiting Mary Higgins Clark *by Linda De Roche*

Louise Erdrich *by Lorena L. Stookey*

Ernest J. Gaines *by Karen Carmean*

Gabriel García Márquez *by Rubén Pelayo*

Kaye Gibbons *by Mary Jean DeMarr*

John Irving *by Josie P. Campbell*

Garrison Keillor *by Marcia Songer*

Jamaica Kincaid *by Lizabeth Paravisini-Gebert*

Revisiting Stephen King *by Sharon A. Russell*

Barbara Kingsolver *by Mary Jean DeMarr*

Maxine Hong Kingston *by E. D. Huntley*

Terry McMillan *by Paulette Richards*

Larry McMurtry *by John M. Reilly*

Toni Morrison *by Missy Dehn Kubitschek*

Walter Mosley *by Charles E. Wilson, Jr.*

Gloria Naylor *by Charles E. Wilson, Jr.*

James Patterson *by Joan G. Kotker*

Chaim Potok *by Sanford Sternlicht*

Amy Tan *by E. D. Huntley*

Anne Tyler *by Paul Bail*

Leon Uris *by Kathleen Shine Cain*

Kurt Vonnegut *by Thomas F. Marvin*

James Welch *by Mary Jane Lupton*

Tom Wolfe *by Brian Abel Ragen*

SCOTT TUROW

A Critical Companion

Andrew F. Macdonald and
Gina Macdonald

CRITICAL COMPANIONS TO POPULAR CONTEMPORARY WRITERS
Kathleen Gregory Klein, Series Editor

Greenwood Press
Westport, Connecticut • London

Library of Congress Cataloging-in-Publication Data

Macdonald, Andrew, 1942–
    Scott Turow : a critical companion / Andrew F. Macdonald and Gina Macdonald.
       p. cm.—(Critical companions to popular contemporary writers, ISSN 1082–4979)
    Includes bibliographical references and index.
    ISBN 0–313–33115–4 (alk. paper)
    1. Turow, Scott—Criticism and interpretation. 2. Legal stories, American—History and criticism. I. Macdonald, Gina. II. Title. III. Series.
PS3570.U754Z76   2005
813'.54—dc22   2004028233

British Library Cataloguing in Publication Data is available.

Library of Congress Catalog Card Number: 2004028233
ISBN: 0–313–33115–4
ISSN: 1082–4979

First published in 2005

Greenwood Press, 88 Post Road West, Westport, CT 06881
An imprint of Greenwood Publishing Group, Inc.
www.greenwood.com

Printed in the United States of America

The paper used in this book complies with the
Permanent Paper Standard issued by the National
Information Standards Organization (Z39.48–1984).

10 9 8 7 6 5 4 3 2 1

Contents

viii   <u>Contents</u>

Series Foreword

The authors who appear in the series Critical Companions to Popular Contemporary Writers are all best-selling writers. They do not simply have one successful novel, but a string of them. Fans, critics, and specialist readers eagerly anticipate their next book. For some, high cash advances and breakthrough sales figures are automatic; movie deals often follow. Some writers become household names, recognized by almost everyone.

But, their novels are read one by one. Each reader chooses to start and, more importantly, to finish a book because of what she or he finds there. The real test of a novel is in the satisfaction its readers experience. This series acknowledges the extraordinary involvement of readers and writers in creating a best-seller.

The authors included in this series were chosen by an Advisory Board composed of high school English teachers and high school and public librarians. They ranked a list of best-selling writers according to their popularity among different groups of readers. For the first series, writers in the top-ranked group who had received no book-length, academic, literary analysis (or none in at least the past ten years) were chosen. Because of this selection method, Critical Companions to Popular Contemporary Writers meets a need that is being addressed nowhere else. The success of these volumes as reported by reviewers, librarians, and teachers led to an expansion of the series mandate to include some writers with wide critical attention—Toni Morrison, John Irving, and Maya Angelou, for example—to extend the usefulness of the series.

The volumes in the series are written by scholars with particular expertise in analyzing popular fiction. These specialists add an academic focus to the popular success that these writers already enjoy.

The series is designed to appeal to a wide range of readers. The general reading public will find explanations for the appeal of these well-known writers. Fans will find biographical and fictional questions answered. Students will find literary analysis, discussions of fictional genres, carefully organized introductions to new ways of reading the novels, and bibliographies for additional research. Whether browsing through the book for pleasure or using it for an assignment, readers will find that the most recent novels of the authors are included.

Each volume begins with a biographical chapter drawing on published information, autobiographies or memoirs, prior interviews, and, in some cases, interviews given especially for this series. A chapter on literary history and genres describes how the author's work fits into a larger literary context. The following chapters analyze the writer's most important, most popular, and most recent novels in detail. Each chapter focuses on one or more novels. This approach, suggested by the Advisory Board as the most useful to student research, allows for an in-depth analysis of the writer's fiction. Close and careful readings with numerous examples show readers exactly how the novels work. These chapters are organized around three central elements: plot development (how the story line moves forward), character development (what the reader knows of the important figures), and theme (the significant ideas of the novel). Chapters may also include sections on generic conventions (how the novel is similar or different from others in its same category of science fiction, fantasy, thriller, etc.), narrative point of view (who tells the story and how), symbols and literary language, and historical or social context. Each chapter ends with an "alternative reading" of the novel. The volume concludes with a primary and secondary bibliography, including reviews.

The alternative readings are a unique feature of this series. By demonstrating a particular way of reading each novel, they provide a clear example of how a specific perspective can reveal important aspects of the book. In the alternative reading sections, one contemporary literary theory—way of reading, such as feminist criticism, Marxism, new historicism, deconstruction, or Jungian psychological critique—is defined in brief, easily comprehensible language. That definition is then applied to the novel to highlight specific features that might go unnoticed or be understood differently in a more general reading. Each volume defines two or three specific theories, making them part of the reader's understanding of how diverse meanings may be constructed from a single novel.

Taken collectively, the volumes in the Critical Companions to Popular Contemporary Writers series provide a wide-ranging investigation of the complexities of current best-selling fiction. By treating these novels seriously as both literary works and publishing successes, the series demonstrates the potential of popular literature in contemporary culture.

Kathleen Gregory Klein
Southern Connecticut State University

Acknowledgments

We owe a debt of gratitude to a number of people who made this book both possible and better. First of all, our deepest thanks go to Scott Turow, himself, for not only kindly granting an interview but generously giving of his time to provide information that helped make this text more informed, accurate, and up-to-date about his life and work than it would have been otherwise. Mr. Turow is a charming raconteur but also a dedicated professional committed to social justice, and it was indeed a pleasure to have him share his political, creative, and personal views. Our thanks also go to Kathy Conway, assistant to Mr. Turow, for arranging the details of this interview.

We also wish to give a special thanks to the representatives of our universities who provided funding to facilitate the Chicago interview with Scott Turow: Larry Howell, who at the time was serving as Interim Academic Vice President of Nicholls State University, and Gary Talarchek, Grant Supervisor at Loyola University New Orleans. Nicholls colleagues Patricia Gabilondo and Mabel Illidge provided psychological support and interesting sidebars.

The Life of Scott Turow: The Making and Shaping of a Literary Lawyer

Novelist, lawyer, and humanist Scott Turow, also known as Scott F. Turow and (L.) Scott Turow, has repeatedly been called "the father of the legal mystery/thriller," or the inventor of "the contemporary lawyer-turned-novelist school of thriller writing." Although others before him had written in the genre, the highly acclaimed *Presumed Innocent* (1987) spawned a plethora of imitators who have made the legal mystery a modern phenomenon. Turow has managed not only to balance legal and writing careers but to excel at both, turning out a complex and challenging novel every three years and trying cases that raise significant legal issues and test the justice of current law. Critical reviewers sing his praises. According to them, with almost no exceptions, his books are relentless/suspenseful/mesmerizing/riveting/compelling/gripping; they are also sensitive/subtle/psychologically true/utterly convincing. Dramatically paced and richly detailed, they take readers into the labyrinth of the mind; his portraits are deft, and his courtroom dramatics are realistic but gripping, setting new standards for and transcending the genre and producing thought-provoking literature that will endure. In "Presumed Guilty," *New York Times Book Review* critic Wendy Lesser calls Scott Turow not only "one of our best crime novelists," but also "one of our better novelists," giving readers both "page turner" mysteries and "pleasing literary artifacts" that delve into "complicated social questions and complex human emotions" (November 3, 2002, 8). In book after book, Turow reveals the moral ambiguities that afflict both accuser and accused, and challenges readers to reconsider preconceived notions of justice. In doing so, he fulfills both of his callings, as a lawyer committed to judicial reform and as a novelist crafting words that will teach, entertain, and even change readers' thinking. Perhaps more than any other current popular writer, Turow bridges practical and professional concerns with civic, literary, and humanistic values.

BIRTH AND CHILDHOOD

On April 12, 1949, Scott Turow was born in the city that has dominated his writing, Chicago, Illinois, fictionalized as Kindle County, a tri-city area in an unidentified midwestern location. His parents were the children of Russian-Jewish immigrants from Byelorussia, the region and village of Turov, a location from which the family gets its name. There were Jewish families on record in the Turov region south of Minsk in the seventeenth century, a period of pogroms, and in the eighteenth century the Turov Jewish community of over 300 people was a significant presence, taking an active part in agriculture (105 farmed, in addition to peddling and some trade in wood and fish). By 1925 there were over 5,000 Jews in the Turov region, numbers horrifyingly diminished when the Nazis occupied the area in July 1941, and the Jewish and Gypsy population was massacred; the dead were piled in anonymous mass graves. Those Turovs who survived the Holocaust immigrated at the end of the war, some to Cuba and Argentina, others to New York and Chicago. Scott Turow notes that there were Spanish and Italian Turovs as well (with variant spellings). One Americanized version of Turov is Turow, Scott Turow's family name.

Turow's father, David D. Turow, was a dedicated physician, an obstetrician, who was often called away from home to deliver babies at all hours of the day and night. His strong work ethic laid the foundation for the drive that characterizes his son, but the elder Turow, on call around the clock, had little time free to spend with his family. Like Turow's fictional defense lawyer Sandy Stern, as the breadwinner, his life centered around his work, and his family had to simply endure his absence. Thus, the task of raising the young Scott Turow fell to his mother, Rita Pastron Turow, a writer of children's books, who spent much time cultivating his language skills. The Turows raised their son in the Jewish faith he continues to practice today. Both of Turow's parents had high ambitions for their son, hoping he would follow his father's calling and become a physician. In order to push him in this direction, they emphasized the value of hard work and dedication to tasks. They placed great worth on reading and writing and made them important family values. The results were telling. Turow told interviewer Kathy Stevenson of *Writer* that he tried to write his first novel at age 11, plagiarizing heavily from seventh-grade reading texts, but that the process of imitation was the first step on the journey to his present literary achievements (23).

The Turows lived in downtown Chicago during young Scott's boyhood. The city reflected its immigrant population, with different sections readily distinguished as Irish or Slavic, Jewish or African American. The Turows lived in a heavily Jewish section, where Yiddish was the idiom of the street and orthodox religious practices were commonplace. Turow says his neighborhood was so solidly Jewish that he and his friends joked about the few African American neighbors really being Jews—just with darker skin.

However, Turow's parents, striving for greater assimilation into the American mainstream, moved to the suburbs, an affluent neighborhood in Winnetka, Illinois, where David Turow's medical practice drew a wealthy clientele. In this neighborhood at that time, the population was unabashedly WASP (White Anglo-Saxon Protestant), and Jews were very much outsiders. Turow suffered from the cruelty of difference when he attended New Trier High School. The change in schools was traumatic; Turow mourned the loss of childhood friends and of the comfortable neighborhood life he had shared with likeminded people of a similar ethnic, cultural, and economic background. His grades suffered (he even flunked freshman English), and he felt betrayed by his parents' decision. For this reason, Turow has a genuine sympathy for his youthful readers. Grateful for their interest, he hopes that their reading is not the forced march he remembers from his own school days, but if it is, he advises them not to worry because time brings change and choices (Macdonald interview, 2004). In terms of his later writing, these adolescent traumas have since enabled him to very effectively capture the estrangements that occur between parents and offspring, the dichotomy between parental expectations and the dreams and hopes of young people.

During these teenage years, his parents' medical ambitions for him pushed Turow in directions quite different from the medical profession. The dreams of writing that had begun in his youth continued to dominate his plans for a future career. A high school journalism teacher who told the class, "You will learn to write under inclement circumstances," paved the way for the industrious persistence that has characterized his adult writing accomplishments (Stevenson, 24).

His love of writing eventually led to his becoming the editor of the New Trier school newspaper. His decision to enroll at Amherst College in Massachusetts as an English major was the final rejection of his parents' plans for him. He wanted to be a writer. "I didn't want my father's life," he told a *Washington Post* reporter who interviewed him on October 2, 1977, about his first published work, *One L.*

HIGHER EDUCATION AND EARLY WRITING EFFORTS

Turow attended Amherst College, working on a B.A. degree from 1966 to 1970. At age 18, after completing his freshman year, he got summer employment as a mail carrier in Chicago. He could complete his route in less than the five allotted hours and spend the remaining hour and a half as he wished (mail carriers reached a quiet consensus about their use of downtime before returning to the post office). The public library was the only air-conditioned public building in town at that time. While there, Turow read significant works of fiction that influenced his thinking and his writing (at taxpayer's expense, the lawyer in him makes him confess). When back at the university, his required writing and literature courses engaged his native skills and interests, and he began producing short stories and novels, toiling away in the evenings, honing his craft. Rarely do undergraduates publish much beyond college-sponsored venues, but a few of Turow's short pieces were printed in such literary magazines as the *Transatlantic Review*. He titled his first novel, about Chicago teenage runaways who had witnessed a murder, *Dithyramb* in tribute to James Joyce, whose work he had been reading. In 1970 Turow received writing awards from the College English Association and Book-of-the-Month Club. On the strength of such publications and awards and the fact that he graduated with high honors, he received an Edith Mirrielees Fellowship for two years (1970–1972) to the Stanford University Creative Writing Center.

While at Stanford he met and, on April 4, 1971, married painter and art teacher Annette Weisberg, with whom he eventually had three children: Rachel, Gabriel, and Eve. When the fellowship ran out, Turow taught creative writing as a Stanford E. H. Jones Lecturer until he completed and received an M.A. degree in 1975. One of Turow's teachers, Wallace Stegner, a realist writer in the tradition of Henry James and Theodore Dreiser, proved a major influence on Turow's thinking about audience and content. Stegner stressed the need to represent real, everyday experiences in fiction. Yet, in the main in graduate school, the writing emphasis was on innovation, creativity, and personal expression—discovering new forms and stretching the boundaries of what had already been done. During this time Turow began working on a Chicago story about a rent strike called *The Way Things Are*, which, as he reports, was "steeped in the intricacies of real estate law," and, hence, like *Dithyramb*, remains unpublished (*New York Times* on the Web, www.nytimes.com, November 22, 1999). Twenty-five rejections later, he was forced to reevaluate his career plans. Looking back on that time, Turow defines those early novels as "academic" and as not meeting "the taste of any publishers in the known universe" (*Guilty as Charged*, 1–2).

As a married man with plans for a growing family, he needed a reliable source of income, and only one publisher of the many that he contacted (Farrar, Straus and Giroux) was even slightly positive about his writing potential. His Master's degree in creative writing meant little if it did not translate into sufficient earning power to survive. His vision of himself as a budding novelist thoroughly undermined by such critical rejections, Turow made a pragmatic decision: to choose a career at which he could make a living, one that would provide the income to support his efforts to improve his writing and move toward writing serious fiction on the side. Looking back on that decision, he says that writing *The Way Things Are* had made him see in himself "a previously unrecognized passion for the law," to which he adds, "I startled everyone, even myself, by abandoning my academic career in favor of law school, vowing all the same to live on as a writer" (*New York Times* on the Web, www.nytimes.com, November 22, 1999). However, he admitted to *Observer* interviewer Robert McCrum in "To Hell with Perry Mason" (2002) that he lacked a scholar's attitude: "The great break of my literary career was going to law school." Although he eventually employed a few paragraphs from *The Way Things Are* in *The Laws of Our Fathers*, Turow has no plans to ever go back to his early books. He says, "Unfortunately, I don't judge any of my early manuscripts to be *The Naked and the Dead* [one of Norman Mailer's early works]. Those novels are done with; they were stepping stones to what I do now" (Macdonald interview, 2004).

Indeed, Turow had already found himself taking an interest in legal issues. An English degree prepares one well for the quantity of reading and for the close examination of texts required of lawyers, so Turow made a career move in keeping with his training and interests, one that provided him with the life experiences and raw materials he needed to instill his prose with passion and with a complex vision of harsh realities. He entered Harvard University in 1975 and immediately secured, through his literary agent, a contract for a short personal account of the law school experience, a sort of insider's look at the law school process in action: what to expect, how to cope, and so on. Written from the perspective of a newly admitted law student, this coming-of-age story walks readers through the first-year experience. Turow felt that the first year of law school was a meaningful journey into new territory, a journey experienced in the company of verbally facile super-achievers.

The writing of this book parallcled the reality as Turow took hurried notes on his classroom activities and observations, even as he was experiencing them. He captures the nightmare of the Socratic method of teaching—being called upon at random to expound on the nuances of case studies and being exposed to public ridicule for failure to do so coherently. Turow joined a study group, participating in harrowing intellectual melees that grew more harrowing as exams drew closer. The summer break provided the time needed to complete the work, published by Putnam in 1977 and titled *One L: An Inside Account of Life in the First Year at Harvard Law School.* The closeness of the writer to the experience he describes assures a sense of immediacy and captures the partial insanity and shared pathos felt by all newcomers to such a highly competitive, supercharged program as that of Harvard Law, a proving ground aimed at weeding out those not intellectually or emotionally suited for the verbal parrying and trials of endurance, understanding, and wit that would thereafter characterize their professional work. Turow called the experience a psychological and intellectual "roller-coaster" and "merry-go-round," full of exhilaration and dread as law students learned "a grimly literal, linear, step-by-step process of thought" aimed at fostering suspicion and distrust, and learned to take nothing at face value, to question every premise, to cultivate skepticism. Though it sold modestly initially, its compelling and accurate vision of the tensions, panic, fears, and competition of the first year have made *One L* standard reading for would-be law students, frequently recommended to eager students in LSAT prep classes along with guidebooks on briefing cases. In a 1977 review, *New York Times* critic P. M. Stern called *One L* even more "important" for its look at what law students don't learn and who they are not equipped to represent when they graduate. *Christian Science Monitor* critic Seth Stern appropriately titled his October 2000 review "A Survivor's Tale" (13). Turow says that law school confirmed his attraction to the life of a working lawyer, particularly a criminal lawyer. He once again graduated with honors three years later (1978), this time with a J.D. degree, and he passed the Illinois bar exam soon thereafter the same year. Officially a lawyer by education, he moved quickly to be a lawyer by trade.

OPERATION GREYLORD: A GOLD MINE OF JUDICIARY SOURCE MATERIALS

In his last year of law school, Turow worked as a clerk in the Suffolk County District Attorney's Office in Boston, Massachusetts, getting first-hand experience in the legal profession. Upon graduation from Harvard, Turow returned to Chicago and immediately began to practice law. He became a member of the Chicago Council of Lawyers and of the Chicago Bar Association. From 1978 to 1986, he served as an Assistant United States Attorney in the U.S. Seventh District Court of Appeals, Chicago, Illinois. In this position, he participated in the famous "Operation Greylord," a federal investigation of corruption in the Illinois judiciary. Acting as government counsel with other prosecutors in a series of trials connected to this widespread investigation, he helped convict former Illinois Attorney General William J. Scott of tax fraud and Circuit Court Judge Reginald Holzer of judicial malfeasance. As a neophyte to the courtroom, working prosecutor Turow was astonished to find himself facing "the same old questions about how to address an audience" that he had found himself dealing with as a neophyte creative writer in graduate school. As he points out in his essay in *Writers on Writing*, the tasks of a trial lawyer and of a novelist, are, in unexpected ways, "shockingly similar," with both involving "the reconstruction of experience, usually through many voices, whether they were witnesses or characters"; however, a trial lawyer who loses his audience also loses his case. (*New York Times* on the Web, www.nytimes.com, November 22, 1999). Turow drew on the experiences of colleagues who had been in the business far longer than he, gleaning advice about how to engage a jury, how to tell a good story, how to keep them waiting, fascinated, for the next vital piece of information. He says, "There were plenty of good stories told in the courtroom, vivid accounts of crimes witnessed or conspiracies joined. The jury hung in primal fascination, waiting to find out what happened next. And so did I" (*New York Times* on the Web, www.nytimes.com, November 22, 1999).

The federal government had an early computer-research system on which Turow could "literally do the research of three or four lawyers," an advantage the opposition lacked (*Inc. Technology*, 1994, 42). Such a rich source of materials on judicial corruption, intrigues, and legal wrangling was irresistible to Turow the writer, who began to keep notebooks of intriguing real life details that would bring his fiction to life. He had been tinkering with a draft of a novel unrelated to law, but the realities he was discovering about bribery of judges and witnesses made him start in a new direction, a story about an attorney. Moreover, the courtroom imperative to tell a good story helped Turow overcome the block that had afflicted the writing of his early novels; learning to tell a good story in the courtroom gave him a sense of audience that enabled him to tell a good story in a novel. He found he had important ideas to communicate, ideas that ordinary people needed to understand, and he now had a vision about how to communicate these ideas. "The practice of criminal law had set me to seething with potential themes," Turow says, and he goes on to enumerate a few of them: "the fading gradations between ordinary fallibility and great evil; the mysterious passions that lead people to break the known rules; the mirage that the truth often becomes in the courtroom" (*New York Times* on the Web, www.nytimes.com, November 22, 1999). From 1982 to 1986 he supervised new recruits to the Attorney General's office and, consequently, had occasion to attend court as an observer of his younger colleagues, judging whether they could "structure a direct examination, . . . put a leading question on cross, . . . address a judge with appropriate deference" (*Guilty as Charged,* 1). In doing so, he discovered how spellbinding even routine trials could be as courtroom contenders struggled with elusive truths (the result of "shady recollections," "suspect motivations," or "the simple parallax of different viewpoints," [*Guilty as Charged,* 1]). The "universal drama" and "moral imperatives" of trial by jury explored issues ordinary citizens, untrained in the niceties of law, could nonetheless understand and respond to (*Guilty as Charged,* 2). Turow's recognition of the power of legal themes set him on the track that led to his first legal thriller. Furthermore, he had inspiration from a colleague, the chief deputy prosecutor in Boston, who was not only a gifted trial lawyer but also a poet, and who consequently convinced Turow that he too could have a dual career as writer and lawyer (www.scott turow.com).

Before he began, however, he had some vital decisions to make about how he would approach this new novel. One of the things he wanted to do was "sort of kick back and write in what I took to be my own voice" (www.scottturow.com). Turow's decision to focus on plot and on "the tenacious emotional grip" he felt in "contemplating crime" led him to the mystery genre, which, though not highly esteemed in academic criticism, persists, nonetheless, as a powerful storytelling form. The mystery reader's compulsion to know what happens next fit with Turow's need to tell a story as he would in a courtroom and also to build on some of the values he had learned from Wallace Stegner about the traditional realist novel. He wanted to explore his characters in psychological depth in a prose style that went beyond mere plot considerations. Faced with the genre conventions of the mystery, he decided to invert the traditional detective perspective by having the investigator accused of the crime and on trial for his life.

By 1985, the very high profile nature of his prosecutorial duties in Operation Greylord made Turow see the virtues of the suburban life that his parents had once enjoyed, and he chose the familiar territory of Winnetka, Illinois, as a safe haven, ironically sending his children to the same school he had once so vehemently rejected, New Trier High School. A prosecutor's salary enabled him to purchase a comfortable suburban escape. The demands of work, commuting, and a growing family kept Turow too busy to write very much. He rose early to get some writing in before catching the commuter train into the city, and the train to and from work served as unofficial office as he edited chapters of his new novel. Weekends and evenings provided blocks of time for writing. Of necessity, he wrote in isolation, having no time for contact with other writers. Finally, his wife convinced him to take a chance, quit his job, and concentrate on finishing his novel. Having been burned once, he hedged his bets by accepting a partnership at the prestigious downtown Chicago firm of Sonnenschein, Carlin, Nath & Rosenthal but with the condition of a three-month hiatus from the firm in order to finish his legal novel. In this way he would be furthering his legal career while enjoying a brief respite to work at his writing career full time. It had taken him eight years of part-time writing to complete *Presumed Innocent*, in longhand, mainly on the commuter train. He mailed his finished manuscript to a New York agent only two weeks before his new job started.

TWO SUCCESSFUL CAREERS

Turow's life became the stuff of fantasy when he found himself a major success in two careers, with a solid position in a high-powered law firm and with immediate success as a first-time novelist in the legal mystery genre. Turow's legal background and daily immersion in the realities of the legal system provided an inherently interesting subject matter for fiction that dealt with the key issues of his time and questions of life and death, truth and justice, social inequities, and judicial fairness. His work as a prosecutor not only supplied Turow with a ready source of material, it also influenced the manner in which he would present it. The building of a case takes place in two ways: (1) linear and chronological, an impersonal acquisition of facts, some misleading and perhaps irrelevant, some vital to the outcome of the case; and (2) skewed and Byzantine, the intuitive leaps that connect the seemingly disconnected in kaleidoscopic patterns that change with the addition of new evidence or new memories, as lawyers and investigators theorize and speculate, respond to gut feelings, and put totally personal spins on information that may be fact or fiction.

Yet a courtroom presentation must be lucid. A prosecutor must build a case that seems airtight, indisputable, and credible. The narrative story line the prosecutor creates must compel a jury toward belief. In contrast, a defense attorney must create alternative scenarios that introduce ambiguity and doubt. Turow notes that every trial lawyer knows that if you are not telling the jury a good story you're going to lose them: "I think this is very hard for defense lawyers. They want to sit down. But the best defense lawyers I know also want to get up and tell jurors their story—an alternative version of the facts. It's not enough to just say your client is innocent. There's got to be a story" (Macdonald interview, 2004). He provides the following example as typical of such a story:

> It may look like an arson case to you, but the truth is that my poor client hired a guy who, little did he know, turned out to be, not an arsonist as the government is saying, not an arsonist for hire, but a firebug, someone who likes to set fires, and that is what this case is really about. My client is a victim just like everybody else whose plant burnt down. . . . It's just coincidence that the plant was insured for a hundred million dollars the week before. Just a coincidence we'll talk about later. I'm pushing this a little, but this is the type of story I hear in court every day. (Macdonald interview, 2004)

In addition to telling a good story, lawyers, like writers, should be open to the deeper significance of a particular situation. The argument in law always depends on being able to draw analogies, says Turow, but they are usually analogies in terms of facts. The use of precedents is, in fact, the legal equivalent of literary analogy, forcing lawyers to think in terms of connections between two situations that are superficially different but similar at their core.

Turow relies heavily on figurative language both in writing fiction and in addressing the court because doing so is an instinctive part of his thinking. "It's who I am," he says, and adds, "I think that the process when we dream at night is that we are making metaphors; we are collecting our experience. The secret of metaphor is the secret of memory going back to Proust and the teacake. So I give in to that—the idea of association of images" (Macdonald interview, 2004). Besides this personal affinity for analogies, however, metaphor is an inherent part of legal rhetoric integral to clear storytelling, a shorthand for clarifying for the jury with commonplace images such as "you can't unring that bell" (i.e., words said in public cannot be recalled) or "fruit of the poison tree" (i.e., evidence acquired from illegitimate sources remains tainted). Seeing connections and drawing analogies in this way is instinctive to lawyers and to Turow.

Serving at various times as both prosecutor and as defense provided Turow practical experience in crafting a narrative from different sides of an issue. Because lawyers are indeed storytellers who must tell a good story in court, picking and choosing from the information available to them to produce a credible interpretation of events that a jury or a judge can respond to, Turow's decision to continue his law practice never became a decision not to write. Rather, it was a decision to gather unique materials from his occupation to feed his private (and fast becoming public) passion for writing—telling a good fictive story with the same complexity lawyers must consider a natural part of their job. However, the lawyer in him made the private storytelling aim at public repercussions: a rethinking of the justice system, of how our courts function and of what happens to people caught up in the system. Being a lawyer nurtured Turow the writer. As *Time* reviewer Paul Gray contends in "Who Killed Carolyn Polhemus?" Turow's fiction, though entertaining, aims at far more than entertainment: its goal is "the healing of society"—to which Gray adds, "Bestsellers seldom get more serious than that" (71). Moreover, for Turow the healing process involves a recognition that something is terribly missing between the ideal and the reality of the justice system.

Turow's *Presumed Innocent* caught the attention of New York's biggest publishing houses and started a bidding war over publication rights. Turow, simply hopeful his novel would be published, was met with offers whose sums exceeded $200,000. Turow remembered that the only encouragement he had received for his first, unpublished novel came from Farrar, Straus and Giroux, so he accepted its bid, even though it was not the highest one offered. The firm's literary reputation confirmed for him that this was the best choice for a writer who wished to continue to publish, and he has remained faithful to Farrar, Straus and Giroux ever since,

publishing all of his novels with the company in hardcover and then selling the paperback rights to Warner Books. For Farrar, Straus and Giroux,
the contract was a major financial commitment: the $200,000 they offered
Turow was the largest sum the company had ever paid for a first novel.
Writer critic Kathy Stevenson reports that, when asked about his writing,
Turow told a group of fellow writers at a luncheon, "The principal ingredient in having a successful bestseller is . . . luck. Mere merit is never
enough. I spend a lot of time puzzled and confused about how I became
a writer. And I decided if you don't write, you are not a writer; if you do,
you are" ("Author Events Let You Learn from the Best," 24). With the
publication of *Presumed Innocent,* Turow proved he had luck, but also that
he is a very good writer—a writer audiences wish to hear from again and
again. Instead of aiming at innovation, he followed the lawyer's cue and
aimed at accessibility, coherence, and clarity.

Ironically, with two careers Turow found himself in exactly the same
position as his father—engaged in compelling work that kept him from
his family. When *Presumed Innocent* came out, his older daughter Rachel
was already nine, but his son was only six, and his youngest daughter
had just been born. Turow says that each of his children has been affected
in different ways by his success. "A lot of children have busy parents, but
fewer children have parents who are well known, and it is," he confirms,
"the notoriety that really made a great difference" in his children's lives.
At nine the eldest already had a lot in her life set, but for his youngest
her father's success has been a constant presence: her teachers ask, "Is
your father . . . ?" and her response is "Forget about him. I'm here. I'm
the one to be taught" (Macdonald interview, 2004). That kind of daily
notoriety is hard for children, and as a father Turow is very protective.
His family has had trouble with stalkers from early in his career, and that
has kept him reticent about his family's private life.

Another family note related to his first book is Turow's dedication of
Presumed Innocent to his mother, to whom he attributes his literary ambition. The dedication is a thank-you for the early education she helped
provide him that turned him in a literary direction, ironic in part because
his writing diverged so greatly from her own and much that he does is
quite the opposite of her approach to writing. With the exception of one
book she wrote on the children of divorce—"a subject with which she has
no first-hand acquaintance," observes Turow—she has published articles
in the *Chicago Tribune* and writes children's books. In 2004 she was writing
a quasi-autobiographical "memoir" and delighting in making things up
as she went along. This difference in subject matter and writing methods

occasionally leads to clashes. Her first writing advice, upon reading Turow's novels in manuscript was a blow-by-blow critique, a reaction that made Turow conclude, "It's very hard for parents to give children advice they want to hear," but his wife Annette clarified the role of family-member readers with her comment, "Scott's got a really good editor. That's not really our role. He wants us to read it so that if he has questions [we can help]" (Macdonald interview, 2004). Since that time, that has been the family's role as readers. Turow's wife, Annette, is his first reader, and in his recent books both Annette and his eldest daughter, Rachel, read the first versions in manuscript. Both, says Turow, are "very discerning readers" whose feedback he values.

Presumed Innocent

In the novel *Presumed Innocent* (1987), a conflicted deputy prosecutor assigned to investigate the murder of a female colleague with whom he, his superior, and possibly the judge in his case, have had sexual relations, finds himself on trial for her murder. Turow captures the complexity of personal and professional relationships and the incestuous nature of public institutions to suggest not only the elusiveness of truth but also to show a conspiracy of court officials and politicians connected to the judicial system to protect their own dirty secrets. Turow asks how effective the criminal-justice system can be as a truth-finding mechanism when everyone involved in a case is guilty of something. The truth that Turow learned as a prosecutor and that he dramatizes so effectively in *Presumed Innocent* is that "we all do things we wish we hadn't done and that we're not necessarily proud of" (*Authors and Artists for Young Adults*).

The large fee *Presumed Innocent* brought Turow was justified by reader response. According to *Contemporary Authors*, the novel was more than 43 weeks on the bestseller list, went through 16 hard-cover printings, and sold 4 million paperback copies; as of November 1987, 700,000 hardback copies had already been sold (Osborne, 1). *USA Weekend* reviewer Mei-Mei Chan declared, "*Presumed Innocent* won the literary lottery" (June 1, 1990), as she reported Turow getting $3 million for the paperback rights and another million for the movie rights. Turow received the 1988 Crime Writers Association Award for *Presumed Innocent*. A 1990 film adaptation was one of the 10 top-grossing movies of that year, starring box-office attractions Harrison Ford, Raul Julia, Bonnie Bedelia, and Brian Dennehy. Turow published his second novel to coincide with the film debut of *Presumed Innocent*. The cover of *Time* magazine featured his picture, making him the 92nd writer to appear there (other *Time* cover authors include Ernest Hemingway, J. D. Salinger, and Alex Haley). The book was translated into Spanish, Portuguese, Hebrew, Japanese, Korean, and Chinese, and was read on audio tape by John Heard. Turow was, in his own words, "staggered" by the success of his novel. He says that his only goal had been finally to publish a novel, that he was not even sure that he personally liked most best-sellers, which he had always thought of as "short on imagination" (*New York Times* on the Web, www.nytimes.com, November 22, 1999).

Sonnenschein, Carlin, Nath & Rosenthal

Although the income from *Presumed Innocent* could have freed Turow to retire from the law and write full time, the close ties between his literary achievements and his law career have made the pursuit of both right for him, with his creative efforts growing out of his law practice. Sonnenschein, Carlin, Nath & Rosenthal is an international law firm with over 400 lawyers. Turow's practice within the firm has mainly dealt with white-collar criminal litigation—the representation of individuals and companies in all phases of criminal matters—but his *pro bono* work has extended into far less savory corners of society as he has taken on high-profile cases that raise important legal issues about personal rights. As a half-time partner, Turow charged $250 per hour for his services as defense attorney (Kucherawy, 43).

Practicing law in Chicago has provided Turow a solid legal foundation on which to construct his insider studies of the justice system. First of all, having to appear in a courtroom in front of a jury affects the way one thinks of a case. A lawyer has to make sense to 12 jurors from diverse social, economic, and ethnic backgrounds and with varying degrees of intellectual ability, verbal competence, and education as well as divergent political alliances and personal prejudices. Often these are people with only a faint understanding of the law involved, so they must be guided step by step through the legal intricacies at work. Yet a lawyer must never insult or talk down to a jury; there must be eye contact and some means of making jurors listen to an argument and respond in predictable ways. Thus, courtroom practice demands from Turow a clarity of perception and an ability to pull together disparate threads of an argument to create a credible whole for a diverse audience. Turow told *Wall Street Journal* interviewer Joanne Kaufman, "getting a difficult case ready for trial and organizing a novel have never seemed that different skills" ("Legions of

Lawyers Turned Novelists," August 1, 1991, A10). In fact, Turow added, "Organizing a case is fundamentally an issue of narration." "Witnesses are like narrators, and you have to figure out how to make it [the case/ the story] interesting to an audience, in this case an audience of twelve who are the jurors" (A10).

Second, the court experience provides an endless source of information and images, as well as brings together professionals from a number of fields. Thus, Turow has the opportunity to capture the diversity of experiences found in the courtroom. His novels explore the behind-the-scenes, day-to-day realities of the legal trade, the inevitable deceptions as clients and witnesses tell partial truths and defense lawyers block both professions of innocence and intimate confessions of guilt, the competition between lawyers within and among firms, the way in which money and politics drive "justice," the trade secrets of police and prosecutors, defense attorneys, and judges. His books portray the role of personal and professional loyalties at all levels of the legal system and the various psychologies and motivations that drive investigations from crime to conviction.

Third, the nature of the legal profession forces Turow to consider very different perspectives of the same issue. As a prosecutor for the United States Attorney's office, Turow learned the strategies and routines of one side of the legal equation; as a defense attorney protecting clients for Sonnenschein, Carlin, Nath & Rosenthal, he learned the strategies and routines of the opposition, so that he writes convincingly of the psychology of court officers on both sides of the legal joust. He captures both the tedium and significance of daily routines and trial procedures, as well as the high potential for error. In his introduction to a collection of legal short stories titled *Guilty as Charged* (1996), Turow asserts that in his books "the questions asked, objections offered, and rulings made," to the best of his ability, are "accurate, typical, and in conformance with the rules of evidence," unlike the "jarringly inaccurate" Perry Mason television trial scenes (8). His courtroom encounters are quite purposefully very different from the Perry Mason tradition. Turow and his imitators focus more on legal details, the mechanics of the court, the legal stratagems, the complexity of the judge's rulings, the rationale that determines rulings. Furthermore, his courtroom scenes are lower key and far more subtle and fluid, driven by personalities and the personal insights of individual lawyers. Even when the final decision is handed down, Turow has set readers up to question the justice or appropriateness of that decision, given the murky ambiguities that surround it.

Moreover, his courtroom experiences have driven home for Turow the difficulty of ever fully knowing the truth. When witnesses and clients lie in ways both small and large, when perception is skewed by prejudice or by past experience, "truth" breaks down into multiple "truths," and right and wrong moves from black and white to multiple shades of gray. Evidence is lost or misinterpreted, and behind-the-scenes investigations do not provide firm answers but instead are hit-or-miss, doubtful, and subject to interpretation.

Finally, Turow's Kindle County legal mysteries further gain depth and interest from his vivid portraits of those caught up in the justice system, characters ranging widely from street cops, FBI investigators, and pathologists to cynical, befuddled, or personally motivated court officials, sad, lonely wives, rebellious youths, corrupted judges, and ruthless politicians. In other words, in the practice of law Turow has found a gold mine of complex and ever changing material with all the subtle variations of meaning necessary to explore the changing contours of the human terrain. In an October 11, 1999, *Publishers Weekly* interview, Turow confirms the value of his law career, observing that his law practice has already given him "stories enough for a lifetime," and that he practices law because he enjoys doing so, not to develop new material for his books. In a November 2002 interview with Robert McCrum of *Guardian Unlimited*, Turow observed that criminal law deals with the "ambiguities . . . beneath the sharp edges of the law," "human beings in extremis," and "definitions of evil"—the central concerns of his novels ("To Hell with Perry Mason," http://books.guardian.co.uk).

The Burden of Proof

While on a promotional tour for *Presumed Innocent*, Turow began writing his second legal novel. Wanting to write carefully, at a speed that would accommodate his style and topic, he refused to sign a contract committing him to deliver another potential blockbuster by any particular date: He told a *Maclean's* interviewer that he wanted to write the book he wanted to write without someone having a gun to his head: "You can't practice law and meet deadlines that easily. I wanted to be free to be the writer I want to be and not the writer five million readers—whom I was grateful to have—may want me to be" (Kucherawy, 28). He continued writing between 6:15 and 8:15 each morning for a year and a half, but by then realized that his law practice was so consuming that he would have a hard time finishing this book. Finally, Turow worked out a balancing act that enabled him to continue two careers alongside each other. He arranged with his firm, case load permitting, to spend mornings at home writing, but kept in contact with the downtown firm by telephone, computer, and fax machine in case he (or his feedback) was urgently needed; he used the commute time to edit his manuscript. The result of this arrangement was that three years after *Presumed Innocent,* in the summer of 1990, *The Burden of Proof* appeared on bookshelves nationwide. Turow had signed a contract only upon its completion, and within two weeks after its release the novel topped several best-seller lists.

Self-described as a guilt-ridden workaholic, like the best of his characters, he established a writing routine that he would continue with future books: writing several hours a day, in between the practice of law. The new technologies of the late twentieth century, in fact, made this juggling act more and more feasible. *The Burden of Proof,* another complex, multi-layered study of human beings compromised and bereft, returns to the enigmatic defense attorney from *Presumed Innocent,* the middle-aged Sandy Stern, who returns home from a business trip to find his wife dead, an apparent suicide, and $850,000 missing from her bank account. Despite its exploration of insider stock trading schemes and confrontations with prosecutors, the intrigue of this novel is family centered: Stern's wife's private life, inescapable family ties, unspoken family codes, alienated children and relatives, and Stern's own emotionally complicated sense of loss and human frailty. Betrayal, misunderstanding, personal vanity, and personal sacrifice play out behind the scenes of a brother-in-law's grand jury indictment for business fraud in a commodity-futures firm, as Stern re-evaluates his life, explores a sexual side of himself that had lain latent, and establishes meaningful human relationships.

As a creative writer, Turow has tried, with great success, to avoid the trap that many popular writers fall into, self-imitation: to be forced by audience and publisher expectation into repeating the same pattern ad infinitum. The departure of *The Burden of Proof* from the pattern of his first novel and the variety of the works that followed confirm his self-conscious attempts to avoid cloning *Presumed Innocent* and to fulfill his artistic obligation to lead his readers in new, more satisfying, or at least more challenging, directions. While a few critics, like the June 30, 1990, *New York Times* reviewer, expecting a repeat of *Presumed Innocent,* were unhappy with the results, others (like Jonathan Yardley of the *Washington Post*) noted the high literary quality of this second novel and its foray into new territory. *The Burden of Proof* was listed number one on the *Publishers Weekly* best-seller list (June 22, 1990), with 800,000 copies in print. It spent

29 weeks on the *New York Times* best-seller list. It has been translated into Spanish, Portuguese, Italian, German, Hebrew, Japanese, and Vietnamese.

An Important Death Row Case

While producing novels at a steady rate in the early 1990s, Turow, as a *pro bono* attorney, helped overturn the 1984 death penalty conviction of Alejandro Hernandez, who had been found guilty of the kidnapping, rape, and murder of a young girl, and whom Turow represented in 1991. Hernandez, whose IQ was only 75, was sentenced to death, along with codefendant Rolando Cruz, and was kept on death row despite the 1985 exonerating confession of a convicted child murderer. Turow told Terry McCarthy of *Time* that when he read the evidence (which rested largely on a single sentence in English spoken in the middle of a Spanish conversation) and the confession of the other inmate, he could not believe that such an injustice was happening in America (64). Hernandez had already spent 11 years in prison, many of them on death row, when Turow finally won his release. Elements of this real case paralleled and inspired the later novel *Reversible Errors,* whose character Rommy Gandolph has an IQ of 73, has been found guilty of murder, is accused of sodomy, and spends 10 years on death row before release.

Pleading Guilty

With *Pleading Guilty* (1993), Turow turned away from the courtroom to produce an Elmore Leonard–style detective story narrated in a laconic diary/report format (six tapes transcribed over a one-month period). Therein, when a star litigator and partner in a prestigious midwestern law firm suddenly goes missing (as does some $5.6 million designated to settle a class action suit against the firm's largest client), the morally ambiguous firm, fearful of scandal and lost business, sends Mack Malloy, a former policeman turned lawyer, to investigate. The hard-boiled detective genre conventions (including a corpse in a refrigerator, embezzlement, bookmaking, offshore banking, a missing man, cutthroat alliances, a sinister nemesis, plenty of plot twists, lots of hardboiled talk, and a sleazy corporate culture) combine with powerful, imagistic descriptions to lead Charles Champlin of the *Los Angeles Times Book Review* to rank Turow with such genre greats as Dashiell Hammett and Raymond Chandler (June 13, 1993, 11). As with Hammett and Chandler, it is a world-weary, aging maverick, a tough loner, fiftyish and street-wise, a recovering alcoholic whose usefulness to his firm has been questioned, who makes this novel so engaging. The first-person narrative voice is personable and credible, a fitting addition to the contemporary *noir* genre. On April 19, 1993, *Publishers Weekly* reported 876,000 copies sold in the first printing (47), with copies sold in Russian, Spanish, Hebrew, and Portuguese by the next year (Russell). TNT bought the rights to *Pleading Guilty*, scheduling filming for the spring of 2003, but the project has not been active.

The Laws of Our Fathers

The Laws of Our Fathers (1996) begins with an African American gangster and a grim inner-city slum and moves to the shooting death of a state senator's aging wife to explore the hold the past has on the present, for the death brings back together a group of 1960s radicals, past friends who had gone separate ways and were leading very different lives from those they had envisioned more than 30 years earlier. Despite a murder, a "bench trial" in which the judge alone hears testimony and evidence, and a good bit of legal conniving, Turow is more interested in character in this story, the way in which past lives and loves led to the present moment and new realities. His novel depicts the deeply felt conflicts that caused generations to clash during the Vietnam War era and a different kind of generational conflict in modern times. Assistant Prosecutor Sonia (Sonny) Klonsky of *The Burden of Proof*, now a judge, presides over a court peopled with interconnected lives, including those of newspaper columnist Seth Weissman, black defense lawyer Hobie Tuttle, sixties leftist Loyell Eddgar, now a state senator, and his hapless son. The judge, herself, was a member of this group, and the case makes the judge recall her wildly idealistic communist mother and consider the future of her own young daughter, as Turow captures the revolutionary fervor of the 1960s and the compromises that generation made with time and age. Seth's father (a Nazi death camp survivor) also figures in the retrospective of the past.

The 1960s part of the story is set in a fictional California university town with elements of Berkeley and Stanford, the latter where Turow studied in the creative writing program and observed firsthand the turbulence of his contemporaries in the baby boom generation. The events 20 years later occur in Kindle County, where the compromised idealism of the flower children and counterculturalists has been worn down by the realities of the Midwest and age. The funeral elegy for Seth's father is a particularly moving statement of generational conflict and misunderstanding; Seth in the 1960s segments is a cruel adolescent but becomes a grieving middle-aged son, a father himself. *New York Times Book Review* critic Michiko Kakutani finds the resulting story "by turns moving and manipulative, compelling and contrived," with Turow continuing "to break new ground" (October 8, 1996, 4). The movie rights have been sold to Universal Studios.

By this time, Turow had moved away from the handwritten manuscripts of his first efforts. As with many writers, the computer changed his writing for the better, so much so that he says he doesn't know whether he would have continued as a writer without the technology. As a novelist his method is "gathering" or compiling information, writing a paragraph here, a section there, out of sequence, with no linear order, just scattered bits and pieces that he then cuts and pastes and stitches together into the story he wants to tell (*Inc. Technology*, 42). In precomputer days this meant lots of note cards arranged and rearranged laboriously. On the computer, it simply means a lot of cutting and pasting. Bookreporter.com (2004) notes Turow's enthusiasm for shifting large blocks of text on the computer, a practice evident in the increasingly complex and innovative narrative development of the later novels, beginning with *The Laws of Our Fathers.* As a young man, Turow could not understand why the great author Vladimir Nabokov depended heavily on note cards to organize and write his books, but now he realizes that he writes in the same way—only electronically. Turow admits, "I don't think I could have given my books such intricate plots if I hadn't had the liberty to go back over my work again to sort of monkey around, experiment, tinker with small details"—"a monumental task of stitching . . . together" (*Inc. Technology*, 42).

Creative Method

Basically, Turow's creative method has remained consistent since *Presumed Innocent.* The process takes him approximately three years. He starts with an idea, usually a very broad idea. For example, with the book following *Reversible Errors,* he knew that he wanted to write about World War II because the war loomed very large in his life and in his imagination, partly because his father's war stories had had a large impact on him. He wanted to tell those stories somehow in a novel but make the story his own. He ended up making the story about a court martial so he could draw on his own legal expertise and legal interests. By the summer of 2004 he had the very vague outlines of a plot, which he felt very happy with.

At this stage he starts his research. Throughout the process ideas come to him—then maybe a line of text. He describes the process as follows:

> I may look out the window and think I have an original way to describe the sky that day. It may be characters or pieces of an argument. Usually, it is something that strikes me in the course of the day and I think, "Oh yeah. That will fit that character." And I'll write it down. Eventually, when I have a sense of the plot, I begin to realize where these pieces fit, but I keep threatening to try to keep it chronological. Inventory! And publish a book that way. The utter chaos of a random mind! Just call it experimental fiction! Structures become very formalized, and elaborate, and to some extent the elaboration is in order to accommodate all these diverse pieces. I sit there and think, "And how am I going to get that in?" (Macdonald interview, 2004)

As a result, he ends up with a lot of sidebars and seeks ways to include this detail or that anecdote. For example, while working on *Pleading Guilty,* he attended a birthday party for a friend turning 40 held in the downtown Chicago Russian baths. As this fun party progressed, Turow became more and more aware of how interesting the baths were, so he made several trips back there (before, he notes, they "sadly" closed). After that he thought, "I've just got to get this in my book" (Macdonald interview, 2004).

Despite the wealth of details in his novels, Turow does not keep a journal. Everything he observes as relevant goes directly into the novel he is working on, or, as he puts it, "All that impressionistic, reflective stuff we all have on a day-to-day basis I just throw in the work. . . . When I have a project, I know what will fit and what won't so I don't have to have a journal" (Macdonald interview, 2004). The early writing often takes the form of scenes without regard to chronology or plot. In one instance a lawyer told him a story about a coroner's inquest and he sketched out the scene with no idea where that scene would fit in the book.

As to building suspense, Turow employs strategies that have served others well, observing that all good writers lay the groundwork for dramatic developments and noting, as Chekov pointed out so clearly, that if a gun is hanging on the wall in Act I, it had better go off in Act III or the audience has been misled and will not be happy. "You have to hang the gun on the wall," says Turow, "and you have to do it in a way that is not terribly obtrusive" (www.scottturow.com). With time and a consideration

of dramatic intent, the pieces fit into place and the details provide resonances that carry the reader beyond simple questions of "Who done it?"
and "Will s/he get away with it?" to a strong sense of place, of irony, of
complexity and complicity, of frail humans trapped in unforgiving systems, alienated and even tormented, but often finding the ways and
means not only to survive but also to create family relationships and values. Turow admits that he doesn't have a lot of fixed rules about exactly
how he will write, but he definitely postpones constructing an outline
until the later stages—usually the second or third draft (www.scott
turow.com).

Personal Injuries

Turow's next novel, *Personal Injuries* (1999), grew directly out of his
earlier experiences with Operation Greylord, and, as a result, the nuts and
bolts of the sting depicted ring with authenticity. The story turns on the
contradictory character of con-artist Robbie Feaver, a sleazy personal injury lawyer who never passed the bar exam and who, caught by the FBI
for bribery and tax evasion, has turned federal witness and is selling out
almost every co-conspirator he ever had. A womanizer whose once beautiful wife is slowly and pitifully dying from Lou Gehrig's disease, Feaver
is corrupt, scheming, and offensive, yet, at the same time, charismatic,
human, big-hearted, and likeable. Lesbian FBI agent Evon Miller can
barely resist Feaver's charm, and her understanding and ultimate forgiveness of Feaver confirm the ambiguities of the human heart. *New York
Times Book Review* critic Gary Krist in "When in Doubt, Lie" asserts that
watching Feaver and Miller "gradually probing the multiple veils, curtains, and trapdoors of each other's personalities, penetrating a little
deeper each time," brings "the kind of reading pleasure that only the best
novelists—genre or otherwise—can provide" (October 24, 1999, 7). The
narrator, Feaver's lawyer, George Mason, is the fly on the wall, advising
Feaver on how to beat the rap and outwit the feds, even as he deplores
what Feaver has done. Feaver makes credible the human frailties that
thwart a carefully planned sting operation, as self-righteous prosecutors
step over the line in their fervor to convict. R. Z. Sheppard argues that,
while all Turow's novels explore "the space between legal necessity and
reality's messy urgency," *Personal Injuries* goes much further than his previous works toward explaining why Turow "splits his time between satisfying clients and pleasing readers"; he concludes, "In law there must be
a deal or a judgment. In literature the jury can be hung thoughtfully be-

tween matters of head and heart" (*Time*, 114). *Personal Injuries* pulls readers in both directions.

In 2001 Turow received the Writer for Writers award, and in the summer of 2001, Dustin Hoffman bought the film rights to *Personal Injuries* and plans to produce, direct, and star in it. Turow, who is looking forward to the final product with great enthusiasm, has called Hoffman "one of the transcendent figures in American movies, a genius as an actor and not merely a star" (*Book*, Nov.–Dec. 2001, 14). The film was scheduled to be in preproduction in 2003, but no action had been taken by early in 2005.

With the production of each book, the publicity machine at Farrar, Straus and Giroux moves into high gear, setting up interviews for Turow with key magazines and newspapers, arranging television and radio spots. The November 1999 *Publishers Weekly* reviewer notes that online coverage for *Personal Injuries* included an Amazon.com interview and a live chat on www.bn.com; it also pointed out the regularity with which the publisher sends Turow on nine-city tours with, for example, special breakfast and dinner appearances at New York Is Book Country or a reading at the Miami Book Fair to publicize *Personal Injuries.* All this publicity produced problems for Turow's family and led him to finally sell the home they had lived in since before *Presumed Innocent* came out and move into a home on Lake Michigan with better security.

A Workaholic Schedule

Turow's schedule remains daunting. Celebrity status has meant a steady regime of nine-city publisher-arranged lectures and interviews and has subjected him to the constant calls and programming of various media. However, Turow thrives on pressure. The excitement of law school had been, in part, the excitement of tight deadlines. He told *New York Times Magazine* reviewer Jeff Shear that he runs on "a combination of fear, anxiety, and compulsion" and has to control his impulse "to work all the time" (June 7, 1987). Of course, the downside of such a public life shows up in the lawyer's private office. Clients prefer privacy, and, with Turow as their lawyer, sometimes, inevitably, they fear that he will not give their case the attention it deserves or, as he told Joanne Kaufman of the *Wall Street Journal*, that he will be "a lightning rod on a particular case," bringing disaster to a client because of his own notoriety (August 1, 1991, A10).

He continues to practice law even though his books are such large successes. His office is on the 77th floor of the Sears Tower, and his fee has risen to over $450 an hour. Given the enormous popularity of his books, making money is no longer a concern, so he can opt to do what he enjoys. He enjoys writing, but writing alone without the immersion in the lives of others could become boring for someone used to the high pressure of balancing careers. Besides, lawyering enables him to deal where it counts with issues that drive his fiction. Then, too, as he notes in a piece on technology for a 1994 issue of *Inc. Technology,* computers, fax machines, and E-mail have become the "daily tools" of lawyers, in his case enabling access to his firm's database and documents by modem and making clients and colleagues accessible from home (42). Without leaving his home office, he can discuss documents and drafts with people in different parts of the city. His schedule in the late 1990s and at the beginning of the new millennium has continued to include an early morning writing session and a break or two to deal with legal or personal issues. If he starts writing by 8:00 A.M., he might finish by 1:30 or 2:00, at which time he deals with the legal work at hand, although inevitably this schedule must be flexible, because judges, colleagues, and clients take precedence. Turow told Robert McCrum, in a November 24, 2002, *Observer* interview, "To Hell with Perry Mason," that his creative writing teacher Wallace Stegner taught him that writing a novel cannot be "done in a sprint," but instead is "a marathon" in which the writer must pace himself, writing perhaps two pages a day with a day off at Christmas (as Stegner did), so that at the end of a year, there would be at least 700 pages, some of which would be "worth keeping."

In reply to questions about maintaining two careers, Turow laughingly observes that the idea that artists cannot have mainstream lives was probably first dreamed up by intellectuals who sought this alienation for themselves, but he notes that the concept is very agreeable to the mainstream as well. "The bourgeoisie were very happy," he says, "to get rid of those [artistic] people rather than have them in their midst questioning conventions and such hokum" (Macdonald interview, 2004). However, for him the two careers are inextricably bound together. The writing enables him to reflect on and distance himself from his experiences with the legal system. By tackling in prose some of the major issues raised in his legal work, he strengthens his commitment to the values that have led him to provide *pro bono* legal service. As is so clearly evident with *Reversible Errors* and *Ultimate Punishment,* his writing career is in many ways an extension of his legal career, with each complementing and enhancing the other. Besides, as he told Adrienne Drell for "Murder, They Write," he didn't want to be "locked up all day with a pencil" (46).

Turow also occasionally teaches a creative writing course, as he has done at Stanford University and Northwestern University. When asked if he thought it possible to really teach writing, he replied that he had indeed taught very talented would-be creative writers at Stanford, among other places, and he believes it is truly possible to teach talented young people to write. However, he qualified that remark by noting that his most famous student, Michael Cunningham, who won the Pulitzer Prize in fiction, demonstrates the exception. Turow modestly muses: "The only thing I taught Michael of any value was how talented he was, because I don't think I taught him a damn thing besides that. The week he won the Pulitzer Prize, I happened to be in New York, and he made a migration to pay me a visit, which was very flattering, but he was so good that I didn't realize until then that my class was his first writing class. So who knows [whether one can truly teach others to write]" (Macdonald interview, 2004). Turow has no plans to teach creative writing in the near future.

With time, Turow the overachiever has worked hard at learning to have fun, taking pleasure in Chicago sports and in playing golf.

PUBLIC SERVICE

Turow has given his time to such charitable causes as Literacy Chicago. An active member of the Authors Guild, the national membership organization for professional writers, he was president for the 1997–1998 year and continues to serve on its governing board. He is a Trustee of Amherst College.

According to www.bookreporter.com (2004), Turow has been appointed to a number of public bodies. These include:

1. A member of the United States Senate Nominations Commission for the Northern District of Illinois (1997–1998), which recommended appointment of federal judges;

2. A member of the Illinois State Police Merit Board (2000–2002), which determines matters of hiring, promotion, and discipline for members of the Illinois State Police;

3. One of 14 members of the Commission on Capital Punishment (comprised of lawyers and criminal justice experts), appointed March 2000 by Illinois Governor George Ryan to review the state's death penalty policy (particularly its death penalty law and death row policies) and to consider reform of the capital punishment system; as a result of the Commission's report, delivered April 2002, in January 2003, Governor Ryan commuted the death sentences of every resident of death row in his state;

4. Chair of the Illinois State Appellate Defender's Commission, charged with over-
   seeing the state agency that represents indigent criminal defendants in their
   appeals (2004).

DEATH PENALTY ISSUES

Turow has been quite vocal in his exploration of death penalty issues—
in the press, on television, and in his books. His intense examination of
case studies provided no evidence that "killing a killer makes murder less
likely," only that it somewhat consoles the victim's relatives, but it also
acquainted him with the behavior of "twisted creeps" who could change
ordinary lives forever (McCarthy, 64). Ultimately, it was the mounting
evidence of sloppy defense counsel, prejudiced juries, forensic errors, and
unfair application of the ultimate penalty to minorities that made him
decide that the present system perverts justice.

Reversible Errors

Reversible Errors (2002) came after Turow's work on the governor's commission and, as Turow himself confirms, represents his continued investigation into the issue of capital punishment. Turow told *Publishers Weekly*
critics Jeff Zaleski and Adam Dunn, "The death penalty is an unbelievably
rich subject, certainly the richest subject in the law. It asks questions about
the value of life, the nature of punishment, the power of government—
and, of course, it's inherently dramatic because the stakes are so high"
("New Novel Considers the Death Penalty," 65). Turow told *People Magazine* that he does not think the death penalty is immoral, but he believes
death penalty cases are more prone to error than other cases and that we
cannot really construct a legal system that will deliver the ultimate punishment in an unfailing way. "The death penalty tests the very limits of
the law," says Turow: "It doesn't function as a deterrent, at least not in a
way that's provable. Its effect is symbolic. That's well and good, if you
can convict the right people. But the nature of law is that it is prone to
error" (September 15, 2002, 126).

Turow's fictional death row inmate Rommy Gandolph, nicknamed
"Squirrel," is borderline mentally retarded, a minor scam artist convicted
for a 1991 triple murder touted as the Fourth-of-July Massacre. Shortly
before his execution, an inmate who is dying of cancer, Erno Erdai, confesses to the murders, but Gandolph's court-appointed defense lawyer for
his final appeal, Arthur Raven, initially doubts the truth of this confession,
especially since Gandolph had originally confessed his guilt to the police

interrogators. However, against his will, Raven slowly comes to believe that his client really is innocent. He tries to enlist the aid of the presiding judge in the original case, Gillian Sullivan (first encountered in *Personal Injuries*), who has just finished a prison sentence for bribery. However, he is thwarted in his defense efforts by Muriel Wynn, the ambitious prosecuting attorney, who has personal reasons for wanting Gandolph's conviction upheld, and by her sometime lover, the lead detective on the case, Larry Starczek. As the novel alternates between the original 1991 investigation and the 2001 appeals case, Turow explores the complex way in which personal lives and relationships impede justice and make proof of guilt a dubious exercise. As noted, his personal experience with capital cases informs the novel with a palpable credibility about how people behave in the countdown to execution.

Turow received the 2003 *Chicago Tribune* Heartland Prize for fiction for *Reversible Errors*, an award presented in November at the Chicago Humanities Festival.

Ultimate Punishment

Turow's interest in indigent criminal defendants and the death penalty remained unsatiated, so he sought another venue for exploring questions raised both in his *pro bono* work and in his investigative duties for Governor Ryan's capital punishment commission. The result was a nonfiction work titled *Ultimate Punishment: A Lawyer's Reflections on Dealing with the Death Penalty* (2003). The study records his personal reflection on his service on the commission and on the events and reasoning that transformed in just four years the formerly pro–death penalty governor into an anti–capital punishment advocate who took the unprecedented step of commuting the death sentences of the 167 death row residents in his state a week before he left office in January 2003. Before setting the commission to work, the governor had first imposed a stay of all state executions to be in effect until after the report. Turow himself began his work on the commission without a strong conviction one way or the other, having argued the case for both sides in court. However, the commission's investigation of the enforcement of the law in Illinois since its enactment in 1977 revealed serious flaws: more prisoners had been released from death row because of wrongful convictions than had been put to death in the state. Turow gravely and methodically examines the question of capital punishment, not on the basis of morality, but from the logical and limited perspective of whether the criminal justice system can fairly and correctly decide those cases in which the death penalty is appropriate and still protect the innocent. After due consideration, Turow answers as did the majority of the governor's commission, that such absolute certainty is impossible; the innocent cannot be protected. Critic Stuart Shiffman in a bookreporter.com review (2004) concludes that the seriousness and honesty of Turow's investigation and his carefully considered support materials lend his conclusions unusual weight and value.

Looking back on his experiences, Turow realized that while he was writing the novel *Reversible Errors* at the same time as the nonfiction work *Ultimate Punishment,* he really had become persuaded that murder "takes us all to the land's end of the law": "These crimes are so far beyond our imagining and our ability to cope with them that there is an inherent anxiety when somebody abducts, rapes, and murders a little girl; such an act really does test the law's ability to cope and it invites and asks for restoration" (Macdonald interview, 2004). "People want to feel that the world they know, the safer world, has been restored, but it can never really be restored by taking someone out and killing him," he asserts. "It takes a long time to understand that truth and the fact that part of what is making people upset is the human condition." In reference to the Oklahoma City bombings and the debate over Timothy McVeigh and Terry Nichols, he asks, "What do you do? All those dead and no restoration is possible. That whole second trial ended up being pointless, a gigantic exercise in waste of money" (Macdonald interview, 2004). When asked whether he felt comfortable being described as decidedly anti–death penalty now, Turow replied that he had come to rest on this issue, even though he understands and often feels the emotional momentum that leads people to think that the death penalty is an appropriate punishment. To capture the quagmire of the question, he repeats a story his mother told him of a young African American man—a student at the University of Illinois—accosted by an equally young but very poor urban youth who demanded the starter jacket he was wearing; the college student gave it to him, but the other youth killed him anyway. Turow says that one's natural initial reaction is, "God, that's savage," but, of course, the reality that lies behind the incident is the poor youth saying "give me your jacket" because he wants to be like the college student, and then shooting him when he realizes that the jacket changes nothing: 'I'm still not like you'" (Macdonald interview, 2004). This real incident was one of many that affected Turow's vision of Rommy Gandolph's plight in *Reversible Errors* and of death penalty issues in *Ultimate Punishment.*

TUROW'S FUTURE PLANS

In interviews and on his Web site, Turow has repeatedly confirmed his desire to continue balancing his two interlocking careers. Although the soaring profits from his books and the films based on them mean he need never work again, he has no intention of retiring from his law practice or from writing. His personal sense of self is inextricably bound to both occupations. A February 16, 1990, *Chicago Tribune* review of *The Burden of Proof* confirms that dual sense of identity. After spending his undergraduate and graduate years defining himself as a writer, he at first felt he was faking it when he became a lawyer. At some point, though, that feeling changed, and he underwent an identity shift that now makes him, when asked, identify himself as a lawyer rather than a writer. Psychologically, he feels that calling himself a writer is "a grandiose claim for somebody who spends sixty hours a week doing something else." Nonetheless, he still finds writing very fulfilling, and every three years like clockwork he produces another blockbuster novel. Speaking to Kathy Stevenson of *Writer*, Turow discussed the isolation of most writers, who, in their daily lives, "rarely come into contact with other writers" (24). Yet he personally finds value in writers' conferences and in those occasions when he can meet and talk with other writers. He told Stevenson that it "nourishes my writer's soul to steal away from my computer and hear stories about the writing life from others who are doing the same thing," even if those authors are "light years ahead of me in publishing credits," because each and every one faced the blank page and "sat down and wrote the first sentence of their first book, just as we all must do" (24). In a Malcolm Jones/Ray Sawhill *Newsweek* article, "Publish or Perish," Turow argued that publishing pressures for mainstream writers who will produce multiple books "drowns all of the smaller and more diverse voices" (June 12, 2000, 68–72), not a problem Turow has personally experienced. Turow's books have been translated into more than 20 languages and have sold approximately 25 million copies worldwide. He considers himself lucky but expects to "fall off the mountain" sooner or later (*Washington Post*, June 9, 1990).

Writing remains an exciting challenge for Turow. In an essay titled "An Odyssey that Started with *Ulysses*" in *Writers on Writing*, from the *New York Times* on the Web (www.nytimes.com, November 22, 1999), Turow concludes his discussion of his writing by saying, "I have, frankly, learned to enjoy all the rewards of best-sellerdom, but none more than the flat-out, juvenile thrill of entering so many lives. I love my readers with an affection that is second only to what I feel for my family and friends, and I would be delighted to please them with every new book." He feels "blessed" to have discovered what Graham Greene describes as a writer's "ruling passion," for "as individuals we can only dig toward our ruling passions, uncover them and desperately hope, as we fail, to be heard." At the end of May 2004, the CBS miniseries *Reversible Errors* aired, with William H. Macy as the *pro bono* corporate attorney stuck defending a death row inmate, Felicity Huffman as the corrupt judge who presided over the condemned man's original trial, Monica Potter as the politically ambitious prosecutor, and Tom Selleck as the original police investigator who elicited the murder confession. Turow, caught up in the excitement of seeing his complex novel honed to a fast-moving four-hour, two-part television film, reflected on the way the boom in television procedurals like *Law & Order* and the various *CSI: Crime Scene Investigation* series have transformed audience understanding of forensics and legal niceties and made writing legal fiction a very different task from what it was when he wrote *Presumed Innocent*. "There was a time when I actually had to explain in my novels what a sidebar is, and you wouldn't think of doing that now." The downside, he adds, is that many people think DNA can solve every case nowadays, when it obviously cannot (Walker, 7). Part of the continuing thrill of deliberately told crime stories, says Turow, is that "it's part of life to want to find out definitive answers to things that seem unknowable" (Walker, 7).

The accolades of his reviewers and critics suggest the skills he has honed and the quality readers can expect from future Turow works, whatever direction they take. As early as his first published novel, critics recognized his writing as a cut above that of the usual mystery. The August 30, 1987, *Washington Post Book World* reviewer called *Presumed Innocent* "a book of considerable intelligence and style," one that provokes as well as entertains. Turow is to be ranked with Dashiell Hammett or Raymond Chandler, notes R. Towers of the *New York Times Book Review of Books* (45), or with those special authors who know how to hold reader attention—Jane Austen, Tolstoy, Rex Stout—asserts the *Vogue* reviewer. The *Detroit News-Free Press* (1999) says of *The Laws of Our Fathers*, "No other novel this year is likely to be as thoughtful, as timely and richly detailed, and as satisfying to read . . . a *tour de force*." The *Chicago Sun-Times* reviewer calls it "a richly nuanced story of crime and punishment that is bound with sinews of generational strife, of the loss of idealism, and of love lost and won again." The reviewer goes on to praise Turow's books overall as "densely plotted, their characters of great psychological complexity, their themes deep ones of corruption, venality, and human weakness," all executed with such "great skill and compassion" that "the details all ring with vivid truth . . . empathy . . . imagination." *New York Times Book Review* critic Gary Krist in "When in Doubt, Lie" says *Personal Injuries* sets "new standards for the genre," in the "depth and subtlety" of characterization (7), while the *Chicago Tribune* reviewer calls Turow "the closest we have to a Balzac of the *fin de siècle* professional class." In "The Last Word," *Newsweek* reviewer George F. Will sums up the consensus of his colleagues: "Turow's novels are not quite entertainments. They transcend their genre. They are literature that will last."

As a mature writer, Turow speaks to the crucial civic issues of our time, including public corruption, justice versus mercy in the punishment of public servants and others convicted of malfeasance, the public face of investigation against the insider's view, and so on. Yet, although attorney Turow is clearly immersed in the law, his novels are highly accessible to outsiders, as their vigorous sales and film versions attest. Turow has the rare knack of being able to make highly technical and potentially tedious topics gripping and dramatic. His best works achieve literary excellence, yet retain the ability to speak to a wide and serious audience far distant from legal or civic issues. He looks forward to a satisfying future of exploring more legal questions that compel public attention and relate directly to events ongoing in our culture. Politically, Turow's vision shares the complexity and morality associated with America at its best. He is a committed democrat, politically engaged in making the world a better place through challenging Americans to think more deeply about the legal issues—which are the human issues—of our time.

In his introduction to *Guilty as Charged*, Turow argues that, more than ever before, the law has become "the forge" for shaping national values, providing answers to questions that in the past would have been the business of religious leaders: questions about "the propriety of abortion, of surrogate motherhood, of unwelcome sexual advances, of discrimination on the basis of sexual preference" (4). His legal fiction serves the "educational function," says he, of responding to reader curiosity about the law and the values it upholds (*Guilty as Charged*, 4).

Turow's official contact address remains: Sonnenschein, Carlin, Nath & Rosenthal, 233 South Wacker Drive, Sears Tower, Suite 8000, Chicago, Illinois, 60606-6491.

2

Scott Turow's Literary Heritage

All good writers are, to some degree, a product of their reading, learning from other writers how to address an audience, present an argument, explore an idea, and bring to life a story. As a fiction writer, Turow is quite forthcoming about the important role reading quality literature has played in his life and in his art, giving credit to a broad spectrum of writers and works from which he learned. He began reading and writing at an early age and has persisted throughout his lifetime, even while practicing law, raising a family, and conducting a public life. Postmodern pastiche may be an overused phrase for the nature of the readings that have influenced currently working writers, but Turow's wide-ranging reading has allowed him to draw on a great variety of sources.

CHILDHOOD FAVORITES

Like many American youths, Turow read Ian Fleming's James Bond series with great enthusiasm. Before Bond, one his favorite characters, he told Robert McCrum of the *Observer* in "To Hell with Perry Mason" (November 24, 2002), was the protagonist of *The Count of Monte Cristo*, although the first serious novel to interest him was Stephen Crane's *The Red Badge of Courage*. Ernest Hemingway also appealed to him as he grew older because Hemingway was "accessible" and also because "he defined a kind of masculinity that was the prevailing view in the USA when I was a youth—James Bond gone serious" (McCrum interview).

Saul Bellow

Later Turow became a fan of Saul Bellow, a fellow Chicagoan and a "gargantuan influence," whom he saw as the voice of his parents' generation. He liked Bellow's interest in ideas and his good sense of the vernacular, but most of all Bellow helped him examine himself as a future writer. Over time, reading Bellow influenced Turow in multiple ways but most of all by helping him identify his points of disagreement with Bellow as a writer and as a thinker ("Scott Talks" on www.scottturow.com).

Charles Dickens

Turow says that, as a child, he read a number of novels by Charles Dickens, but with neither relish nor appreciation, even though Dickens's articles in *Household Words* (1850–1859) created positive images of resourceful, hardworking police (like Inspector Field), entering slums and adopting disguises in order to track down criminals and criminal conspiracies and serve the public good. Yet, as an adult, Turow looks back on the formative influence of Dickens with pleasure and recognizes the profound influence Dickens had on him despite his early lack of enthusiasm. Today, he sees in Dickens an artist with the power to create robust characters and at the same time concentrate on his principal storytelling mission, and Turow invokes him as a model of how to achieve a literary end through character. Both writers people their novels with dozens of characters, some memorable because of their convincing literary "roundness" (they seem full and complete, like real people), some quirky and odd, and some almost grotesques. Dickens also based his works in part on real criminals or real criminal acts as a springboard to his fiction, an approach Turow has used from the start of his legal procedural writing career. Both writers share an interest in the demimonde, the dark underworld, as seen from the point of view of middle-class propriety. They also, says Turow on his Web site, share a "view of the novel as . . . governed principally by plot," with characters developed "within the conditions that the plot provides . . . like building on the land between the streets." Turow most admires Dickens for creating robust characters "without giving up his principal mission as a storyteller."

Harper Lee

The trial book that Turow responded to most emotionally in early adolescence was Harper Lee's *To Kill a Mockingbird* (1960), a classic (and highly popular) courtroom story in which the lawyer is the best educated member of his rural Southern community, with keen insight into the prejudices that drive his fellow citizens and with respect for upholding the law and justice against personal biases, in this case, racial hatreds. Set in a racially segregated Alabama, the story centers around an African American man (Tom Robinson) falsely accused of raping a white woman and nearly lynched by a rabid mob of locals who are faced down by the man's lawyer, Atticus Finch. Gregory Peck, playing the part of Atticus Finch in the popular film version of the novel (1962), captured the high moral resonances of the case. Turow told McCrum, "Atticus Finch is so perfect it's beyond belief": "a widower caring in a loving fashion for two wonderful children," "a man of courage, principle, deep intellect," and "the best shot in the county!" His children sit in the "colored balcony" with the town's black citizens as their father lays out the clear-cut evidence to the all-white jury. Respected in his community and in the courtroom, Finch forces the jury to look into their hearts and to see with clearer eyes the truths he proclaims, the lies and false accusations born of fear, the absence of a crime, the conspiracy of silence to save reputation. Despite the power of Finch's summation and the strength of defense evidence of innocence, the all-white jury convicts the accused. Later, when Tom Robinson tries to escape, he is shot to death, and readers share in Finch's son Jem's loss of faith in justice. Plot and character in *To Kill a Mockingbird* provide an idealistic model of the role of a lawyer, a model untouched by modern skepticism and cynicism.

HIGH SCHOOL AND COLLEGE INFLUENCES

In an essay titled "An Odyssey that Started with *Ulysses*" in *Writers on Writing*, from the *New York Times* on the Web (www.nytimes.com, November 22, 1999), Turow describes the public library volumes that molded his thinking and writing style as an undergraduate and a would-be novelist. One major influence was James Joyce, whose *Ulysses* and *Portrait of the Artist as a Young Man* made Turow want to be an experimental novelist. He still calls *Ulysses* "magnificent" and was most taken by T. S. Eliot's 1923 praise of the book as "the most important expression" of its age—although, at the same time, it was far ahead of its time in form and concept. In tribute to Joyce's use of Greek mythology, Turow called his first novel *Dithyramb,* the name of a Bacchic dance, a title Turow says had only a very allusive relevance to his story of two teenage runaways from Chicago, witnesses to murder.

So impressed was Turow by *Ulysses* that he began to be bothered that no one else seemed to check out the library volume and read it carefully and enthusiastically each day. That youthful experience raised questions about the relationship between writer and audience that still affect his fiction. Turow wanted to be a success as a novelist, but he asked himself whether *Ulysses* could rightly be called a great work of literature if its leisure-time readership was so small and if those few who dared to tackle it found it so taxing. Thinking about *Ulysses* also made him think about the obligations of writers to readers, what readers are entitled to ask of writers, and how easy or how difficult writers can make their works, be true to their ideas and goals, and still communicate effectively. Clearly, all writers must ask themselves on a regular basis, "What concessions must I make of vocabulary, style, and content in order to reach my audience?" "Do I write for an elite, a small cadre of fellow thinkers capable of understanding great ideas and maybe changing culture as a result of them?" Turow reports that "the radical democrat . . . running amok" in his soul in the 1960s did not think so. Instead, he thought of the reader–writer relationship as more of an "I-thou relationship," with the artist offering "a special vision that reframes experience in a way that, although intensely personal, reverberates deeply among us all." Yet, as a neophyte novelist he had no clear conception of how to deal with significant ideas and issues in ways that would appeal democratically to a universal audience of ordinary readers, not an academic elite.

The arguments of would-be writers at the Creative Writing Center at Stanford University echoed these same questions, with some of his fellow students horrified when he asserted that his conception of the ideal novel was that it "would be equally stirring to a bus driver and an English professor." At this stage in his reading life, Turow was most interested in realistic writers like Theodore Dreiser and Saul Bellow, with Bellow a particular favorite. Thus, Turow's decision to settle on the mystery genre, and particularly the legal mystery, was a decision about voice and audience, about realism, and about the genre conventions and traditions on which he would build. When he opted to write in the mystery genre, he brought to his writing a rich, popular history, with a variety of conventions readily at hand, conventions that enable the handling of serious issues in formats accessible to wide readerships.

The crime novel and its subgenre, the murder mystery, have a long and honorable history, including writers as diverse as Edgar Allan Poe, Wilkie Collins (whose *The Moonstone* is often named as one of the first murder mysteries), and Raymond Chandler. In England in the middle of the twentieth century, the crime novel/mystery became one of the means by which esteemed novelist Graham Greene explored a wide variety of serious themes, some in a detective story like *Brighton Rock*, some in novels with detective conventions. From the 1960s through the 1990s, P. D. James also brought the crime novel enormous literary respectability, with her nuanced and grave analyses of character and action. Both Greene and James balance fallen human nature and the corruptibility of institutions set up to govern and control human nature, a theme Turow also explores.

CRIME FICTION, DETECTIVE FICTION, AND MYSTERIES

The broad genre of crime fiction, detective fiction, and mysteries includes both short stories and novels, but all have in common the investigation of a criminal problem, whether by an amateur or professional detective, a police officer or other representative of the judicial system, an insurance claims investigator who goes beyond his or her purview, or a nosy neighbor who wonders what happened to the reclusive widow next door and decides to find out. Crime fiction focuses more on why events happened, (that is, on the character and psychology of the criminal) and on the repercussions: crime and punishment. Crime fiction often asks why A would want to kill B, or what made a situation so intolerable that it resulted in violence (see Tony Hilfer's *The Crime Novel*, 1990). Patricia Highsmith's *Strangers on a Train* (1950), with its focus on criminal psychology and the process of reasoning that leads to the criminal act, is a good example of a crime story. In contrast, detective fiction and mysteries focus on the sleuth/investigator and the investigative process to discover the guilty party or parties once the crime has been committed. The term *mystery* is a general category encompassing crime and detective fiction, but the term emphasizes in particular the puzzling and mysterious events that eventually lead to the discovery of a crime and a perpetrator. A typical mystery unravels deceptions, whether mechanical (a locked room murder puzzle), verbal (misleading or erroneous testimony or lies), or forensic (fake fingerprints, misleading semen, ballistics that don't match up). Often the crime story begins with the back story and moves forward to the crime, while the detective story or mystery usually begins with the crime and looks back to determine how and why it occurred. *Thriller,* another term used for this genre, is broader, and describes any story that promises excitement and action, the pursuit of a criminal (or a spy), with the chase figuring importantly in the process and with the potential for danger inescapable (a mass murderer, for example, with the detective or a friend of the detective in line as the next victim). A thriller may be a spy story or a murder story, but "thrill" is the key distinguishing word. The genre plays with the emotions of the readers, taking them on roller-coaster chases like those in the Robert Ludlum international suspense stories or the James Patterson cat-and-mouse pursuits with the unknown and monstrous serial killer interacting with the detectives who pursue him.

Conventions of the genre include the investigator observing more closely than do ordinary citizens, gathering evidence, interviewing witnesses, checking alibis, discovering clues as well as means and motives, setting up and testing hypotheses against facts, eliminating suspects, and—through some intuition and much more reasoning and logic—discovering the truth and unmasking the murderer, usually by answering the questions of who did what and why. For this reason, books in this genre are called "whodunits." Often the investigating detective has a sidekick or companion to ask the right questions and make the detective's logic shine. The detective may be a scientist applying empirical reasoning, a psychologist unraveling the workings of the human mind, a hard-boiled pragmatist caught up in the politics of events, a gentleman who amuses himself with intellectual puzzles, and so on. The storyteller inserts red herrings to misdirect readers or may bring all the suspects together in a single room so the truth will come out.

As a lawyer, Turow is particularly partial to misdirection. In *Presumed Innocent*, for instance, he guides readers through sets of clues that suggest very different scenarios depending on one's perspective. An armchair detective never leaves his or her own home but uses pure reasoning to determine guilt and innocence and to solve the puzzle of the crime (murder in a locked room, for instance, is a conventional puzzle). The murder often occurs in an isolated setting, with suspects confined in a limited space, and the solution to whodunit depends on the investigator developing a timetable to pinpoint who was where when. Turow plays variations on this formula with the murder in *The Laws of Our Fathers*, whose triggerman is known but whose instigator becomes the issue at trial. The murder mystery often includes a map of the house or neighborhood in which the crime occurred, as we see in the graphic of Kindle County in *Personal Injuries*. Coroner inquests can play an important role in defining the nature of the crime and in directing or misdirecting readers. Writers such as

John Feegel (*Autopsy*, 1975), Patricia Cornwell (the Kate Scarpetta series, beginning with *Postmortem*, 1990), and Kathy Reichs (the Dr. Temperance Brennan series, beginning with *Déja Dead*, 1997) have made the coroner-as-detective story a showcase of technological wonders, as applied science provides answers about rigor mortis, DNA from fingernail scrapings and hairs, the testimony of carpet threads, and so on. These are features Turow makes use of with the occasionally incompetent Japanese American Kindle County coroner, "Painless" Kumagai, who muddles evidence in *Presumed Innocent* and appears briefly in *Reversible Errors*.

Hard-boiled Detective Stories

The hard-boiled detective story is a typically American type of mystery or detective story. The hard-boiled detective is a tough guy on the fringes of the law. He belongs to the sordid atmosphere of a dusty, cluttered, rundown office located in a broken-down building in a tough neighborhood on the edge of the city's business district; he is a marginal professional who has chosen his milieu as a form of rebellion, a rejection of the ordinary concepts of success and respectability, reports John Cawelti in *Adventure, Mystery, and Romance: Formula Stories as Art and Popular Culture*. Cynical and frustrated, this type of detective knows how to handle himself in violent situations and is willing to use violence, himself, in order to solve the crime he investigates; he won't be pushed around by the police, government officials, or criminals. Such detectives act as hired guns; they take as clients the rich, the powerful, and the seductive, all of whom try to draw the detective into their world and use him for their own selfish purposes. However, beneath the facade of respectability lies violence, deceit, and corruption. The criminal frequently turns out to be a close friend of the detective, either a colleague or associate, or a woman who, though romantically or sexually involved with the detective, betrays him and behind the loveliness proves to be perverse, depraved, and murderous. Raymond Chandler, whose writings Turow says influenced his *Pleading Guilty*, describes the hard-boiled detective as a tarnished knight whose idealism has given way but who retains some deeply held principles when faced with temptations and betrayals. The detective must expose a web of conspiracy that connects respected members of the community with the criminal underground.

A hard-boiled detective story usually focuses on a large modern city: a deceptively glittering facade behind which hides a world of exploitation, corruption, and criminality. Raymond Chandler describes it best in the Los Angeles of *The Long Goodbye* (1953):

> Out there in the night of a thousand crimes people were dying, being maimed, cut by flying glass, crushed against steering wheels or under heavy car tyres . . . beaten, robbed, strangled, raped, and murdered. People were hungry, sick, bored, desperate with loneliness or remorse or fear, angry, cruel, feverish, shaken by sobs. A city no worse than others, a city rich and vigorous and full of pride, a city lost and beaten and full of emptiness. (69)

The malignant metropolis became a convention of Chandler's successors and imitators, the city of Dashiell Hammet's Continental Op and Ross Macdonald's California and even John D. MacDonald's Miami. The hard-boiled subgenre features lurking dangers, a fast-moving, frantic pace, and, always, an urban wasteland, decadent and sprawling, like the no-man's-land ghetto area with which *The Laws of Our Fathers* opens: "The air is brackish, although . . . miles from water. The four high-rise towers hulk amid a hardened landscape of brick, of tar and pavement broken by weeds, of crushed coke cups and candy wrappers, of fly-about newspaper pages. A silvery bedding of broken glass, the remnants of smashed bottles, glitters prettily—one more false promise" (4). There is little romance in the hard-boiled cityscape, for the bright lights and excitement are only an illusion. In this view, all the dysfunctions humans in society are capable of are concentrated in the city, feeding off each other but largely invisible except to the detective.

A feature of the hard-boiled genre is the distillation of complex emotions and attitudes into terse one-line summaries. The point of view is tough, no-nonsense, and unsentimental, saying, in effect, "This is the way things are, and there's no use crying about it." These short comments incorporate a whole world view, a *weltanschauung*, and have become a feature of cinema *noir* (literally, "dark" stories) and television police procedurals that ape *noir* attitudes, such as with the hard-boiled detective Lenny Briscoe on the television drama *Law & Order*. Perhaps taking their cues from crime fiction, even real television reporters employ hard-boiled lines. Reporting that the police had shot dead a wanted criminal who had boasted he would never be taken alive, Mike Longman, of WWL-TV in New Orleans intoned, "John Smith got his wish tonight." In another instance, a Miami television reporter led into a description of one man shooting another during an argument in line at a fried chicken restaurant with the hard-boiled statement, "Joe Jones died hungry tonight." Actors as diverse as Clint Eastwood and Arnold Schwarzenegger have made the *noir* style their own, often with signature catchphrases like Eastwood's "Make my day" or Schwarzeneggar's "I'm back." The hard-boiled refusal to indulge emotion is a quintessentially American style, a culturally powerful genre convention.

Even though academics sometimes look down upon the quality of the mystery genre as inferior, as Turow observes, "it enthralls people," and in unique ways "delivers answers that life and certainly the courtroom cannot." Yet, despite the potential of the mystery genre to capture the ironies of real life, Turow finds the conventions limiting to some degree. "Only in the mystery novel are we delivered final and unquestionable solutions," and, yet, "The joke to me is that fiction gives you a truth that reality can't deliver" (www.scottturow.com).

Turow has read widely in the mystery genre, reporting "I've read everybody," and citing as his favorite thriller writers Harlan Coban, Michael Connelly, Dennis Lehane, Robert Park, and Colin Harrison (Macdonald interview, 2004). He reveres English cozy mystery writer Ruth Rendell (who depicts the murderous and violent passions hidden behind the picturesque façade of the quiet English village) and hard-boiled American writer Elmore Leonard, with his Detroit-bred working-class heroes. He has read widely in the legal mystery genre as well but tries not to comment on favorites since many are friends and acquaintances, some of whose books he has reviewed for *Playboy* and *New York Magazine,* among others. Such reading has given him a solid sense of the parameters of both the mystery genre and the legal mystery subgenre and of the degree to which he can vary his repertoire to experiment with additional forms and techniques to provide variety and depth and a broader thematic, dramatic, and intellectual range than found in the genre at its most narrow.

THE LEGAL PROCEDURAL

The legal procedural belongs in the category of detective fiction but is narrower in focus, a subgenre of crime or detective fiction. It concerns itself most specifically with the business of the courts and the legal system, just as a medical mystery concerns itself with crimes involving doctors, hospitals, and the treatment of patients. Turow's legal procedural novels are extensions of the familiar hard-boiled police procedural, which examines the mechanics of law enforcement. Where the traditional detective story features a private detective or a police inspector as investigator and concentrates on the gathering of evidence in order to determine "whodunit," the legal procedural concentrates on the activities of lawyers, whether defense or prosecution, and on the business of the law: the preparation of a legal case, the drama of the courtroom, and the behind-the-scenes activities through which the legal processes are carried out. Its focus on attorneys and the court system may be tempered by insights into the personal and emotional lives of the lawyers and legal staff who deal with the higher reaches of the legal system. There may be police or private detectives involved in the case, but they are usually peripheral to the actions of the judge, the jury, the legal teams, and the points of law, the rules by which justice is dispensed and petitions are filed. The legal procedural can be found in both British and American popular fiction, although, of course, the rules of the court and legal procedures are somewhat different. Such stories are most intriguing when they turn on points of law or challenge readers to rethink the laws and the justice system to better protect the innocent and enable a fairer, more just determination of guilt or innocence.

The English and Scottish Legal Procedural

Historically, the legal procedural has its roots in England in the nineteenth century with novels preoccupied with the law and its processes and featuring lawyers discharging their duties to their clients both in and out of court. Charles Dickens, for example, captured the nightmare intricacies of the law courts at Chancery in *Bleak House* (1852–1853) and the legal obfuscations that took a mental, physical, and monetary toll on all those caught up in the system, including the lawyers (Lady Deadlock's blackmailing solicitor Tulkinghorn is actually murdered). Dickens's powerful imagery of the ominous fog enshrouding all those drawn into the case of Jarndyce versus Jarndyce set the precedent for the dense imagery Turow much later employs to suggest significances beyond a single case or single event. *Bleak House* was the earliest English novel to make the ins and outs of the law (in this case inheritance law) a fictive focus, featuring an elusive and ever busy Inspector Bucket, who investigates the murder of Tulkinghorn and searches for a missing Lady Deadlock. The sketchy and incomplete *The Mystery of Edwin Drood* (1870) laid the groundwork for close-up psychological studies of criminals (in this case John Jasper) and introduced the prototypical family solicitor, a feature of future legal procedurals. Dickens also captured the psychological horrors of prisons, of despairing men in claustrophobic cells. Dickens's novels provided writers interested in crime fiction not only inspiration but also concrete techniques for using the mystery genre conventions to demonstrate the virtues and vices of police procedures, to criticize the court systems, and to develop vivid portraits of individuals caught up in the legal system—for good or for ill.

Wilkie Collins's innovative novel *The Moonstone* (1868), featuring the theft of a stunning and exotic Indian moonstone with a bloody history, employs multiple points of view to guide readers through events. Collins's skill in weaving diverse materials and various plot threads into a convincing study of unexpected truths paved the way for complex different perspectives leading to surprising explanations in modern crime fiction. Furthermore, one of the significant voices in Collins's novel is that of the lawyer, whose perspective is essential to the narrative.

In the twentieth century, many British authors have made legal niceties the heart of their mysteries. A sampling includes

Dorothy Sayer's *Clouds of Witness* (1926), a trial by peers in the House of Lords

Margery Allingham's *Flowers for the Judge* (1936), with its jury inquest

Cyril Hare's 1940s coroner's inquests, circuit judges, and provincial assizes

Agatha Christie's *Witness for the Prosecution* (1948), in which a lying witness turns a jury

Josephine Tey's *The Franchise Affair* (1948), with defiant Robert Blair standing on principle against the community

Anthony Gilbert's 1950s crusading Cockney lawyer Arthur Crook

Edward Grierson's *Reputation for a Song* (1952), in which the presumption of innocence frees the guilty

Sara Woods's 1960s investigating lawyer Antony Maitland, who unravels intriguing puzzles with a trial in progress

Julian Symon's *The Progress of a Crime* (1960), with its grimly realistic legal process

John Mortimer's *Rumpole of the Bailey* (1978), and other novels in which the scruffy, egalitarian Rumpole defends petty criminals with wit and humanity

Sara Caudwell's five barristers and a law professor, all occupied with trust funds and tax planning in *The Shortest Way to Hades* (1985)

Reginald Hill's *Recalled to Life* (1992), in which justice miscarries.

Jury deliberations sometimes take central focus, as they do in Eden Phillpott's *The Jury* (1927), Dorothy Sayer's *Strong Poison* (1930), George Goodchild and C. E. Bechhofer Roberts's *The Jury Disagree* (1934), Raymond Postgate's *Verdict of Twelve* (1940), Donald MacKenzie's *The Juryman*

(1957), John Wainwright's *The Jury People* (1978), Michael Underwood's *Hand of Fate* (1981), and B. M. Gill's *Twelfth Juror* (1984), in which a juror's insider knowledge taints his judgment. Michael Gilbert's *The Queen Against Karl Mullen* (1991) turns on the British system of jury selection. Such writers established a pattern of lawyers crusading for justice; challenging witnesses; questioning evidence; participating in inquests, hearings, and court scenes; and uncovering lying witnesses, manufactured evidence, and corrupt judges. The books study the role of jurors in determining the outcome of a trial, the power of judges to control and manipulate proceedings, the intricacies and loopholes of the law, the strategies of the prosecution and defense attorneys, and the investigative activities of not only the police but also the legal teams as they put together a credible case. John L. Breen's *Novel Verdicts: A Critical Guide to Courtroom Fiction* (1984) provides an overview of some of the top names in British and American courtroom fiction.

The American Legal Procedural

Although the subgenre of the legal procedural began in England, it quickly became popular in America as well. American culture has long been fascinated with lawyers, legal niceties, and the interpretation of religious and civic texts. (Famously, the United States has 10 times the number of lawyers per capita as Japan, and other cultures have a similar impoverishment of attorneys by American standards.) Perhaps one of the reasons for this emphasis on court officers and arguments about legal language lies in America's origins, with the religious values of the Puritans and the attempts of other colonials to shape compromises about the American identity during the Revolution.

The Puritans, as did many Protestants, found their truth in their Good Book, but often refused to defer to human authority in their reading of the Bible. Their priesthood was of competent interpreters, and the habits of exegesis, with its values of close attention to words, to syntax, and to the process of parsing meaning, carried over into secular texts as well. Less religiously driven Americans were also often readers and debaters about texts and language, their disputes fed by the hosts of printers who worked in Philadelphia. At the time of the Revolution, most colonial households supposedly owned at least two books, the Bible and Tom Paine's *Common Sense*, each read with a fine attention to detail.

There was much to argue about in questions of faith and politics, with numerous religions coexisting without government sponsorship and countless competing visions of what the new American identity should be, both in government and in culture. Many of the founding fathers were enthusiastic readers trying to promote a common destiny for their emerging nation, and they had the assurance of critics and explicators, people who value the power of language to shape reality. They read text as the beginning of a process of creating meaning, not as the end. The compromises hammered out in the Declaration of Independence and the Constitution represented an innovative approach to governance, one based on written documents that could in theory be interpreted by any literate citizen.

Later immigrants also found the American identity in texts for their children if not for themselves. Being American meant learning English, a task accomplished very well by the public schools of the nineteenth century. Noah Webster's speller sold 40 million copies, as acquiring literacy in American English became a great leveler for new Americans whose children would have remained unschooled in Europe. As a nation founded on a creed—that is, a set of beliefs epitomized in the Declaration of Independence, the Constitution, and the Bill of Rights—rather than on a common religious or racial identity, it is not surprising that those with the skill to understand texts should be valued and respected. Thus, secular rather than religious exegesis of the law has a special role in American society.

Moreover, the habit of finding the common American identity in texts is an ingrained habit, a consequence of the nation's deep-seated habit of exegesis. Lawyers, explicators by trade, held prominent positions in American life throughout the nineteenth and early twentieth centuries, defining civic obligations and penalties. In frontier areas, literacy was often a privilege of the medical doctor and the village lawyer, the intellectual and civic leaders of many small towns. A depiction of this phenomenon in fiction, one mentioned by Turow as influential on his own conception of the law, is Harper Lee's *To Kill a Mockingbird*. Atticus Finch is not simply a defense lawyer, a technician for hire; rather, he is one of the few in a small community ready to stand for principle, an exemplar of personal courage in the face of community pressure and even personal threats. Who will defend core American values in small towns or isolated areas? Church leaders are often divided by denominations, and the training of doctors is scientific and technical. It falls to lawyers to draw on their understanding of civic issues, the ethics of the social compact. Contemporary real-life American lawyers like the controversial Erin Brockovich and Jan Schlichtmann have played this role.

In the American literary tradition, the first lawyer-detective, Melville Davisson Post's Randolph Mason, was a shyster who used his wits to find loopholes that would help his clients escape legal retribution for their deeds in *The Strange Schemes of Randolph Mason* (1896) and *The Man of Last Resort or, The Clients of Randolph Mason* (1897). According to B. A. Pike in "Legal Procedural," American fictional lawyers in the 1930s were frequently hired to protect the rich from unwelcome police attention, as were Mr. Archer in Leslie Ford's *The Clue of the Judas Tree* (1933), Eldridge Fleel in S. S. Van Dine's *The Kidnap Murder Case* (1936), Chester Begilow in Barnaby Ross's *The Tragedy of Y* (1932), Mortimer Peabody in Rufus King's *The Lesser Antilles Case* (1934), and Judge Ephraim Peck in August Derleth's series (*Oxford Companion*, 261).

In the 1930s and 1940s the most widely read American series was the Erle Stanley Gardner Perry Mason books, beginning with *The Case of the Velvet Claws* (1933) and ending with *The Case of the Postponed Murder* (1973), a 40-year run. Gardner's image of the lawyer dominated both the written and televised genres, with 86 novels (plus five more published posthumously), hundreds of television episodes starring Raymond Burr, and some 26 television movies (from 1985 to 1993). The television depiction expanded on the image in the books, including a defense team of investigators/assistants who regularly tested the limits of the law and courtroom pyrotechnics (rapid-fire cross-examinations; unexpected revelations—often a witness or spectator jumping up to spontaneously reveal the truth—mystery witnesses; spectacular demonstrations; and sudden, last minute, confessions of hatreds, lies, and even guilt). These dramatic events overwhelm the prosecution and, ultimately, expose the truth. The judge in a Mason trial never questions Mason's methods or results, simply banging his gavel to mark a judgment of "sustained" or the end of a case. In *The D.A. Calls It Murder* (1937) Gardner added a sympathetic district attorney, Doug Selby. Although Turow and other modern writers of legal procedurals consciously write in direct opposition to the Perry Mason scheme, the formula persists as a genre staple. Andrew Macdonald's *Beachum Encyclopedia* entry on *"Personal Injuries"* (300) cites a number of American trial novels that follow the Gardner tradition, including C. W. Grafton's *The Rat Began To Gnaw the Rope* (1943), Ellery Queen's *The Glass Village* (1954), Robert Traver's *Anatomy of a Murder* (1958), Al Dewlen's *Twilight of Honor* (1961), William Harrington's *Which the Justice, Which the Thief* (1963), and Robert L. Fish's *A Handy Death* (1973). Traver's *Anatomy of a Murder* is notable for dramatizing the effects of the

Michigan insanity defense, a defense not possible in other states and one the author sought to reform.

Recent years have seen an explosion of American legal mysteries, with authors sometimes specializing in a single aspect of the court experience. For example, some focus on jury selection, jury duty, jury bias, jury tampering/corruption, or jury debate, as do the following: Harvey Jacob's *The Juror* (1980), Parnell Hall's *Juror* (1990), Vincent S. Green's *The Price of Victory* (1992), Steve Martini's *Compelling Evidence* (1992) and *Prime Witness* (1993), William J. Coughlin's *Death Penalty* (1993), and John Grisham's *Runaway Jury* (1996). Some legal mysteries feature biased judges like the one in Barry Reed's *The Verdict* (1980). In fact, in keeping with this tradition, the judge in Turow's *Presumed Innocent* (1987) has not recused himself despite a close personal relationship with the victim, and the speed with which he censures deviations from accepted protocol is in fact a cover up of his own involvement with the victim. Other popular authors of legal procedurals include Clifford Irving (*Final Argument*, 1993, a Florida death row argument, with prosecutor error at fault), Brad Meltzer (*The First Counsel*, 2001, on a White House lawyer), Philip Friedman (*Grand Jury*, 1996, on a grand jury investigation of a drug conspiracy in Chinatown), and John Lescroart (*Nothing But the Truth*, 1999, on a grand jury murder investigation), among so many others.

THE (PERRY) MASONIC MYTH: THE ATTORNEY AS JUSTICE DISPENSER

The lawyer television series *Perry Mason*, based on California attorney Erle Stanley Gardner's series of over 90 novels about his eponymous Los Angeles attorney, was on the air from 1957 to 1976. It still survives on cable television rerun channels such as Court TV and the Hallmark Movie channel. As a cultural touchstone, its conventions and general outlines of plot and character are familiar to viewers far too young to have seen the original broadcast versions or to have listened to Gardner's popular 1940s radio series. The Perry Mason series is significant for a number of reasons beyond its longevity and romanticizing of lawyers. Gardner systematically conflated the lawyer story with the detective story, creating a new genre that still thrives in the twenty-first century and often redefines the role of the fictional attorney. Gardner moved the professional legal advocate from an officer of the court, an important but still subsidiary figure in the drama whose central characters were the judge and jury, to center stage as the activist master of ceremonies, a lion tamer (or a Prospero) who takes control of a dangerous situation and imposes order much as fictional investigators and detectives have always done.

Whereas lawyers have traditionally, and accurately, been associated with legal scholarship and libraries (employing scriveners and now copy machines), dusty offices, and the minutiae of esoteric judicial procedure, the detective figure in prose and on screen is an activist, a man (the Mason-style lawyer-detective is almost always male) street-savvy about criminal behavior and haunts, one adapted to surviving in the underworld. This street-toughness is particularly true of the American hard-boiled detective—a tough, working-class character epitomized in the writing of Raymond Chandler, Dashiell Hammett, and Mickey Spillane—a solitary warrior for rough justice that verges on vigilantism. Hundreds of American hard-boiled detectives have operated in print and on screen, creating in the popular imagination myths of how the lower spectrum of the justice system works, with the full force of popular literature and film shaping even the self-images of practitioners of the investigative and policing trades depicted. (Real cops have famously been ardent consumers of police fiction on theater and television screens, from *The French Connection* to *Law & Order,* sometimes even admitting how art has driven their own behavior.) Attorney-author Gardner's contribution was to create an upscale version of the detective story by combining it with courtroom drama, sanitizing some of its less-appetizing elements and providing order through selected judicial rituals, but retaining some investigative elements. In effect, Gardner "opened up" the courtroom and law office.

The Mason series on television, even more than the books or radio shows, had enormous influence. Any successful long-running series allows the consumer of popular culture an opportunity to get to know characters and prototypical plots with an intimacy no single novel, film, or television special can provide. The recurrence of character and plot pattern allows growth and variation, creating an experience directly analogous to our encounters with friends and acquaintances, leading to a sense of realism often different in quality from that achieved by even ultra-realistic single works of film or text. It is common knowledge that characters in soap operas and other recurring works draw stalkers and other obsessives who cannot distinguish between fact and fiction, but such pathological cases are only extreme versions of a much more common phenomenon. The predictable presence of series characters creates a solidity that we associate with real life rather than fiction. Thus, the 271 television episodes of *Perry Mason* have had a power far exceeding their technical worth or quality as storytelling. They have shaped and defined how many Americans think about the law, lawyers, and the justice system in general.

Mason's defense practice bears only a tangential relationship to that of a real law office. While his clients come to his office and are interviewed and deposed by Mason and his vibrant and wonderfully named secretary/assistant Della Street, readers also get to know a regular cast of characters who exist in opposition to the defense, especially prosecutor Hamilton (Ham) Burger and his various police minions. Mason's private investigator Paul Fleming is the opposite number to the prosecution's constabulary, but he bears little relationship to the hard-boiled Mike Hammers, Sam Spades, and Philip Marlowes also operating the mean streets of fictional U.S. naked cities. While Gardner's Mason stories reel in both police and private eyes to circle Mason as satellites, they also spruce up the tone of affairs considerably, avoiding violence entirely or stylizing the shootings and fisticuffs into bloodless ballet, lifting the level of language from the vulgarities of the street to the niceties of the court, and broadening the role of defense attorney to include investigation, manipulation and coordination of events, and sometimes the identification of the true miscreants. This new genre of lawyer-as-private-investigator has inspired countless imitators and some fascinating distortions of the justice system as depicted by popular culture.

In keeping with the Perry Mason model, legal thrillers turn the lawyer, or the lawyer's assistants, into an investigator/detective or detective team uncovering whodunit. Typical is Lisa Scottoline's *Moment of Truth*, which includes no major trial scene, but instead has its lawyer heroine Mary DiNunzio investigate her client's innocence. *Wall Street Journal* reviewer Cameron Stracher, in "Taste: The Case of the Legal Thriller—The Law Is Dull; So Why Are These Books Popular? A Cross-Examination" (W13), finds legal thrillers like those of John Grisham and Lisa Scottoline shifting the burden of proof and suggesting that truth is the best defense (while real practicing lawyers understand that truth is often the least effective defense). If the lawyer is also an investigator, then she or he will inevitably face physical peril, a thriller genre convention which any sensible real lawyer seeks to avoid, but which made the Mason series so effective. Thus, Grisham's Mitch McDeere (*The Firm*) tackles the mob head on, while Scottoline's DiNunzio takes a bullet for her client. Another genre convention that has grown out of the Mason series, says Stracher, is the idea of lawyers in thrillers outwitting criminal masterminds or out-thinking police detectives. Then, too, a convention most writers of legal thrillers have adopted to add a sense of realism to a genre that has, through Mason's television influence, become stylized and unrealistic, is the authors' claims of real-life experience to certify the authenticity of their fiction, noting number of years spent as trial lawyers, judges, legal investigators, or (as in Turow's case) a U.S. district attorney.

THE MESSAGE STORY

In contrast to the plot-driven Perry Mason model of the legal procedural is another type of story entirely, one intended to force readers to rethink serious issues, to confront the implications of and discrepancies in our laws, and to promote reforms. The message-driven legal procedural aggressively confronts legal issues much in the public eye, such as the Supreme Court *Roe vs. Wade* abortion decision and various states' capital punishment laws. The legal pattern of determining right and wrong by reducing morality to simple black-and-white questions leads to interesting dilemmas and raises fair questions about human complicity, behavior, and responsibility.

Roe vs. Wade

Typical of these message-driven works is Harvard Law School graduate and California civil rights lawyer Stanley Pottinger's first novel, *The Fourth Procedure* (1995). The book combines medical suspense with legal conflict in a speculative story of how new medical procedures might be used to protect the *Roe vs. Wade* decision from reversal by an anti-abortion Supreme Court. Although it is not fully credible, it is clearly message driven. Therein, an outspoken feminist surgeon transplants the complete uterus and living fetus of a female volunteer into the abdomen of an overweight, zealous, anti-abortionist male who is soon to be sworn in as a new Supreme Court Justice, one who will have the swing vote in attempts to overturn *Roe vs. Wade,* the court ruling that made abortions legal. The surgeon has attempted to do so before with three other men active in destroying abortion clinics, doctors, and other personnel. The judge is in her care for a kidney problem that she has corrected with a viable transplant, but she goes beyond the legal limits of her medical power when she turns him into a mother-to-be. When the surgeon is finally arrested and on trial for her life (three men have died under her knife for a variety of medical reasons), she acts as her own defense lawyer, and Pottinger puts into her mouth a strong feminist argument that is obviously the heart of his novel and the civil rights message it carries. Asking what the all-male jury would do if forced to bear children against their will, to carry to term a child that is the product of rape, or to simply turn over to the courts, the church, or even some other individual the right to decide what could or could not be done to their bodies, she answers that their response to oppression historically has been to fight back aggressively, from the American Revolution to the Civil War, to the World Wars: "if you lost the most basic freedom of them all—the right to your own body—is there any doubt what you would do? I don't think so" (520). She defends her surgical transplants as viable attempts to help men understand a woman's perspective on the abortion issue. Her summation speech to the jury is high rhetoric, first suggesting the motives that might have driven other women to similar acts and then ending with her own motives:

> I was not raped by a madman. I was not spit upon or cursed for entering a church while menstruating. I was not held down while old women cut off my clitoris. My vagina has never been sewn shut or ripped open. I was not forced to burn myself to death on the funeral pyre of a dead husband. I was not drowned in the Yangtze River because I was born without a penis. I was not sold into a harem in Khartoum. I was not stoned for touching the Torah. My throat was not slashed for sleeping with a man not my husband. I have never been beaten by a pimp. I was not held prisoner in a closet for seven years. I was never made to bless the size of a whip before my husband beat me with it. I was not dismembered with a chain saw. I was not stabbed to death by Richard Speck. (522)

Her list of atrocities she has avoided (but obviously others have not—worldwide) continues for five more paragraphs, with the acts committed against women growing closer and closer to home: " I was not fired because I refused to give sexual favors to a boss. I was not rejected from medical school, or excluded from a club I wished to join, or deprived of the chairmanship of my department, or denied the Medal of Freedom. I was never forced to sew buttons on a man's shirt. I was not even sent to my room for conduct unbecoming a lady" (524). Her conclusion is that she acted because any such heinous acts might have happened to her, as they happened to others, and because, at age six, she watched her mother "die on an abortionist's table." "Although I didn't know it at the time," she notes, "that was the moment I crossed over from your rules to mine" (524).

In creating a strong female character, who, in terms of the detective story, is the killer everyone seeks, and yet in giving her so strong a voice in court and a cool, reasoned assessment of motive during her final defense speech, Pottinger makes the voices of the court and the final legal decision dramatize his message about the inadequacies of the law in this legal and civic territory and the need for female voices to challenge laws born of male-centered perspectives that deny to women the basic freedoms that men take for granted.

Another interesting abortion message novel using the courtroom as a vehicle is Howard Fast's *The Trial of Abigail Goodman: A Novel* (1993). Like Pottinger's *The Fourth Procedure*, which is built around the idea, "If men could get pregnant, abortion would never be illegal," *Abigail Goodman* is short on credibility but long on provocativeness, imagining as its premise the equally unlikely possibility that abortion could be prosecuted as murder, a crime equal to a street shooting. An unnamed southern state has taken the "abortion is murder" argument completely literally, and the centerpiece of the book is the trial of Abigail Goodman, a 41-year-old mother of three and a college professor, under a new law that makes abortion punishable retroactively as a capital offense. The trial includes as star witnesses for the prosecution a Catholic bishop, a Hasidic rabbi, and an obstetrician now opposed to abortion. The vehicle of the trial allows a fervent debate difficult to imagine anywhere else.

Fast's point, of course, is that, rhetoric aside, only assassins of abortion doctors really take the "abortion is murder" argument literally, acting with violence to stop what they see as premeditated homicide. Everyone else, even people sincerely and forcefully opposed to the procedure, mentally classify it quite differently from murder. The context of a trial makes Fast's readers consider just how people of varying ideological stripes really do define abortion.

Death Row Novels

Death row stories date back to the origins of the crime novel, to the works of William Godwin (*Caleb Williams,* 1794, wherein Williams discovers evidence of a murderer guilty of a crime for which another man was hanged), Edward George Earl Bulwer-Lytton (*Zanoni,* 1842, in which the hero goes to the guillotine in place of the heroine), and lawyer Honoré de Balzac (*Un Drame dans les prisons,* 1847). These novels examine crime within the broader context of the human comedy. For these early writers, stories about crime were a form of radical social protest, combining, as George Woodcock points out of Godwin in *Twentieth-Century Crime and*

Mystery Writers, "moral complexity, political lessons, and much suspenseful excitement" (1528). For them, the criminal was a victim of social injustice. They assumed that society was cruel and unjust, especially in its treatment of the underprivileged, the lower class, and the down-and-out; they also assumed a corrupt or ignorant judiciary. Balzac drew on the character of Eugene François Vildocq, a redoubtable former convict and multiple escapee turned policeman in charge of organizing the Paris brigade de Sureté, for his own Vautrin in *La comédie humaine* (1842–1848), translated as *Comedy of Human Life* (1887–1896). His novels and stories feature the loss of a legal identity (*Le Colonel Chabert,* 1832), disputed legacies (*Le Cousin Pons,* 1846–1847), marriage settlements (*Le Contrat de mariage,* 1835), petitions in lunacy (*L'Interdiction,* 1836), and bankruptcy proceedings (*César Birotteau,* 1837; *Illusions perdues,* 1837–1843). Some critics have found affinities between the works of Scott Turow and those of Balzac in particular, but Turow, though flattered, finds this a reach, saying that Balzac's impact, like Tolstoy's, has been so large on so many that "it is in the soil by now; all realist writers are in his debt" (Macdonald interview, 2004).

A classic of the death row genre is George Orwell's short essay "A Hanging" (1945), which depicts an East Indian prisoner of the colonial British as a pathetic victim, a tool of larger forces. He, among others, has been convicted of some crime or another and locked away in a cage of prisoners, all Burmese, awaiting the moment of execution. For Orwell, who had served as a military police officer in Burma from 1922 to 1927, the crime is not the issue, nor is the question of guilt or innocence. The man committed some crime whose penalty under the law was death by hanging, he was convicted, and quite possibly was guilty, though as readers we never find this out. Instead, Orwell captures the dichotomy between the British legal procedure and justice, for in Burma, British justice was basically a vehicle by which the colonialist state imposed its will on a subject people. Orwell purposely describes the prisoner and his situation with animal imagery to establish the British point of view: the natives are less than human. He begins by describing the condemned cells as "a row of sheds fronted with double bars, like small animal cages" to suggest the distance in treatment from the human/humane. Later, he has the six warders handle the prisoner with "a careful, caressing grip" as though he were "a fish which is still alive and may jump back into the water." The warders, keeping a psychological distance from him, equate the prisoner with a slippery subspecies of life. Not until paragraph 10 does the narrator speak of the condemned prisoner as a fellow human being, one who steps aside to avoid a puddle even as he marches to his death. The early animal images prepare the reader to share in the narrator's wonder at discovering the prisoner's humanity. Orwell hopes the images and emotions he relates will move the reader to understand, along with his narrator, the tragedy of destroying "a healthy, conscious man," "the unspeakable wrongness of cutting a life short when it is full tide."

Truman Capote's *In Cold Blood: A True Account of a Multiple Murder and Its Consequences* (1967) also argues the wrongness of capital punishment, but in a very different way. It employs a documentary style narrative that provides a sense of distance and objectivity to tell the story of two murderers, who, on a November night in 1959 killed a wealthy Kansas farmer, his wife, and their two teenage children. The two young murderers admitted the crime and were eventually hanged for it. Capote spent six years researching and writing his study of their acts and motivations to raise questions about the justice of capital punishment. He juxtaposes and dovetails the lives and values of the victimized Clutter family and those of the killers, Perry Smith and Dick Hickock, to produce a stark image of the deep duality of American life. He poses questions of social justice with his focus on the murderers coming from the lower classes of society, with Perry Smith in particular having been abused and neglected, the product of a broken, violent home of suicides and alcoholism. However, Capote's focus is also on the inadequacies of the justice system, as his description of Perry Smith in prison confirms:

> In the disposition of capital cases in the United States, the median elapsed time between sentence and execution is approximately seventeen months. Recently, in Texas, an armed robber was electrocuted one month after his conviction; but in Louisiana . . . two rapists have been waiting for a record twelve years. The variance depends a little on luck and a great deal on the extent of litigation. . . . even an attorney of moderate talent can postpone doomsday year after year, for the system of appeals that pervades American jurisprudence amounts to a legalistic wheel of fortune, . . . somewhat fixed in the favor of the criminal, that the participants play interminably, first in the state courts, then through the Federal courts until the ultimate tribunal is reached—the United States Supreme Court. But even defeat there does not signify if petitioner's counsel can discover or invent new grounds for appeal; usually they can, and so once more the wheel turns, and turns until, perhaps some years later, the prisoner arrives back at the nation's high-

est court, probably only to begin again the slow cruel contest. But at intervals the wheel does pause to declare a winner—or, though with increasing rarity, a loser: Smith's lawyers fought to the final moment, but their client went to the gallows on Friday, November 30, 1962. (359)

Thereby Capote makes his crime novel not just the study of two confirmed killers but an indictment of the American system of justice.

More than four decades after *In Cold Blood*, the issue still generates anti–death penalty books focusing on the crime and its consequences. A contemporary death penalty book was written by Sister Helen Prejean, famous for her opposition to capital punishment and a regular guest on talk shows, arguing against the death penalty. She worked in the St. Thomas housing project in New Orleans and became so entangled in the lives of death row prisoners that she felt compelled to write *Dead Man Walking* (1996). The book is the result of her visits to two death row inmates at the Louisiana State Penitentiary where she serves as a spiritual advisor. Although she documents the inequalities of the judicial system that has condemned these men, her main point is that a society that carries out this extreme punishment should, itself, be perfect. This anti–death penalty work, while not shying away from the horror of murders, shows the killer as a human being and argues against his execution on the basis of common humanity.

When director and screenwriter Tim Robbins decided to make the book into a film, he purposefully and carefully made the film more balanced than the book. He, Susan Sarandon (the actress who plays Prejean in the film), and Prejean all oppose the death penalty, but they agreed to balance the arguments and emotions on opposing sides of a profoundly troubling issue. Prejean worked daily with Robbins on the script and together they made it into a complicated study of the death penalty. The killer, Matthew Poncelet, is a composite based on two real-life death row residents whom Prejean counseled, Robert Lee Willie and Elmo Patrick Sonnier, the latter a convicted killer of two rural teenage lovers, the former the killer of a young woman. Robbins told reporters, "I don't have any romanticized notion of criminals. I wanted to show Poncelet for what he was—a real badass, a mean person, and almost unredeemable" (Grundmann, 8). He makes Prejean's Sonnier character much more contemptible than she does in her book because he felt it was absolutely essential that the person be guilty and not particularly likable. He did not want to do a typical Hollywood treatment of a probably innocent nice guy. Robbins shot his film on death row at the Louisiana State Penitentiary in Angola, with Sean Penn playing Poncelet.

Turow's *Reversible Errors* is a product of the death row debate and takes a lawyerly approach to an emotionally charged issue. If the defendant says, "I'm not guilty," and maintains that innocence until the very end, the lawyers present the case for each side and the jury finds the facts. However, Turow says, "all they're doing is making educated guesses," because "you know beyond a reasonable doubt, but you don't know beyond any doubt at all that that's what really occurred" (www.scott turow.com). Turow's reservation is similar to Prejean's point about society being less than perfect. It is in this territory of doubt that the legal thriller writer can deal with significant questions of justice and social truths. In *Reversible Errors*, the defendant, an innocent but illiterate man, confesses out of confusion and embarrassment about an irrelevant personal matter, and when he finally asserts his innocence, no one believes him, and the police and prosecution have strong personal reasons to have him executed.

FICTIONAL LAWYERS IN THE NEW MILLENNIUM

A number of writers compete with Turow for an audience of readers interested in legal thrillers. These include, among many others, John Grisham *(The Firm, The Partner, The Client)*, Lisa Scottoline *(Final Appeal, Legal Tender, Moment of Truth)*, David Baldacci *(The Absolute Truth, The Simple Truth)*, Steve Martini *(The Attorney)*, John Martel *(The Alternate)*, George Green *(The Juror)*, David Guterson *(Snow Falling on Cedars)*, and Nancy Taylor Rosenberg, whose *Mitigating Circumstances* (1993) came out the same year as Turow's *Personal Injuries* and is mentioned positively in Turow's book. (John Grisham, too, receives a nod in Turow's Hotel Gresham, "a towering space constructed in the Gilded Age" in *The Law of Our Fathers* [333].) These are just a few of the many writers who turn out legal thrillers on a regular basis. *Wall Street Journal* reviewer Cameron Stracher in "Taste" asks how legal procedurals could have become so popular, given the fact that "the law itself is about as thrilling as the Internal Revenue Code, that lawyers are among the unhappiest of professionals, and that copying machines play a major supporting role in most litigation" (W13). Her answer is limited: mainly, they have the appeal of fast reads with "courtroom derring-do" in the Perry Mason tradition, but they occasionally lack legal realism. Stracher finds only a few writers of legal fiction striving for greater realism, deeper characterization, and legal reform, but she points to two effective works by non-lawyers who demonstrate the moral depth possible in the genre: Chris Bohjalian's short story "Midwives," about a midwife accused of murder, and Jonathan Harr's *A Civil Action*, a nonfiction account of a lawsuit filed by citizens of Woburn, Massachusetts, against W. R. Grace and Beatrice Foods, alleging that trichloroethylene dumping at sites owned by the companies contaminated two town wells and caused leukemia in local children.

Scott Turow's *Presumed Innocent* (1987) began this deluge of lawyer novels. The popularity of the law thriller he virtually invented may be as significant a cultural indicator as the dominance of the earlier popular genres of the cowboy/Western and the detective/police procedural. If the enthusiasms in entertainment of a culture are self-revelatory, as they surely are, readers might well ask what has happened to bring lawyers to the fore at the end of the twentieth century and the beginning of the twenty-first. True, people in the United States employ the services of legal professionals on a high per-capita basis, but what, beyond an enthusiasm for courtroom combat and a great deal of linguistic wrangling over agreements and contracts, does this plethora of advocates reveal about us at the start of the new millennium?

Verlyn Klinkenborg, in a March 14, 1994, *New Republic* review of Turow's *Pleading Guilty*, writes an extended, thoughtful analysis of current American attitudes toward the law. He points out that the ideal of the "lawyer-statesman . . . like Earl Warren or Daniel Webster or Abraham Lincoln" (33) is countered by the modern reality of hired guns like Joseph Flom, of Skadden, Orps, Slate, Meagher and Flom, whose ethic is simply the profit motive (Klinkenborg quotes Flom's response to being called a sewer rat: "I can live with that," 33). This disconnect between the idealized lawyers of the past and the pragmatic self-interest of many present-day practitioners has a number of causes. One is growth: from 296,000 lawyers in 1965 to 800,000 in 1990, 4 times the population growth, with the ratio of representation per capita shifting from 1 in 600 to 1 in 350, a growth pattern that has continued into the 2000s (all Klinkenborg quotes are from the *New Republic* Web site, www.tnr.com). Klinkenborg aptly concludes, "No profession experiences this kind of growth without losing a sense of itself, without seeing its traditional values opened up for examination." In response to this growth, large law firms have sprung up, some employing over 1,000 lawyers, mirroring the expansion and dominance of corporate organization in all aspects of American culture from the 1950s on. Growth of law practices also led to specialization, the decline of the generalist lawyer as large law firms obeyed the logic of rationalized corporate organization. Legal education naturally responded to the legal marketplace, creating a multiplicity of new specialties and subspecialties such as environmental law, entertainment law, and immigration law, and by adopting a case-study approach in which students read court opinions and then argue each side so they can defend any and all positions, irrespective of their moral legitimacy. Turow himself argues this point more fully in *One L:* "Legal thinking is nasty . . . you believed nothing . . . and to preserve long-established rules . . . would accept the most ridiculous fictions—that a corporation was a person" (75–76). The charge is not new; Plato condemned the Sophists of ancient Greece for teaching the technical skills of rhetoric while ignoring the uses to which the argumentation would be put.

Yet the growth in the number of lawyers and their power and prestige probably reveals less about the legal community and more about the decline of other authoritative institutions in U.S. society in the last three or four decades of the twentieth century. Watergate, the Pentagon Papers, the prevarication about the Vietnam War, the assassinations of such idealistic leaders as the Kennedys and Martin Luther King, Jr.—all the usual suspects can be rounded up and charged with causing the general distrust of government and the decline in faith that afflicted all institutions during this period. Even religious faith shifted toward the personal, with fundamentalist and charismatic movements growing and trust in orthodox organizations declining. On the western frontier, the absence of trustworthy organizations led to the hiring of gunfighters, and a similar phenomenon may be at work today. Whereas before Americans might have sought justice or arbitration from local government leaders, churchmen, or corporate leaders, now they flip through the yellow pages to the burgeoning "attorneys" section. Such specialists know the rules and the lingo and can thus protect an individual's interests in a world that is increasingly technical and complex and basically untrustworthy.

The resulting problem, of course, is that hired guns are not only hard to love, but they might be aiming their weapons at their former employers in the next case. As Klinkenborg points out, the legal thriller genre has an "uneasiness about the anthill quality of large law practices" (4), which can drag us with a lawsuit into the maws of the social contract, a limiting agreement we do our best to ignore most of the time. Perhaps as with Congress and local government, Americans treasure an advocate who looks out for an individual client's interests but scorn the institution as a whole. Like the spy and detective novels from which legal thrillers derived, suggests Klinkenborg, the genre celebrates the power of the dedi-cated individual against the corporate masses. Paul Newman as the drunken Boston lawyer in *The Verdict* (1982) finds redemption by acting as the lone advocate for a deserving victim of a medical malpractice suit against a large corporation. John Grisham's works also show this phe-nomenon at work, and the John Travolta film of the nonfiction work *A Civil Action* is another excellent example of myth-making at work: the complexities of the real, nonfictional case are trimmed and cut to make Travolta's attorney into an urban version of *Shane*. The text of *A Civil Action* makes legal investigation exciting, but at the same time carries a highly effective message about the difficulty of making large companies pay for the damage they do to the environment and to communities (par-ticularly to the health of children) through illegal dumping practices.

For all that Americans long for the perhaps mythical lawyer-statesman of the past, we are as a culture certainly aware of the dangers in having multiplying numbers of interpreters of texts among us, exegetes uncom-mitted to any particular philosophy or social ethic apart from the weak-ening constraints of bar association rules and state regulations. The freedom to advertise opened the gates to the more vulgar of hucksters and forced attention on the driving force of the profit motive. Klinkenborg convincingly argues that Americans are perplexed by lawyers, believing the law noble but lawyers debased. Certainly, the number of lawyer jokes on the Internet suggests the truth of this view. However, it may be more accurate to say that most people see other people's lawyers as debased and see their own lawyers as saviors, though saviors to be handled warily. Author Howard Fast tells the story of being called before the House Un-American Activities Committee for having Communist sympathies. Fast fulminated noisily about the government's lawyer: "He's a son-of-a-bitch, nothing but a son-of-a-bitch." Fast's defense lawyer finally had enough, saying, "Howard, you hate him because he's *their* son-of-a-bitch, but I'm *your* son-of-a-bitch" (*Howard Fast*, 19).

The growth of lawyers and lawyering in this country and the moral issues raised by the behavior of corporate legal firms has helped create an audience for an ideal medium through which modern writers can grap-ple with the significant moral, ethical, and political issues of our day: the legal mystery. This form, like the Cold War spy novel, lends itself well to the exploration of clashing philosophies and to the place of individuals in organizations indifferent to or destructive of what the main characters, the little people of the story, hold dear.

TUROW'S EXPERIMENTAL MIXES

In order to lend his writing greater depth, strengthen the force of his themes, and add a complexity of the sort reviewer Cameron Stracher wishes for in modern legal fiction, Turow extends the genre to create an experimental mélange of patterns, conventions, and forms. Unlike that of most of his predecessors in legal fiction and of his contemporary competitors, Turow's legal fiction conflates genres, creating a mix of conventions to enrich his works and lend them greater depth of characterization and of social applications. In keeping with his strong literary foundation, this mix includes both modern and historical forms.

Typical is the combination in *Pleading Guilty* (1993). It is nominally legal fiction, a thriller that focuses on the activities of members of a large legal firm and their response to a crime involving one of their members. However, it also draws heavily on the conventions of both the hard-boiled detective story in the attitudes and methods of its central character and of the police procedural in its focus on action taken in chronological order as the investigation progresses. Within the context of these genres, the protagonist's escape at the end is most disturbing, until one realizes that Turow also draws on the conventions of the spy novel, and the final action is in keeping with the amorality of the spy-pawn betrayed by his own organization after putting his life on the line. Unexpectedly, too, Turow draws on the conventions of the epistolary novel to complicate readers' understanding of the main character and of the events in which he is engaged—the entire novel is supposedly a taped "report." The complexity and the resultant intellectual depth produced by such overlapping of genres make Laura Lippman of the *Baltimore Sun* place Turow's works closer in spirit to those of John le Carré than those of John Grisham, who reduces legal complexities to a simple story everyone can follow. In like manner, *The Laws of Our Fathers* combines the reunion story of modern drama (the film *The Big Chill* is a defining example) with the film convention of ghetto stories, a slice-of-life subgenre showing the underclass struggling to survive against the white establishment (John Singleton's *Boyz N the Hood* is an example); it also brings together the headline murder trial whose participants bridge generations with a poignant, nostalgic study of family and friends, lost ideals, and values betrayed. This mix is an unlikely combination, but Turow erases the seams between the genres and conventions, making his story both credible and engaging.

Through these means Turow goes beyond the literary heritage of crime, mystery, and legal fiction to infuse his legal stories with a breadth of vision and a depth of characterization that places him in a long tradition of serious literary social critics from Jane Austen and Honoré de Balzac to Theodore Dreiser. As a writer, Turow has refused to be compartmentalized by his success. By drawing on a wide variety of storytelling conventions and genres, including those of film and drama, he brings together characters and values in collision and thereby carries on a serious debate about modern issues and a study of individual responses to the normal setbacks of the human condition. His novels encompass the human comedy—exploring social manners and social behavior, raising questions of political and social justice, defining the place of the beleaguered individual in corporate America. One sees in them the disparate literary influences that make the whole—the flair for striking descriptive satiric detail of Charles Dickens, the comedy of manners and social satire of Jane Austen, the broad social vision of Honoré de Balzac, the driving social realism of Theodore Dreiser, the self-irony and family portraiture of Saul Bellow.

3

Presumed Innocent (1987)

Presumed Innocent was a blockbuster novel, one that received enormous attention even before its publication when a number of companies bid for its publication rights. Reviewers repeatedly described the novel as "absorbing," "suspenseful," "compelling," "stunning," "full of shocking betrayals," and said it plumbed the hidden depths of the human heart and of consuming human obsession. Fellow attorney and crime novelist George V. Higgins praised *Presumed Innocent* as a "beautifully crafted tale," finding it so "packed with data, rich in incident, painstakingly imagined" that "it snags both of your lapels and presses you down in your chair until you've finished it" (*Chicago Tribune*, 1987). Toronto *Globe and Mail* correspondent H. J. Kirchhoff found it "surprisingly assured" for an author's first published novel, adding, "The prose is crisp and polished, every character is distinct and fully realized, and the dialogue is authentic" (1987). He goes on to say, "Turow has blended his experience in the rough-and-tumble of the criminal courts with a sympathetic eye for the vagaries of the human condition and an intimate understanding of the dark side of the human soul." Jeff Shear of the *New York Times Magazine* concludes that the criminal justice system *Presumed Innocent* portrays, "without tears or pretense, has seldom appeared in literature quite like this" (June 7, 1987). *Contemporary Authors* observes that it will "hold" and "haunt" readers long after its "shattering" conclusion.

KINDLE COUNTY

In *Presumed Innocent* Turow creates a fictitious county through which he can explore the type of municipal and judicial corruption with which he had been dealing in his real workplace. Turow's Web site (www. scottturow.com) explains the logic behind this decision: the desire not to get stuck with a geography he could not alter and the general "hokey"-ness of "novels set in real places, involving fictionalized historical events." Turow concludes that he would "rather make the fictional cut at the first level" and admit that "this is a nonexistent place . . . [and] nonexistent people," so that readers can move on to agree about how true-to-life the story is rather than argue about the accuracy of the setting. Kindle County frees him from particular details, like remembering whether a particular downtown street is one way or whether it runs north or south. Turow admits that he fell into Kindle County with *Presumed Innocent*. At one point his model for this fictitious setting was Boston, familiar to Turow because of law school, but he later drew more on his own Chicago. Since Chicago in many ways epitomizes the tough, direct midwestern spirit, Turow has it both ways, reflecting the essence of the authentic city and region in a more provincial tri-city "county" described as hundreds of miles from the Windy City.

Kindle County is a highly detailed creation. A lovingly particularized map by Robert Clyde Anderson appears inside the front and back covers of the Farrar, Straus and Giroux hardback edition of *Personal Injuries*. This illustration depicts a far-flung metropolitan area of the American midwestern kind, several middle-sized cities or series of interlocking towns strung along an extended "S" curve of the Kindle River, with farms still operating not far from the city center and with low hills looming on the northwestern horizon. One million people inhabit the central area, with another two million in the county area.

The Burden of Proof provides the origin of the name Kindle in an interlude in which Sandy Stern contemplates the river from his office windows in Morgan Towers, the city's tallest building. When he looks down at the Kindle River, with its tributary connections to the mighty Mississippi, he thinks of the immigrant history of his region: the river first named *La Chandelle* (the candle) by the French trader Jean-Baptiste DuSable, who had come upriver from New Orleans to what eventually became DuSable's trading post. Later, the bend in the river became home to the nearby towns of Moreland, settled by the English, and Kewahnee, once an Indian encampment, and finally the modern hodgepodge megalopolis whose citizens came from every corner of the globe (46–47). In various books, Turow often notes the shining brightness of this river and the English mangling of the French word for candle into the present day Kindle. The French influence remains in DuSable, the largest town in the area, a metropolis boasting half a dozen modern skyscrapers, including the headquarters of TransNational Airline, a significant corporation in *Pleading Guilty* and *Reversible Errors*. The city was named after the trader/explorer DuSable, who was later discovered to be black, much to the chagrin of modern city fathers hoping for a romantic European explorer to give their midwestern city Gallic cachet. Turow dryly notes the loss of interest in New Orleanian DuSable after the discovery of his race.

Kewahnee, the second largest town of the tri-city area and home to the older industrial section and river docks, took its name from a Native American settlement on the river. Two bridges span the Kindle at Kewahnee, using for their midpoint an island in the river, home of the public forest where Leon is arrested in *Presumed Innocent*. One of the bridges leads to the third of the tri-cities, Moreland, and its nearby suburb Riverside, on the west side of the river from DuSable. The Callison Street Bridge, in Anderson's illustration a suspension bridge vaguely reminiscent of a small Brooklyn Bridge, leads to the west bank and Lake Fowler, on whose shores lies Greenwood County Club. Nearby is Easton University in its lush verdant setting, just 30 minutes or so from DuSable. Easton is the alma mater of Sandy and Clara Stern, as well as a number of privileged law folk in the books.

Anderson's meticulous map even includes an inset of Rudyard State Penitentiary, where Rommy Gandolph is incarcerated and Arthur Raven and Gillian Sullivan of *Reversible Errors* visit him. DuSable buildings depicted that figure in Turow's works include the Central Branch and Federal Courthouse, the Kindle County Building, the New Federal Building, River National Bank, the Kindle County Jail, McGrath Hall (police headquarters), the Grace Street Projects, the LeSueur Building, and many other names readers will recognize. The railroad lines that stretch from downtown to beyond the university are dug out and "gathered over the belly of the city like a large and tangible scar" (65). The Kindle County Building is a "solid red-brick block dressed up with a few Doric columns," and the Office of the Kindle County Prosecuting Attorney, inside, is characterized by "Dickensian grimness" (19).

Just as a griffin or some other imaginary beast combines parts of real animals into a mythic creature, so this invented city combines authentic features from any number of midwestern cities—for example, Pittsburgh's bridges and Minneapolis–St. Paul's twin downtowns. Kindle County stands in for the prototypical midwestern urban center, and as such its central metropolis could be anywhere from Cincinnati to Kansas City. Turow says, "It has a little bit of everywhere in it. And I got there by accident. But it works well for me" (Macdonald interview, 2004).

Consequently, any number of midwestern, northern, and prairie cities have stood in for Kindle County on film, including Detroit *(Presumed Innocent)*, Kansas City *(The Burden of Proof)*, and Halifax, Nova Scotia *(Reversible Errors)*. Kindle County, of course, echoes the climate, physical setting, cityscape, and ambience of Turow's home city, Chicago, without holding a mirror up to the real place. Actor Bill Macy, amused at the idea of Halifax as Chicago in *Reversible Errors*, joked with Turow, "Boy, Halifax sure does look like Chicago, and every time I look at Tom Selleck I thought to myself, 'Boy, does he look like Eisenhower'" (Macdonald interview, 2004). Turow finds such humor "wry" and very much in keeping with his own sensibility. The point is that Kindle County is as much a state of mind as a particular place. However, Turow is a meteorological determinist in that the midwestern winters he describes shape the character and outlook of his characters. In this regard, Turow comments, "The cold weather drives people inward. Generally speaking there's a lot in my books about the way the midwestern sky looks. In one book I say it feels like a pot lid over you. It has a lot to do with character in this part of the country. The lack of sunlight in winter just makes you unhappy. I feel better in summer" (Macdonald interview, 2004). In the main, however, his characters trudge through the miseries of winter.

Of further literary interest is the pleasure readers often find in this imaginary city, recognizing places and people from book to book with the thrill of recognition. This delight is quite different from the experience of readers puzzling out the routes taken by characters down authentic streets in, say, Ernest Hemingway's Paris of *The Sun Also Rises* or Raymond Chandler's Los Angeles in *The Big Sleep*. Here, the places are completely imagined, and their recollection is wholly based on the reader's memory of a previously experienced fictional universe. Walker Percy's *The Moviegoer* calls the film audience's experience of recognizing a real place seen in a movie a "certification"; there is no term for feeling at home in Turow's created world, but the reaction is real nonetheless.

PLOT DEVELOPMENT AND STRUCTURE

Presumed Innocent might in summation seem a simple tale: Rusty Sabich, a family man and the number-two prosecutor of Kindle County, is handed a politically explosive case—the brutal sex murder of a fellow prosecutor—only to himself become the accused. He is denounced by the superior who gave him the case and attacked by former colleagues until a sharp, intuitive defense lawyer and a loyal associate help him demonstrate to the court the possibility of a frame-up and win his freedom. However, the politics, the human complications, the family betrayals, the power of obsession, the corruption of evidence and of individuals, and the inner workings of a complicated, intelligent, and not fully honest narrator make this novel far from simple.

The novel begins with an Opening Statement, which is just that, Rusty Sabich's standard opening to the jury: "This is how I always start: 'I am the prosecutor. I represent the State . . . '" (1). Sabich's first-person narration includes comments on the short (two-page) statement as he delivers it: "And here I point. You must always point. . . . 'This man has been accused'" (1).

Sabich's idealism and Turow's themes are also touched on briefly, just as an opening statement in court lays out the themes of the prosecution case without providing details and evidence. Sabich calls himself "a functionary of our only universally recognized system of telling wrong from right, a bureaucrat of good and evil" (2). He professes to his readers that he is not uncaring of the accused, but that he has a task to perform, drawing the line between what is prohibited and what is allowed. Returning to his oral presentation, he tells the jurors that, although people's motives may remain "forever locked inside them," the jury's task is to "try to determine what actually occurred," for "if we cannot find the truth, what is our hope of justice?" (2–3).

Through this artful means, Turow establishes the general themes that will be pursued in *Presumed Innocent*. The framing of these ideas in the dramatic form of an opening statement is clever and engaging, and readers will not even be aware until a second or third reading how precisely the terms of this particular case with Rusty Sabich as the accused have been established: the insistence by the law on either guilt or innocence, the confrontation of good and evil, the need to draw lines prohibiting behavior, the obscurity of motive, the need to blame, the necessity of finding out what happened, and the absolute need to determine the truth if anything approaching justice is to be done. Each one of these ideas will be dealt with, and Sabich even casually mentions that he was finger-printed before beginning as a prosecutor, a planted fact that will be important later. The Opening Statement thus truly introduces the story.

The Opening Statement is followed by the first section, Spring, which contains 17 chapters. The next section, Summer, begins with a copy of the grand jury bill naming Sabich for murder, which is followed by 19 chapters. A final short section of four chapters, Fall, is followed by a Closing Statement of Sabich recapitulating the events of the book. Thus, the Opening Statement and Spring establish the offense and the accusation, the characters' back stories, their complex work and home relationships, the details of the crime, the motives for indicting Sabich, and his and others' reactions. The trial is covered in the longest section, Summer, while Fall and the Closing Statement wrap up and move on to the future.

Chapter 1 of Spring begins *in medias res*, in the midst of things, with Carolyn Polhemus's funeral. Prosecuting attorney Raymond Horgan, Rusty Sabich's boss, will deliver the eulogy, and as they drive to the chapel and find their places, a host of characters, all present to pay respects to the murdered deputy prosecutor Polhemus, engage Sabich and Horgan. Rusty spars with Nico Della Guardia, formerly a deputy prosecutor, now Raymond Horgan's election opponent for prosecuting attorney. The scene, a mix of cinematic description and Rusty's first-person commentary, a form of literary voice-over, substitutes dramatic interaction for prose exposition, dropping the reader into the middle of a complex action.

The next chapter begins Sabich's investigation into Carolyn Polhemus's murder. Raymond Horgan has dressed Rusty down, insisting a solution to the crime is necessary for his reelection: if the prosecuting attorney cannot mete out justice for his own assistants, how can he make promises to the public about their safety? Rusty meets with Dan Lipranzer to organize the processing of physical evidence—fingerprints, hair and fibers, bodily fluids, and the like—and to determine who should be interviewed and reinterviewed. In chapter 3 Rusty meets with a psychiatrist, revealing his affair with Carolyn, and chapter 4 shows the effects of the affair on Rusty's wife, Barbara. Rusty works on the investigation but keeps drifting into memories of Carolyn and their affair even as he recalls the case they worked together, the horrific abuse of Wendell McGaffen, whose mother crushed his head in a vise.

Rusty meets with Carolyn's college-age son in chapter 7, evoking the young man's evaluation of his natural mother, that she divorced his father and moved away because he thinks he made no difference to her. Horgan had given a bribery case file to Carolyn for her to investigate—oddly, since she specializes in sex crimes—and Rusty's driving around with Lipranzer takes him past Sabich's deceased father's former business, a bakery, triggering memories of a harsh upbringing by this Serbian refugee and immigrant. An encounter with Tetsuya "Painless" Kumagai, the police pathologist, suggests the doctor is in cahoots with Nico Della Guardia, using deputy prosecuting attorney Tommy Molto, who has been missing from work, as his intermediary. It is becoming clear to Rusty that Raymond Horgan's campaign is in trouble, with defections multiplying. A late-night meeting with Raymond reveals that he, too, had an affair with Carolyn. The last chapters of this section tighten the investigatory noose around Rusty. Phone records show he has been in constant touch with Carolyn at home; his fingerprints appear on a glass found in her apartment; worst of all, he seems to be acting guilty, not following through on standard procedure and thus forestalling the investigation. When Raymond loses the election, Rusty's enemies Della Guardia and Tommy Molto are ready to charge him with Carolyn's murder.

The Summer section is entirely devoted to the post-arraignment period and the trial. Rusty meets with Alejandro "Sandy" Stern and his assistant James Kemp to plot strategy. Judge Larren Lyttle, Raymond Horgan's old law partner, is selected judge by lottery. The glass with Rusty's fingerprints comes up—it is missing from the collection of evidence, although the identification record naming Rusty is on file—and the question arises whether Tommy Molto, who is assisting in the prosecution, will be allowed to testify. Molto wants to report Rusty's "Yeah, you're right" (141), ignoring the clear sarcasm, when Molto asks Rusty if he killed Carolyn. Sabich takes an active role in his own defense, learning how it feels from the other side of the table. He and Kemp search Carolyn's apartment for evidence.

When the trial begins, Rusty is heartened by Sandy Stern's skillful cross-examination of the prosecution witnesses, including Raymond Horgan. Stern keeps bringing up the B (for bribery) file that Raymond gave to Carolyn, much to Judge Lyttle's irritation and Rusty's puzzlement. He also keeps suggesting that Tommy Molto, who has been called a cipher and unimportant in the politics surrounding the prosecuting attorney's office, is manufacturing evidence. An old cop, Lionel Kenneally, who worked in the precinct where Carolyn practiced social work before becoming a prosecutor, reveals to Rusty that Carolyn was then sleeping with Judge Lyttle. Lipranzer testifies, but his clear reluctance to damage Rusty's case works against his friend's interests. However, Kumagai, the police pathologist who conducted the autopsy on Carolyn Polhemus, is a disas-

ter for the prosecution. Sandy Stern ambushes Kumagai, showing that
Carolyn had had a tubal ligation, something the pathologist missed, and
would have had no reason to use a spermicide, which Kumagai said she
did. The contradiction suggests the pathologist has confused his records—
he is "devastated" (335) in Rusty's view.

Rusty and Lipranzer find "Leon," a homosexual mentioned in the B file
as having bribed someone to have his case dropped, and the guilty party
turns out to have been Judge Lyttle when he worked with Carolyn years
before in the North Branch precinct. Miles Robinson, Rusty's psychiatrist,
testifies amidst much wrangling about the doctor–patient privilege, but
in a dramatic moment says that Rusty never said anything about killing
Carolyn. Judge Lyttle dismisses the case without ever requiring a defense
to be mounted—he says there is no credible evidence against Sabich. Della
Guardia, trying to cut his losses, moves to dismiss as well. Rusty is free.

The trial scenes are masterfully described, with Sandy Stern meticu-
lously and skillfully tapping away at the evidence, turning it his way in
tiny increments, while pursuing his larger strategy of suggesting Tommy
Molto has manufactured the case against Rusty. This tack allows Sandy
to keep bringing up the B file, which Judge Lyttle knows would end his
career if it became part of the defense theory that Molto is to blame for
the setup. The strategy gives Judge Lyttle reason to dismiss without
overtly threatening him, and the approach is so subtle even Rusty only
gradually becomes aware of it. The rhythm of the trial, the dramatic highs
and lows as witnesses and evidence loom large and threatening, or peter
out, is wonderfully rendered, perhaps for the first time in fiction with such
intensity. Jamie Kemp has an amusing term for the emotional roller
coaster: "clong"—"the rush of shit to your heart when you see the State's
evidence" (147).

The enormous strain of a lawyer in a trial is made palpable; there is
never enough time to research every issue, track down every possible
witness, exhaust all possibilities of a surprise. The section ends with the
participants unable to believe the trial is truly over. Sandy and Rusty have
a fairly open discussion about Judge Lyttle, but each is holding back,
aware that some things cannot be said.

The section Fall is composed of only four chapters. Raymond attempts
an apology, but Rusty rejects him, even after the offer of a possible judgeship. After trying to make amends, he asks Rusty bluntly who killed Carolyn. Rusty remains impassive but the next chapter reveals the murder
weapon, a "Whatchamacallit" all-purpose crowbar and hammer claw. It
has been secreted in an old toolbox, where Barbara put it after she killed

Carolyn. Barbara and Rusty have a long talk; she plans to accept a teaching job in Detroit and will take their son Nate with her. Barbara claims she killed Carolyn to end Rusty's obsession and left the clues implicating him to let him know what really happened; she says she would have told the truth if Rusty were at risk. Another view is given by Lipranzer, who unsentimentally argues that Barbara meant to set Rusty up all along; she just didn't count on Rusty beating the charge. Rusty counters that if Barbara had confessed, Della Guardia would have said that Rusty set up the whole affair, with Barbara as his fail-safe if it seemed likely he'd be found guilty. Lip says that Barbara as fail-safe for a guilty Rusty isn't true, and Rusty agrees, but a flicker of doubt remains: "What is harder? Knowing the truth or finding it, telling it or being believed?" muses Rusty and his creator (418). The possibility that Rusty is a master schemer remains open—there is no absolute innocence, only the presumption of innocence.

A Closing Argument jumps to the future. Barbara is in Detroit with Nate; Rusty is acting Kindle County Prosecuting Attorney and has a good chance of becoming a judge. But he still thinks of Carolyn and his obsession with her.

Thus, the structure of *Presumed Innocent* follows an innovative pattern vital to Turow's thematic concerns. It starts with outward chaos: Carolyn's murder posed as a sex crime; suspicions rampant, given Carolyn's criminal cases and lovers; and the main character's alienation from his family, his colleagues, and even his sense of self. Rusty's confusion, self-doubts, obsession, and rage reveal his inward chaos. The rigorous rules of trial procedure impose an order on events and begin framing the possibilities of what might have really transpired. However, the novel ends with the possibility of a deeper, almost invisible underlying order: the suggestion that the chaos might be a purposeful illusion, that behind it lies a subtle and intricate plan that manipulates people, prejudices, and situations toward an ulterior end. There is no final certainty, of course, with human motive always layered and unknowable, as Rusty points out in his Opening Statement, but there are inferences and presumptions to be made.

The Sidney Pollock–Alan J. Pakula film starring Harrison Ford as Rusty, Bonnie Bedelia as Barbara, and a sexually menacing Greta Scacchi as Carolyn Polhemus ends with Sabich's discovery that Barbara was indeed the guilty party and that Sabich was either totally in the dark about her deeds until late in the film or even up to his final discovery of the murder weapon in his basement workroom. In this version of events, Barbara Sabich is the cool order behind the seeming chaos. Scott Turow's ending to the book is not so definite, but it clearly suggests the possibility that all is not as it seems. Molto and Della Guardia could certainly believe that Rusty Sabich—knowing the players and the system—might well have manipulated the entire situation from beginning to end, or taken advantage of events, and thus behind the chaos could lie an order planned and staged by a very clever man. Yet the structure also leaves readers with doubts, because just as circumstantial evidence might incriminate an innocent man, so we learn that missing evidence, confused testimony, or private matters played out beyond the courtroom might interact just as easily to free the guilty. The victim is an amoral prosecuting attorney who has slept with Sabich's boss and possibly even the judge on her way to the top, facts that should not affect the outcome of the trial but that nonetheless determine the dismissal of charges. As Rusty says at the beginning, there are no real innocents—only a presumption of innocence. Thus, ultimately, the reader again returns to the impossibility of knowing the truth. Does chaos reign? Has the court been manipulated and deceived? Has Sandy Stern been manipulated, even as he has himself manipulated the judge? He cannot ask his client, and Rusty will never tell.

THEMATIC ISSUES

Presumed Innocent is a dramatic rendering of the themes prosecutor Rusty Sabich lays out in his opening statement. Human beings have a deep need to assign blame; punishing is "one of the great wheels turning beneath everything we do" (2). Yet human culture has never devised an instrument for sorting out good and evil; the court system is the one "universally recognized system of telling wrong from right," but it is a system marred by fallible human beings, and juries must "at least try to determine what actually occurred" (37). Without truth, there is no hope of justice, and truth is a commodity fought over and manipulated in the arena of the courtroom. The inability to determine truth lies behind all the other interlocking themes in the novel, the themes of sexual obsession as opposed to marital obligation, the corruption of officials who use circumstantial evidence to mislead and misdirect.

The Evanescence of Truth

Rusty Sabich's position on truth and justice lies somewhere between the simplistic naïveté of Perry Mason depictions of the law and cynical insistence that the courts are just cat's paws of power and wealth. Sabich, the son of immigrants, retains the hopefulness that new Americans have long brought with them, based on their experiences in places absent the institutions Americans take for granted. (Rusty's baby-faced father escaped death in his Serbian village when the Nazis lined up all the adults against the schoolhouse and shot them.) Yet Rusty, whether because of Slavic gloom or intellectual honesty, recognizes the limitations of the system, the fact that innocence is a rare commodity, and only the presumption of innocence can be counted on as an institutional given. Sabich says he knows exactly how to be a dutiful bureaucrat, but he also knows, after 13 years, how the court system works and how he can manipulate it. The question Turow leaves us with reprises Rusty's opening plea, "what actually occurred" (3). Whether justice has been served is unknowable, for truth remains elusive.

This courtroom issue of the evanescence of truth has its parallel in the domestic arena of the Sabich marriage and in the universal speculation about Carolyn's true nature. Rusty's Opening Statement asserts that human motives may be forever hidden from outsiders. As the court case and the Sabich marriage become more related, readers realize the Sabiches are not what they seem, a prosperous suburban couple with a troubled marriage. In fact, Barbara's real nature is invisible to all but Rusty (Barbara has no friends, only her mother). Like the horrendous Colleen McGaffen, who tortured her son, Barbara, beneath a perfectly presentable surface, remains a mystery, possibly even to herself. Ironically, Carolyn Polhemus is also unknown, displaying a different self for different people. Finally, Rusty, himself, for all his apparent openness and bluntness, remains shrouded in possibility. Is he telling the truth to Lipranzer at the end? Is he the consummate manipulator? As readers, we learn that his exterior calm hides the turmoil of his obsession, but he remains an unreliable narrator, reinforcing through our doubts about him the thematic heart of the book.

The Eternal Love Triangle

Another theme is the eternal love triangle, but in this case the geometry is static and fixed, again in accord with the general idea of the inscrutability of motive which runs throughout the book. What you see is in no way like what you might get, so Rusty and Barbara are frozen in doubtful combat, Carolyn's death and their apparent reconciliation notwithstanding. Rusty's feelings for Carolyn hardly deserve the name *love*; as he confesses to the reader compulsively, he is obsessed, driven, adrift from all anchors, gripped by forces almost demonic in their power. Carolyn, ambitious and manipulative, simply smiles knowingly. Barbara, her reliable husband suddenly missing, looks on with a black despair. Son Nate is a hostage who holds them together; their knowledge of each other's secrets also produces the standoff. Love conquers nothing; it is the despoiler that leaves all in ruins.

Rampant Corruption

The backdrop theme behind the characters involves the Kindle County court and political system, in theory separate institutions but in fact deeply interconnected. Sabich's Opening Statement makes dramatic claims for the virtues of the court system, but in fact he is brought to trial on circumstantial evidence and flimsy accusations by Raymond Horgan and Tommy Molto. Politics drives the indictment with Della Guardia's succession and Horgan's bitterness weighing as heavily as the evidence, and politics also serves to end the case. While courtroom discipline supposedly keeps rumor and innuendo at bay, it is Sandy Stern's repeated introduction of the B file and the potential scandal it could cause for Judge Lyttle that makes the case go away. The munificence of the law, articulated through the lovingly described courtroom decor and architecture, is in some ways as false a front as the Wizard of Oz: frail humans sit on both sides of the bench, and legal decisions may well hinge on bare-knuckle politics.

CHARACTER DEVELOPMENT

In accord with his themes, Turow's characters are never fully knowable. Readers see facets of their personalities, the faces they choose to show the world, and are provided inklings that these surface versions hide the real selves, which are far more complex and perhaps quite different from their facades.

Rusty Sabich

Turow says that Rusty Sabich thinks of himself as "principled" but is "somewhat misled" (Macdonald interview, 2004). He has perhaps inherited from his Serbian immigrant father a certain refusal to compromise his standards and an exactitude about how things should be done, with the result that everyone who knows his work looks at him with suspicion when he is sloppy in the Polhemus investigation—even Lipranzer, since he and Rusty depended on each other to avoid "certain base kinds of stupidity," and Lipranzer would be disloyal to that compact if he failed to communicate that Rusty had "let him down" (81). Sabich's first-person narration acts like a Shakespearean soliloquy, yielding private doubts and embarrassing secrets that make Rusty seem weak, at times almost whiny, especially about his adolescent crush on Carolyn. The rich, metaphorical descriptions of his gloomy melancholy, his despair, play on readers' instinctive trust of the narrative voice. He describes himself as "an island" swept by a wild and "hopeless storm of feeling" and the occasional "cyclonic impact" of human contact (386). He feels as if the people important in his life are "circling . . . like the multiple moons of some far planet, each one exerting its own deep tidal impulses" on him (256). Rusty bares his soul, sharing with readers the depths of his philosophical despair and exploring with them the roots of his anxieties. From the outside, on the evidence of how his colleagues speak to him and treat him, Sabich is stalwart, upright, efficient, a model bureaucrat and politician, the heir apparent to Horgan in all eyes but his own.

Sabich's dual nature, inner and outer, resonates as a very human phenomenon, the disjunction people typically feel between their private insecurities and their more confident public selves. A sense of fraudulence may silently shame even highly successful people; Rusty, who has come from nowhere to near the top of the Kindle County justice system, may be an extreme example. Only Barbara, herself lost in inexplicable "black anger" (43), knows Rusty, who acknowledges his "wife's superior knowledge of my nature" (41). However, Rusty's secret self prevails. He can even maneuver effectively around the wily Sandy Stern, providing him with unexpected material at crucial moments while appearing to follow his lead. Sabich will become acting prosecuting attorney and eventually judge. He calls himself a "museum piece. . . . The biggest bullshit thing you've ever seen" (420), but in fact he is also a consummate politician.

He is a clever man who may well have manipulated events from the very beginning, creating layers within layers of strategies to misdirect not only investigators but his own highly intuitive lawyer. His cynical, loyal, and dogged friend Lipranzer knows him well enough to doubt the exculpatory evidence and to doubt Rusty's handling of it. For Stern, Rusty had laid out the scenario the prosecution would follow, point for point exactly as it played out. For Lipranzer, Rusty lays out another scenario: What if he had blamed his wife, Barbara, for committing murder as a jealous act of premeditated revenge? How would events have played out? He keeps his scenario theoretical, distancing himself from it, but thereby suggesting to Lip the motives that made him, to Lipranzer's eye, seem to behave out of character. Rusty asserts that the prosecution (Nico and Molto) would have argued that he was simply manipulating the evidence to hide his own culpability. They would have reasoned that—with his background in criminal prosecutions, the police investigative patterns, and courtroom procedures—Sabich was capable of committing the perfect crime, one that with one stone brings down two birds: the teasing lover who rejected him for his boss and the wife who despises him for his betrayals. At the same time, he puts himself in an ideal position for both eventual custody of his son and political vindication. The prosecutors would argue that his wife is his fail-safe in case his other ploys failed. Rusty's explanation makes Lip and readers feel as if they have the insider's explanation for Sabich's odd behavior. Yet, for all that readers have been privy to Rusty's private thoughts to the extent that he narrates events, there looms the possibility that he is toying with Lip and with his readers, playing the scenario game as he did with Sandy Stern, and that his inner reality and the reality of events might well be quite different from any explanation yet given. This is why a number of critics, like Jane Spitzer of the *Christian Science Monitor,* find Turow's main character and his ending profoundly disturbing, the moral ambiguity troubling. In Rusty, Turow has created a wondrous character: one who confesses his guilty acts and his struggle to "escape the darkness," yet also suggests his innocence, one who blames others but in so doing leaves a doubt. Who is this man and what is he capable of? Rusty Sabich is the embodiment of Turow's theme, the evanescence of truth.

Carolyn Polhemus

Sabich's overheated descriptions of Carolyn Polhemus reflect his obsessive, almost adolescent fixation on her. He says that she made him feel like Joe College or Beaver Cleaver or today's "boy next door" (285). When they made love, his usual "hum . . . vibrated, sang," transforming her into "a symphonic personality" with a "musical laugh" and the pair of them into a new reality, "like all those gorgeous, poised movietime couples" with "a racing current" between them (33). He envisions her "like some Hindu goddess, containing all feelings in creation," and undamming within Rusty "wild, surging, libidinal rivers" that draw him "over the brink" (60). Although such images make her seem unreal, Polhemus's appeal is confirmed by her many affairs, including her fling with Raymond Horgan, certainly no pushover. Rusty may think of her as his private "treasure box" but that is certainly not how she sees herself.

She seems to have been the self-inventing type of young woman Turow sometimes writes about, a child of limited means and background who, through the force of will and the power of older male mentors, moves up the social ladder in dramatic leaps. Carolyn married her high school English teacher but left him and her young son with few backward glances. She moves from social worker to deputy prosecuting attorney, enjoying the influence of Judge Larren Lyttle and Prosecuting Attorney Raymond Horgan. She moves in on Rusty with the expectation that he will succeed Raymond as prosecuting attorney and name her his deputy, part of her plan to become prosecuting attorney herself, as she confesses to her son. She pulls away physically when Rusty tells her he doesn't plan to run for prosecuting attorney: "I should go to Raymond and tell him his time is up? . . . No way. . . . I'm not gonna bite that hand" (109). From that point on, Rusty has a new image of her as flinty, with a "hard shell manner" and a "little cat's grin," a "darkness" he struggles to escape (34) and of himself as "devastated by . . . passion. . . . shattered. Riven. Decimated. Torn to bits" (105).

Carolyn is beautiful, smart, efficient, complex, kind to children, and surprising—she would be too good to be true were she not so bad as well. Rusty's images provide a sense of her inner complexity, finding in her what "was old and dark and deep," a "Pandora" whose attractively inviting box unlooses a "torrent of miseries" (105). Her manipulation of powerful men might be defended as necessity in the man's world of the court system, but Carolyn also exhibits an almost psychopathic lack of affect, treating her son with civility but little affection and dropping Rusty without regard for damage. Yet she is also capable of real decency toward Wendell McGaffen, the abused little boy whose case she prosecutes. Her sensitivity and emotional skill impress even the psychologist assigned to Wendell. For all her glittering, tasteful exterior, Carolyn is ultimately unknowable, a gathering of contradictions that speaks with no single clear voice.

Barbara Sabich

Sabich's wife, Barbara, is another unknowable woman. Despite her husband's protestations of affection, his images of her are all negative. She has "a savage deadness in her eye" (39), "a look of diamond hardness" (121), a personality with "rocky currents" (123), a passion that is "omnivorous" (123) and "volcanic" (44), moods like "black forests" (121). He resents her mathematical brilliance and, from his perspective, her Ph.D. dissertation lingers "like a chronic disease" (37–38). Although Rusty thinks of himself as dependable, Barbara derides him as a predictable "asshole" (41). Rusty also sees in her expectations of commitments that he feels incapable of meeting. "Barbara hoped I would be like some fairy-tale prince," he says, "a toad she had transformed with her caresses, who could enter the gloomy woods where she was held captive and lead her away from the encircling demons" (123–124). The duty and obligation she takes as a natural part of being married he describes as hard "ore deposits" that replace genuine feeling (2). Even when she loyally stands by him in court he finds the overall effect stilted, "a little like the Kennedy widows" (231). Consequently, his main descriptive word for how he feels about her is rage, "a galvanic anger . . . dark and untamed" (321).

Barbara has isolated herself in an older town that now serves as a bed-room suburb, a location Rusty has come to like for its distance from the chaos of downtown and his work. Now, Barbara finds herself cut off from both Rusty and opportunities for herself. Rusty's affair seems to be the last straw; without him, she has no adult connections (Rusty says she has no friends, only a rocky relationship with her mother). Her culpability in the death of Carolyn Polhemus is indeterminable from the evidence given in the book; she deserves the old Scots verdict of "not proven." Yet her strength as a character can be measured by the fact that the scenario of her guilt seems perfectly credible, even though she has played no more than a supporting role throughout.

Dan "Lip" Lipranzer

Dan Lipranzer is Rusty's best friend and, besides Barbara, his only loyal supporter in his troubles. Rusty, who admires Lip's competence, honesty, and streetwise good sense, amusingly describes him on a questionnaire as "My best friend . . . a cop . . . [with] that look of lurking small-time viciousness . . . seen on every no-account kid hanging on a street corner" (21). A loner "as solitary as a shooting star" (21), Lipranzer has gotten himself assigned as a police liaison with the prosecuting attorney's office, coordinating homicide investigations. This assignment allows him to hang out in bars with miscreants of all kinds, dredging up intelligence as a lone cowboy. Rusty calls him "a scholar of the underlife" (21), and he is exactly that for Rusty: a loyal, reliable ally who stands by his friend notwithstanding his suspicions. It is hard to see how Rusty could have figured out the

B file without Lip, who has no illusions about the justice system and thus sees clearly through its deceptions and misdirections. Lipranzer has a strict code of honor, as his story of another cop—not Lip's kind of police-man, forcing a prostitute to perform oral sex—confirms; his decision to simply not speak up when Molto signs for the glass that Lip has from the crime scene is an indicator of the depth of his loyalty to and trust in Rusty.

Raymond Horgan

Initially Sabich's mentor and even something of a father figure, Ray-mond Horgan, with his "reddened Irish bulk" (264), has been in office far too long. A former partner of Judge Larren Lyttle, who managed his first campaign for prosecuting attorney, Horgan began as a defense lawyer for the down-and-out sixties rebels against society and became a prosecuting attorney who refused to prosecute victimless crimes and persecute mi-norities. Rusty feels his years with Horgan have been "full of authentic loyalty and admiration" (11). However, he feels discontented, especially when Horgan questions his professionalism: "I am thirty-nine years old. . . . I have been a lawyer thirteen years" (55). Despite his reservations about his deputy, Horgan assigns him Carolyn's case because he knows Rusty will protect his mentor's back and Horgan is vulnerable.

Horgan betrays Rusty, telling the new prosecuting attorney Della Guar-dia that Sabich had asked for the Polhemus investigation and recasting Rusty's subsequent actions to heighten suspicion—a body blow to the defense. Horgan may feel competitive about Rusty's affair with Carolyn, especially after being left in the dark about it, and about Rusty's political potential, the protegé replacing the mentor/father figure (others keep say-ing Rusty would have been a better candidate than Horgan). Horgan, in effect, lies in court, "cold as a saber's edge" (263), completely reversing his previous support for Rusty and thereby covering up his personal rea-sons for keeping a lid on the Polhemus investigation. However, he is a born politician and shifts gears again at the end of the book, once again supporting Rusty.

Judge Larren Lyttle

Raymond Horgan's former law partner Larren Lyttle becomes a judge but goes through a bad personal period, including a divorce and a possible affair with Carolyn Polhemus. His life has straightened out by the time of Rusty's trial, but he remains vulnerable because of the events brought up in the B file Horgan gave to Carolyn. Judge Lyttle has a fine legal mind and, as a young lawyer, possessed "a princely style of oratory" (196), a rhetoric of "operatic dimension," ranging from refined to the "round oratory of a pork-chop preacher, or squealing ghettoese" (53). Turow says that the streets of his city have become an "emotional encyclopedia" for him (195). Judge Lyttle provides much of the comedy in the courtroom scenes of the Summer section, with his scathing sarcasm to Della Guardia and Molto. His language code switches up and down the register of formality, reducing complex points to the common sense of street talk and just as quickly reverting to formal judicial discourse. He and Sandy Stern are the most memorable figures of Summer, taking center stage.

Alejandro "Sandy" Stern

Rusty's defense lawyer Sandy Stern, short and soft, with his "brown-eyed spaniel expression" (170) and "odd theatricality" (314), is an Argentine Jewish immigrant who has mastered American legal idiom but retains a Hispanic formality and courtesy. Although often described as "wily," Stern is also honorable and a believer in the law and its standards. He meets Rusty as an equal but takes charge of his case and moves the defense in his own directions. He has under his belt secret knowledge about the political and personal histories of the players—for instance, Judge Lyttle's difficult past. Stern is careful not to ask Rusty questions he doesn't want answered. He is accustomed to lying clients, who misdirect him and who delude themselves, and, as a consequence, Stern has learned to work effectively "in the small open spaces which remain" (157). Rusty admires Stern's courtroom style, his penetrating observations and convincing assertions that compel belief like "sleight of hand" (169). Stern is "a magician . . . pulling rabbits out of hats" (285), "a jeweler, tapping . . . at his themes" (278), a master woodcarver whittling away at the prosecutor's argument and evidence (229), a navigator sailing by "intuition and estimation" rather than following "a charted course" (381). Watching Stern at work in the courtroom is "like tracking smoke, watching a shadow lengthen" (162). At Rusty's trial, Stern carefully works away at the evidence, severing "the knot between what . . . [Sabich] did not say and what . . . [he] did . . . between murder and deceit" (270). Stern's intuitive focus on the B file as he lays the groundwork to influence Judge Lyttle without the court realizing what has happened surprises even the courtroom-savvy Sabich.

GENRE CONVENTIONS

While few authors can be described as inventing a genre, Turow comes close to having single-handedly created the American-style legal thriller. Mysteries with lawyers as protagonists had been around for some time (see the more extensive discussion in chapter 2), but the particular direction the legal procedural took after *Presumed Innocent* was largely due to the influence of this seminal book. The simplistic Perry Mason series of book and television programs so influential in shaping the public view of lawyers and courts was supplanted by a far more realistic, detailed, and modulated portrait. No longer would a participant jump up in court shouting, "I did it!" overcome by guilt and the need to wrap up an episode within 30 minutes. In its place have come shaded, sophisticated understandings of guilt and innocence, a sensibility that insists that, despite the social need for parsing out responsibility and creating closure, even the law and courts can never get things quite right.

In keeping with the requirements of the best modern detective stories, Turow describes realistically the procedures of an ongoing investigation, the gathering of the physical evidence that is at its heart, the coroner's autopsy, the search through files and memories for potential suspects. Rusty ticks off for Sandy the damaging discoveries that point at him: the glass with two of his fingerprints, identifiable from the fingerprints he put in the system when he became the deputy prosecuting attorney; the telephone records of phone calls from his office and his home to Carolyn's home; the malt-colored Zorak V fibers that match samples from carpeting in Rusty's home.

Besides accuracy and authenticity, Turow brought to the legal thriller three other elements from other genres: the family drama that focuses on lovers and family relationships; the emphasis on complexity of motive that characterizes psychologically oriented fiction; and the literary sensibility that finds truth not simply in plot and character but also in prose style, metaphor, and imagery.

Turow writes family dramas, though modern ones, with the definition of family being the nuclear unit, not the extended families of nineteenth-century fiction. Every novel focuses on some domestic crisis, and the smallness of the Sabich family of three should not blind readers to that interest. Turow is always good at exploring father–son relationships, and here Rusty's unhappy experiences with his own father—he considered Rusty a possession of his mother's—extends the connection back another generation. Barbara Sabich is a very modern spouse and mother, a stay-at-home wife who decides to pursue a Ph.D., and Rusty's affair with the socially climbing Carolyn Polhemus is quintessential late–twentieth-century workplace drama. James Gould Cozzens's *By Love Possessed* is the one previous lawyer book that sees love as the core human motive, and Turow follows this precursor's emphasis and extends it, for love motivates all the important events in *Presumed Innocent.*

These tangled relationships (among both family members and coworkers) are approached through the perspective of psychology. Turow knows his Freud, as his frequently tortuous father–son relationships attest; he is equally adept at writing female characters: Barbara and Carolyn are minutely examined and consummately understandable in their behavior, with motives for their overt acts that endure examination even while their behavior is condemned and their murky inner selves remain unplumbed. Finally, Rusty's story has its generic source too; he may be inept and conflicted as an amateur detective, but he is in the tradition of the classic investigator who traces all clues, leading back to . . . himself. When Sandy Stern has him lay out the prosecution's case against him, he is point-for-point on target about the logic of their case. Turow, however, takes the cliché of the self-accusing detective and makes it philosophically sophisticated: what, ultimately, does innocence mean when a crime has been triggered by the bad behavior of another party? Can the categories good and evil really contain murky human motive, which defies linguistic boundaries?

Finally, Turow brought literary value to this newly minted genre. Although some critics have accused him of overwriting, Turow's prose is clearly a reversion to an older, more *belle-lettristic* prose style. Hemingway taught mid-twentieth-century writers that less is more; Turow, though capable of spare sentences, finds his outlet in complex syntax and in long, large books, which, like their nineteenth-century precursors, are not afraid to re-plow tilled fields in search of elusive answers. Turow frequently revisits earlier understandings with fresh character perspectives; life is not unwrapped easily, as in the Hemingway model. The result, says novelist Anne Rice, is "an elegant style and philosophical voice," with "tough-guy speech" a counterpoint to "the narrator's slow, ruminating voice" (*New York Times Book Review,* 1).

Philosophical complexity is also evident in the continual resort to imagery, simile, and metaphor. In the courtroom scenes, Turow uses metaphor to spin out the convoluted interpretive possibilities inherent in the seemingly simplest statement of fact: the prose style is a roadmap providing alternative routes and side excursions on the way to the final destination, a clear-cut determination of guilt or innocence. With the grand-jury room "like a small theater" (154), the witness stand "a glass-and-steel cage" (194), the internal courtroom processes "hedged in" by the formal rules of evidence (292), the police as full of intrigue as "the Medici" (94), and the prosecutor's office so "tangled" that "it would require an archaeological dig to get through the sedimentary layers of resentments built up over the years" (363), Turow's court is like the Roman games with "Christians against lions"—but no one is quite sure who the Christians are (224). Criminal investigators study evil with the same distance and disdain as scientists study diseases through their microscopes (158), but with corruption "a progressive disease" (375).

What is really happening inside or between human beings cannot be captured in the prosaic formulas of ordinary discourse. Metaphor suggests reaching for parallels to enhance incomplete understanding. Thus, Rusty is awash in images that reflect his psychological state. Rejected by Carolyn, Rusty felt as if his judgment were transformed into "the grotesque exaggerations of a cruel cartoon" (133), and he endures his loss "in a fiery pit of shame," "his heart squeezed" (135). His dreams are "like an acid . . . corroding . . . veins and bones" (72). Carolyn's death leaves Rusty feeling emotionally adrift: "like a shipwrecked survivor holding fast to the debris, awaiting the arrival of the scheduled liner" (43). When he looks back on their relationship, he sees her through a darker lens than before: she has "ransacked" his life (152) but has herself become "like a spider caught in her own web" (377). During the murder trial, Rusty feels lost in "the unsolved maze of . . . self," raging as if from "black poison" in his veins (141), on the rim of a "black vortex of paranoia" (151), wanting, "with a desperation whose size cannot be encompassed by metaphor," for all that has happened to have never taken place (151–152). The day's "high-voltage impulse" leaves him so "hollowed out" that he returns home with his shirt encasing him "like a package wrapper" and his spirits "in a sickening spiral, escalating, then instantly descending from elation to bitter lament" (307). No wonder, then, that when Barbara speaks to him "an inner density gathers, a known sensation," as if his veins have "become clogged with lead" (37).

ALTERNATIVE READING

Formalist critics are sometimes known as New Critics, since that movement dominated the reading of literature during much of the "new" twentieth century, from the 1930s until the last quarter of the century. The concern with literary form is an ancient one and may involve anything from genre to character to structure. A major contribution of the New Critics was an emphasis on the linguistic elements of the work, or its "texture." The New-Critical interest in imagery and metaphor brought a fresh understanding of how great writing achieves its literary effects, especially with sets of related images, "tropes" or trains of recurring word pictures and comparisons. This formalist analysis is similar to what a psychologist or psychiatrist perceives in the pattern evident in a given person's language: themes and concerns emerge through repetition of related images and comparisons.

Presumed Innocent makes extensive use of images (word pictures), simile (overt comparisons linked by "like" or "as"), and metaphor (the direct linking of a word picture and an idea to show similarities). For example, when Rusty Sabich discusses his Serbian refugee father, a deeply unhappy man, who "had played in the Olympics of confinement" (276), a Nazi prison camp, he uses adjectives that metaphorically suggest his parent's inability to overcome the damage of his past. The terms refer to the elder Sabich's spirit, not his body—a spirit that has been so damaged that he cannot function properly. He describes his father's soul as "hobbled," "maimed by one of history's great crimes," with "no knowledge of his real prison" (276), while Rusty himself becomes a "sworn enemy of the crippled spirit" (398).

When Rusty as a boy imagined his "maimed" father, he would "paint" him with "a gargoyle's face and a dragon's scaled heart," because, as the adult Rusty understands, "the channels of his emotions were too intricately wound upon themselves, too clotted, strangulated, crowded with spite, to admit any feeling for a child" (72). The elder Sabich regarded his son as "a possession" of his mother, a piece of furniture (72). As a result, the young Rusty concluded pathetically, "my mother loved me, my father did not" (72). The essence of young Rusty's feelings is carried in the imagery, the metaphorical adjectives "gargoyle" and "dragon's scaled," the "intricately wound," "clotted," "strangulated," "crowded" "channels" of the father's emotions, all terms evoking distortion of human normality into literally the monstrosity of gargoyle and dragon, and constricted and twisted "channels" that disallow the elder Sabich from ever expressing an open emotion freely and directly. The metaphors of "crippled" and "hobbled" have moved from visual imagery of unnatural exterior movement to conceptions of the interior, of ways feelings are formulated and made evident. What are the "channels" of the emotions? No such physical ductwork exists, of course, but the power of imagery and metaphor enables us to visualize the ineffable, to give invisible mental and emotional states a physical correlative which explains their motions, or in this case, their failure to move easily. Like a medical scanning device or the electronic equipment used by scientists to study phenomena too small to see or astronomical data too enormous to conceive of, imagery and metaphor never provide one-to-one representation or equivalents of the original— Rusty's father has no "emotional channels." Rather the image, or vehicle, and the idea given, or tenor, are by definition different, for the intent of the technique is to define the unknown through the familiar, to transfer known qualities to an unknown.

Turow, a writer fascinated by interior states, makes copious use of imagery and metaphor. The contrast between Rusty's reaction to wife Barbara and mistress Carolyn is conveyed through the imagery. Barbara is delivering a "drear offensive, a bitterness too tired even to be regret," which Rusty counters by seeming not to notice, showing interest in each remark until "an inner density gathers, a known sensation, as if my veins have become clogged with lead. I am home" (37). The military term "offensive" is ironically modified by the adjective "drear"; Barbara's attack is through emotional flatness, a lack of affect meant to remind and punish. Rusty refuses to take the bait, affecting a false chipperness, an "enthusiasm for every detail." However, Barbara wins, as he begins to feel heavy inside, an "inner density," ending with the wonderful image of "as if my veins have become clogged with lead." This is not simply a physical impossibility; it is an absurd notion, but it captures the heavy feeling of being trapped in a negative relationship with perfect precision.

In contrast to his leaden reaction to Barbara, Rusty responds to Carolyn like a vibrating tuning fork: "Some frequency is heard and everything begins to shatter. A vibration sets in, a fundamental tone, and the whole interior is shaking . . . she seemed such a remarkable mix of things. Symphonic. A symphonic personality" (33). Rusty "gropes around inside" himself (35) for his old, normal self, but the "daily hum" (33) that has been the allure of other women becomes with Carolyn like the "Brownian movement," the action of molecules coursing against one another in the air (32), a sound that Rusty could hear as a child and that "now rises to a pitch, which vibrated, sang" (33).

How does one talk about sexual attraction? The scientifically accurate language of hormonal changes and electrochemical firing of synapses may be true, but conveys nothing of the feelings involved. Here the contrast between lead-filled veins and the vibrating tuning fork sets heaviness against exquisite harmonies, deadness against lively motion.

Carolyn's appeal for Rusty is almost religious: "She seemed like some Hindu goddess, containing all feelings in creation. Whatever wild, surging, libidinal rivers Carolyn undammed in me . . . [her] tender attention [to the abused child] drew me over the brink . . . [and] gave my emotions a melting, yearning quality" (60). Carolyn as exotic goddess lets loose in Rusty a torrent of feeling; we can compare this imagery with what he says about his father's crabbed, "clotted" emotional channels, as well as Barbara's cold, leaden effect. The vehicles (or imagery) of Turow's metaphors convey the truth that Carolyn represents emotional discharge for a man wrapped very tightly.

Formalist or New Critics, then, focus on highly specific literary and linguistic devices to highlight their role in conveying characters, tone, and perspective. In the case of imagery and metaphor, the analysis shows how invisible, though perfectly real, states of mind and feeling can be conveyed.

4

The Burden of Proof
(1990)

The trial section of *Presumed Innocent* delineated the courtroom character of Alejandro "Sandy" Stern as defense lawyer, a consummate professional comfortable with the subtle tools of his profession, a skilled reader of signs that indicate hidden feelings and reactions. The story unfolded at trial and in the headlines, as well as in the mind of the accused Rusty Sabich's voice-over commentary on the action. Defending Rusty, Stern was the intuitive orchestrator of courtroom events and a master of illusion, of smoke and mirrors and sleight of hand, playing a complicated legal game of innuendo and nuance in a case in which the innocence of his client was very much in doubt. In the courtroom, he was calm, self-assured, and inscrutable, a skilled practitioner not only at overt thrusts and parries but also at the seemingly accidental slips that may signal hidden knowledge of fellow players.

The Burden of Proof, in contrast, takes place behind the public scenes, providing more personal facets of Sandy Stern the man—husband, father, neighbor, lover, and friend. Stern the grieving widower must deal with the personal shock of his wife's seemingly inexplicable suicide, the revelation of an embarrassing social disease that may afflict him as well, and a missing $850,000 that somehow connects his wife to his maverick brother-in-law's grand jury indictment for business fraud in a commodity-futures firm. To sort out his shattered personal life, Stern must look at his family in a new way, through the distance of intellect rather than the intimacy of family feeling, in order to unravel the threads that have brought his family and his life to this moment. Stern turns to his past for clues to his present and breaks unspoken family codes to make sense of acts that seem out of character and to reestablish meaningful relationships. While the personal nightmares of *The Burden of Proof* are as intense as those in *Presumed Innocent*, the ending is more positive as Stern reasserts control over his life, devolves himself of guilt, and sees into the human mysteries that have surrounded and enveloped him. Although *The Burden of Proof* is less of a mystery than *Presumed Innocent*, it is an equally compelling portrait of human alienation and the pain family members inflict on each other.

Reviewers call the novel "provocative" and "riveting" (*Chicago Tribune, Kirkus Reviews*), "meaty" and "probing" (*Orlando Sentinel*), "bristling with intelligence" (*Playboy*) and "transcending genre limitations" (*New York Newsday*). "A mystery of the heart," says the *San Jose Mercury News*. "Compelling . . . intelligently and entertainingly crafted," asserts the *American Bar Association Journal*: "Turow's prose is clear, his dialogue real, and his characters sympathetic." Various critics associate Turow's efforts herein with those of the likes of Theodore Dreiser and James Gould Cozzens (Jonathan Yardley of *Washington Post Book World*), Dashiell Hammet and Raymond Chandler (*New York Times Book Review*), John le Carré and P. D. James (*New York Newsday*), and even John Cheever or John O'Hara (*Hartford Courant*). The *New York Daily News* says *The Burden of Proof* is "complex in matters of law, finance, and the heart," "a compelling drama that simmers beneath Turow's accomplished prose," while the *Dallas Morning News* simply asserts "a wonderful read . . . a solid book." The *Atlanta Journal-Constitution* finds everything about the book "exactly right," to which *USA Today* adds, "serious," "ambitious," and "complex." The *Christian Science Monitor* praises Turow as "uncommonly skilled" and "uncommonly eloquent" in this book. Indeed, *The Burden of Proof* is both a satisfying mystery and a satisfying family story. It is an immigrant story about assimilation and conflicts between generations and a love story about self-sacrifice and generosity despite fear, repression, and loss of personal connections.

PLOT DEVELOPMENT AND STRUCTURE

The Burden of Proof is broadly organized into three segments: Part 1 contains chapters 1 through 12, part 2 contains chapters 13 through 30, and part 3 contains chapters 31 through 50. This tripartite division, one

Turow uses frequently, is general and does not frame specific events, which is the function of the chapters. The composition of the parts is (1) exposition of the precipitating event and immediate aftermath, (2) body of the plot, and (3) resolution.

Part 1 begins with the shocking scene of Sandy's discovery of Clara's suicide, and the next 11 chapters show the immediate effects on Sandy and his family and his somewhat desultory efforts at investigating Clara's secrets and beginning his defense of Dixon Hartnell. The particular chapters break down as follows:

Chapter 1: Sandy's discovery of Clara's body, the police investigation begun, the arrival of son Peter

Chapter 2: Clara's funeral, the next three days with the children and Dixon; Dixon's pre-funeral FBI subpoena

Chapter 3: Four days after the funeral: Sandy back to work informally on Dixon's defense; Dixon, Sonia "Sonny" Klonsky; details on futures trading, Kindle County

Chapter 4: One week after funeral: reading of Clara's will, $850,000 unaccounted for; Peter and children, Sandy interact

Chapter 5: A few days after the reading of the will and the weeks thereafter: memories of Clara; neighbor Fiona Cawley and doctor husband Nate's sex video; Sandy's interest in sex reawakened

Chapter 6: Backstory on Sandy and law firm, Rusty Sabich of *Presumed Innocent*; Dixon and Sandy contrasted

Chapter 7: Five weeks after suicide: impromptu dinner with Helen Dudak; Nate Cawley denies treating Clara for a serious condition; Sandy evinces interest in Helen for future

Chapter 8: Sandy to his daughter Kate and son-in-law John's for an awkward dinner; Kate denies knowledge of medical bill; Sandy realizes Peter must have treated Clara

Chapter 9: Forty days after suicide: back story on Stern family emigration from Argentina; Sandy goes to Chicago to examine Maison Dixon (MD) trading records; sleeps with Margy Allison, MD's chief operating officer

Chapter 10: Margy in Chicago explains how Dixon used the error account for illegal trades; phoning Kindle, Sandy accepts Helen Dudak's dinner invitation and asks Lieutenant Ray Radczyk to find out what Clara's lab test was for

Chapter 11: In Kindle, Sandy meets with Sonia Klonsky and discovers her complexity; she reveals John Granum, Kate's husband, is being subpoenaed because of his work at the MD order desk

Chapter 12: Kindle County history. Lieutenant Radczyk reluctantly tells Sandy that Clara's lab test was positive for genital herpes.

In general, then, as we can see from the chapter-by-chapter summary, part 1 traces the first consequences of Clara's shocking act and shows Sandy's immediate responses: guilt, shame, grief, social embarrassment. The later chapters of part 1 record Sandy's adjustments to the dramatic changes his wife's death brings to his life—seemingly no part of his life remains untouched. He begins to understand his own naiveté about those close to him and his escape into overwork. He applies an analytical eye to those around him, initiating a long-delayed process of coming of age, of seeing a complexity in his family he had almost willfully denied, for all his sensitivity to courtroom nuance. His sex life rekindles, and he becomes aware of the limits, emotional and sensual, of his previous life with the closed, repressed Clara. He also comes to understand the prosecutor's case against Dixon.

Part 2 has Stern beginning his investigation of Clara's herpes infection by consulting with his son Peter. Dixon's scam becomes more apparent, and Sandy acts as a kind of amateur detective, delving into Clara's past, scrounging details from Sonia Klonsky about the government's case, and puzzling over the large sum of money missing from his wife's account. Throughout, this section provides the back story of young Sandy and Clara, sometimes as whole chapters, as in chapter 13, and sometimes simply as reminiscences triggered by Clara's possessions or people's references to her.

Sandy moves forward as well, dating Helen Dudak and bedding Margy Allison, Maison Dixon's chief in Chicago, who seduces him when he goes there to examine records. Chapter 20 uses a question from the young Clara to delve into Sandy's family history in Argentina. His life begins to reformulate itself in part because of Helen, in part because of his almost adolescent fixation on Sonny after spending the day and evening with her at her cabin in the country (he breaks up with Helen as a result). Nate Cawley, the doctor neighbor who treated Clara, keeps putting Sandy off about Clara's medical condition before her suicide, but Sandy remains in touch with his daughter Marta, who comes in from New York to sort through Clara's belongings, as well as with his daughter Kate.

In general then, part 2 unfolds in direct synchronization with Sandy's struggles to cope with new challenges: new lovers and a sensuality long suppressed, old memories popping up, unfinished business, evasions by old friends and relatives, new threats from the government. If part 1 was a severe blow to Stern's identity as a husband, father, and even lawyer, part 2 shows elements of his identity being reformulated through confronting old issues long suppressed, such as Clara's near-private relationships with their children, especially Peter and Kate, and through constructing new relationships on his own, rather than as part of a couple.

Part 3 pulls together the shattered parts of Stern's former self and begins to make him whole again. His infatuation with Sonny begins to fade but deepens into a true friendship. Marta returns home to become Sandy's lawyer in his dealings with Sonny and Stan Sennett, and it is clear that now that Clara is gone, there will be no impediment to her returning home permanently and working in Stern's office (everyone seems to find this natural and proper, recognizing Marta as her father's professional successor and Clara as having made Marta's return unlikely). Despite the quasi-comic adventures with the safe in which Dixon has stashed incriminating documents, the futures trading case moves quickly to a head and begins to meld with Stern's personal life, involving Kate, John, Peter, and Clara. Doctor Nate Cawley finally tells most of what he knows, and Peter, caught by Stern *in flagrante* as an informant, grumpily admits his culpability in both the Clara and Dixon disasters. A *deus ex machina* event resolves the Dixon case and brings Stern and Helen together again, but Dixon's end has been carefully prepared for throughout and comes with a sense of inevitability after the initial shock.

With the ending, a new Sandy Stern emerges, certainly sadder and wiser about love and the ways of the world, but also remarried, still the bedrock support for his adored sister Silvia, practicing law with his favorite daughter Marta, and with hopes of some reconciliation with Kate, Peter, and John. Sandy Stern has overcome his attenuated assimilation to American life, his limiting marriage to Clara, and his own reserve to embrace a wider and hopefully more fulfilling life as a husband, father, and professional.

THEMATIC ISSUES

The Burden of Proof examines a number of tightly interrelated thematic issues. These include questions of loyalty and betrayal, of family politics, and the secret lives of neighbors, friends, and family. Suicide's aftermath—the consequences for the survivors—is the particular theme, but Clara's death quickly becomes the matrix for a wealth of family ties and torments, making visible what has long been evident but not to Sandy. Central to the underlying character of the original Sterns are immigrant concerns: the injustices fled, the new lives sought and acquired, the difficulties of full assimilation and acculturation, and the disjunction between first- and second-generation immigrants. Sandy and Silvia Stern show us two responses to the challenges immigrants face, while Dixon Hartnell is, in contrast, another kind of internal "immigrant," a coal-town second-generation American grasping for wealth and respectability. The criminal theme concerns the temptations of risky futures trading, the essence of capitalist gambling, played against the rules and laws enforced by prosecutors. In general, this is a psychologically and emotionally complicated novel about the long-term repercussions of lives lived in secret, of human frailty, and inescapable—because enduring—family ties. Turow elucidates generational differences, especially in degrees of sexual frankness (a new general openness against a former restraint), as causes of Clara's and Sandy's reserve. Reviewer Joseph Feeney sums up Turow's themes as touching "human miseries: the joy and sadness of family, the secrets of marriage, a widower's response to sex, a man's honor and reputation, integrity in law and business and contemporary American values" (*America*, 250), while *Time* reviewer Paul Gray aptly identifies Turow's underlying theme of family as driven by "substantial" characters and as "central to the popular novel from *War and Peace* to 'The Godfather'" (71). *The Burden of Proof* ranks in this esteemed company.

Questions of Loyalty

The novel explores the theme of loyalty with special application to keeping faith with family members, friends, and colleagues. When Sandy's wife, Clara, commits suicide, her unexpected act triggers a minute examination of every family relationship and the other intricate aspects of her life. Sandy has been blissfully unaware of many of the troubles simmering around him, and his investigation into Clara's act is a coming-of-age story for him as well. A bildungsroman is the traditional label for the story of a young person learning how to come to terms with the world and the evil in it; Sandy is far from young, but he has a youthful naiveté that justifies the "coming-of-age" term.

The Immigrant Experience

Sandy is an immigrant, an Argentine Jew seeking a better life free from racial prejudice and the malevolent social limits that are the sad heritage of European religious bigotry. Argentina promised Jews (and other oppressed peoples like the Scots and Irish) a fresh start; in practice, anti-Semitism could be as virulent as in the old country. In Kindle County, Sandy Stern, like many immigrants to the American Midwest, found a refreshing meritocracy at work, a focus on what talent and hard work could achieve, rather than on race, religion, social class, and family background. The great immigrant caldrons of midwestern cities leveled the playing field by providing opportunities for players of many origins: no one group could as easily dominate as in older, more established communities. The practical midwestern ethic also tended to put achievement to the forefront. While prejudice remained (Sandy "did not wade in the same polluted waters they [his clients] did," 412), achievement could go far to counter it. The view of Kindle County's diverse communities and neighborhoods visible from the Morgan Towers is a daily reminder to Stern of the mingling of races that fathered his city.

Yet Sandy Stern, also like many first-generation immigrants, believes too uncritically that the ideals of his adopted nation are essentially the norms of its practice. His investigation into Clara's secrets and his new status as a rich, successful widower expose randy sexuality for which his commitment to work and his married state left no time or inclination. One woman he barely knows calls him after Clara's death with a frank proposition. Sandy eventually succumbs to the blandishments of Helen Dudak, another lonely woman past child-bearing age, and he finds himself experimenting with sex with different partners at age 56. The pursuit of an education, work, and the demands of lawyering had left no time for Sandy, as with many immigrants, to pursue pleasure; the sexual revolution of the 1960s and 1970s passed him by almost unnoticed. He is fairly shocked to see its consequences being played out among people his age.

Sandy is a lot less naive about financial misbehavior. He has been a scold to brother-in-law Dixon Hartnell, a futures trader, continually warning him against his cavalier disregard of rules and the authorities, reminding him, "This is a serious business" (38). Yet even in the economic realm that has been part of Stern's lifelong work, he has much to learn about the financial malfeasance that lies behind the complex of causes that led to Clara's death. He is one of Turow's lawyers for whom the rules are not obstacles to be avoided but rather moral absolutes; Sandy has old-fashioned convictions that go back to his father, and they reflect the dignity and seriousness of his Argentine upbringing. His learning about Dixon's scams is a second coming-of-age.

Family Politics

The other major theme in *The Burden of Proof* is family politics. Families, said one of Turow's law professors, are "the magic circle where the law

ends," or as Turow himself put it, the place where "certain rules, geom-
etries, inclinations" of "given families . . . make them almost ungovernable
universes of their own," despite our hopes for law (Kucherawy, 43).
Clara's sudden absence forces Sandy to confront a hard truth about his
connection to his family: her role as mediator between himself and the
children, a role that developed without Sandy's conscious decisions. The
dynamics of family life have in the past left him mystified and lonely: his
son Peter has always defined himself against Sandy and developed special, private relationships with Marta and Kate while engaging his
mother's intense attention. The roles these family members play seem
partly a consequence of personal nature and partly a result of circumstance: Sandy's 14-hour work days and Clara's upbringing in an emotionally cold family lead them into patterns of separation and alienation
that express the preferences of their basic natures, which are further
shaped by family pressures. Turow's typical interest in father–son relationships is also an issue: Sandy and Peter battle and fall into difficult
silences, two souls unable to connect.

The ultimate trump card in the game of family politics is suicide. Removing oneself from play destroys the integrity of the game and suspends
all responses in a permanent limbo. Clara's quiet pain and inability to see
a way clear lead her to this final act of mutual destruction: the family will
never be the same. Sandy's quest for understanding can only answer some
questions, not make the members whole. Suicide, even when explained,
leaves enormous gaps based on forestalled courses of action, what-ifs that
cannot be acted upon. An admirable goal of *The Burden of Proof* is to mine
this theme, assessing the damage done to survivors.

The Mystery of Personality

Sandy also encounters the mystery of personality. No longer con-
strained by Clara's expectations, he must reinvent himself with old and
new acquaintances as a freshly single man. He wanders the house at night,
discovering long-ignored possessions like a child alert to a new world.
Social life is equally fresh-minted, even as he holds on to the old elements
of identity in his reinvented human connections. He has two sexual affairs
and one impossible romantic interlude. The theme of self-discovery comes
out through these love affairs, as Stern finally constructs his true adult
persona.

Financial Malfeasance

Every Turow novel focuses on an aspect of the law or American life that allows the author to penetrate and expound on a normally closed domain. In *Presumed Innocent* it was the politics and mechanics of a prosecutor's office. Here, it is the arcana of futures trading, a Kindle County and Chicago specialty that offers large financial temptations and numerous possibilities for scams. How can money be made buying and selling not-yet-existent corn, wheat, even the notorious pork bellies? Such commodities have no material substance to traders, only prices, and, although risking huge amounts on a dice toss potentially affected by dozens of variables, all for a product never seen, is the essence of capitalism, few writers have dared to depict the thrills and agonies of this esoteric business. Turow elucidates this complex world with great clarity, enabling readers to see its workings and abuses, through Dixon Hartnell's business dealings and Stern's attempts to keep Dixon out of trouble. We understand clearly its human side, the way Dixon can make the numbers jump his way while his employee, John Granum, for all his competitiveness, crashes and burns.

CHARACTER DEVELOPMENT

The insiders in this book are all family, neighbors, and close friends of Sandy Stern.

Alejandro "Sandy" Stern

The center of this book's universe around which all other characters orbit is Rusty Sabich's enigmatic defense attorney from *Presumed Innocent*, Sandy Stern. Turow based his character partly on an uncle of his, a doctor from Los Angeles, telling Bill Blum of the *Los Angeles Times* that he had always been fascinated by his life and by the fact that when, in his later years, he found himself alone, unmarried, and "not entirely pleased with the way his life had gone," he had the courage to start again: "I always wanted to write a book about a man like that who was starting again" (June 11, 1990).

Stern is a family man whose involvement in his wife's and children's lives has been limited by the fact that he is also a dedicated defense lawyer. Sympathetic to human frailty and driven to understand motive, Stern seeks to make sense of the seemingly senseless death of his wife, Clara.

Like Turow, Stern's father was a doctor, an immigrant to South America who treated Russian Jewish agriculturalist settlers in Santa Fe, Argentina—a rural area distant from Buenos Aires. Stern's sense of personal identity derives from a number of disparate sources.

Stern's core identity derives from his faith, though he admits that "his first faith would always be in the facts" (422). Yet even his pure spiritual center is shaded by other influences, especially his Argentine heritage, his family, and his profession. Fifty-six at the time of the book, Stern was 13 when he emigrated and has spent three quarters of his life in the United States. However, if he left Argentina in 1947, his formative late childhood would have been shaped by a virulent and widespread anti-Semitism, for Argentine dictator Juan Perón, a Fascist sympathizer in World War II, provided a safe haven for the German Nazis after the Allied victory. Such prejudice would clearly make the young Stern very conscious of his Jewish identity, and, aware from an early age of the dangers of the outside world, he would have learned to be very private, secretive, and closed, taking family silence as natural and self-protective. As a result, too, as a lawyer he became "a proud apologist for deviation," for, as Turow's narrative voice asserts: "No person Argentine by birth, a Jew alive to hear of the Holocaust, could march in the jackboots of authority without intense self-doubt; better to keep his voice among the voices, to speak out daily for these frail liberties, so misunderstood, whose existence, far more than any prosecution, marked us all as decent, civilized, as human. He could not abandon the credo of a lifetime" (132).

Yet language shapes us deeply as well. Stern had forsaken Spanish years before the period of the book, but a favored expression would occasionally escape him, and he surprises himself when he automatically speaks Spanish to Silvia. His Spanish accent when speaking English, nonetheless, is inescapable and as a youth, he could not bear the "sniggering" that followed his slightly accented mispronunciation. Turow, ever the careful stylist, plays Stern's stilted, formal English off against the loose-limbed idiomatic chatter of his family and friends, a cultural marker the lawyer would love to acquire. But casual linguistic garb is not Stern: he was also formed by his father, a "quiet, proper man of fragile character" (42) who sought respect and security and found neither. Like many first-generation immigrants forged by horrific experiences in their native lands, Stern, for all his American yearnings, remains a displaced person, a master of the levers of legal power in his profession but a social oddity nonetheless.

The law was another shaping influence on Stern's character, but his choice of profession is also telling: a controlled, formal character, made more so by the threats of his childhood, chooses a controlled, formal professional role, that of courtroom litigator. Sandy is made for this arena, as Sonia Klonsky's almost gushing acknowledgment of his influence indicates: "He [Stan Sennett] has a great deal of respect for you. Everybody there does. You know that. Frankly, he looked very concerned the first time I told him you were involved in this case. I'm not supposed to admit that, am I?" (233). His courtroom demeanor provides elegance and grace to the rough-and-tumble aggression lawyers must practice. Klonsky, and other Stern admirers (there are many for this recurring character), crave just what sets Sandy Stern apart, his old-world elegance of manner. This sensitivity to etiquette, however, does not preclude Stern showing his teeth when angry: one time accusing Klonsky of "leaping unnecessarily" to conclusions (283), another time giving her a "momentary scowl" (138), and then shortly thereafter accusing her of needless "hand-wringing" (139).

Most significantly, Stern is a man who believes the rules matter for their own sake. After escaping a culture where law meant little and raw power ruled, where the *desaparecidos,* or people "disappeared" by the government, might return in a week, a year, or never, Sandy sees the law and his role as defense attorney differently from the perspective of his colleagues. The government must be controlled; human nature makes prosecutors aggressive, high-handed, and arrogant (and "angry," says Turow in the Macdonald interview, 2004). No American optimist, Sandy sees himself as always fighting a rearguard defensive action, retreating while finding a way to win by indirection or subtlety and insinuation as is shown so clearly in *Presumed Innocent.* If some of his colleagues use head-on karate attacks, Stern practices judo and ju-jitsu, the older form of combat in which an opponent's charge is turned against him. Like the best martial artists, he regards the rules as a philosophy of life, a belief system rather than a how-to formula.

Stern's character remains stable throughout the novel—his basic values and beliefs are as firm as bedrock—but his expression of this character undergoes a radical change. Stern's original coming-of-age was foreshortened by isolation as a new immigrant and by the need to work constantly to support himself; from this limited maturation process, he moves into an emotionally constricted relationship with Clara, who allows him to escape into over-work while she rules the emotional arena with the children. Brilliant in court, Stern's polite, formal, evasive persona is a liability in his personal dealings, where he is close only to Silvia and Marta. In his dealings with Helen, Stern takes a certain pleasure in being elusive, and Turow says of him, "He was back to his essential aspect, the foreigner, unknown and hard to figure" (204). His son Peter engages him as an enemy, and his old pal Dixon has a love-hate relationship with him. However, Stern's ethical values and professional commitment are above reproach, as Sonny recognizes even in the midst of Dixon's double-dealing. Sandy must learn to connect emotionally and socially with greater openness and trust.

Clara Mittler Stern

Although she never appears as a living character in the novel, Sandy's wife, Clara Stern, is a presence throughout, in Sandy's memories of her, in recollections by their children and friends, and in the physical and social environment she created: her house and furnishings, her garden, her charities and financial bequests. It is this pervasive presence that Stern must work through, all the while realizing Clara had a secret life he was unaware of: "he would never really know what lay inside" (226).

Clara, who is 58, was the daughter of an extremely wealthy lawyer who remained suspicious of impoverished immigrant Sandy's intentions, to the point that Sandy declared he and Clara would live off his salary, and did so. (Clara had worked briefly as a grade-school teacher at a ghetto school, but she didn't stay long.) Clara's cool reserve was possibly a product of her father's upbringing and certainly in accord with his expectations of a young woman of her class and time period, but with her own children she practiced complete devotion. She has an intense relationship with her son Peter, perhaps unwittingly aiding him in shutting his father out of his life. She is heavily involved in her girls' lives, to the point Sandy wonders about women like her: "But certain women, married women, mothers prototypically, became too involved with the dense network of their activities—the nurturing, organizing, doing, and attending—to broadcast any ostensible sexual interest" (170). Although Clara has confined herself to house and children, she has been engaged in her synagogue (her family helped found it) and her charities and teaching music appreciation at an impoverished Kindle County inner-city school. But she is nonetheless quiet, reserved, and private, a woman of taste and gentility. Clara's suicide is all the more shocking because she has seemed a mere appurtenance of Sandy's life, like the house or children before they grew up. Her act forces Sandy to consider her as her own person and to reevaluate their entire history together.

Clara's name means "clear" in Spanish, and the masculine form *claro* is a confirmation of understanding, yet Clara, her actions, and her motives are most unclear, even murky, and the facts that begin to emerge at first only cloud our image of her even more.

Marta Stern

The Sterns' older daughter, Marta, is important because she is so much like her father, a budding lawyer (working for legal aid in New York), a thoughtful, serious person, and, eventually, Sandy's partner in later books. (She has a small part in *Reversible Errors*.) Unfortunately for Marta, she has also inherited Sandy's (not so good) looks, for both are "short, with a tendency to gather weight in their lower parts" (26). Nonetheless, she is bright and memorable and connects with Sandy in ways his other children are unable to do. In fact, Marta is Sandy's one true child, a quick learner like her father, and, if not a soul mate, at least someone on the same wavelength, professionally and personally. Sandy is proud of her legal prowess when she acts as his lawyer, and Marta is praised warmly by friend and foe alike. She is a younger, more American version of Sandy, but retains some of his graciousness, though not his reserve. Tellingly, she seems to have been Clara's least favored child (Clara believed Kate was the brightest and clearly held Peter in special regard). Sandy has always felt close to Marta, and Clara's demise brings her home.

Peter Stern

The Sterns' son, Peter, was his mother's favorite, but his typical way of relating to his father is combat: "Peter had located all of his father's foremost antagonists and joined league with them" (472). Peter, a medical doctor, chooses not to help Sandy understand Clara's problems until he is forced to; the lines of communication were active between mother and son, but their closeness shut Sandy out. Peter is more like his mother than his father, but he trades Clara's reported gentility and refinement for a prickly, unpleasant, even misanthropic personality, a character flaw his siblings shrug off as Peter just being Peter. He is high-strung, and Sandy even worries that Peter will upset the police investigating Clara's death. When Peter and Sandy go to dinner, their conversation soon lapses into silence. When Peter checks his father for herpes, secretly knowing the truth of his mother's condition, he takes pleasure in embarrassing his father, remarking "Life is full of surprises" (172), as if he has just made a nasty discovery about Sandy. By the end of the book Peter and Sandy reach a point of termination: their father–son intimacy is severed, so they would meet in the future as acquaintances only (477). Sandy has hopes, however, that he may someday make peace with Peter.

Kate Stern Granum

Sandy's younger daughter is married to John Granum, her high school sweetheart and a former football player who works as a futures trader for Maison Dixon, Dixon Hartnell's firm. Kate announces her first pregnancy on the day of her mother's funeral. Although John and Kate figure importantly in the plot, they remain cipher-like, uninteresting as personalities. One character insight is that their marriage is across religious lines— John is Gentile and has been "gently" opposed by the Sterns, but Kate married John anyway, perhaps suggesting a rebellion against the Stern clan. She certainly does little to justify her mother's claim that she is the brightest of the children, and her decisions with John about his Maison Dixon activities inspire little confidence. Turow describes John Granum as "a sweet Gentile hunk, an almost laughable prototype, a football player and a paragon of blond male beauty with his apple-pie face and hapless manner" (20). The union to an all-American-jock type can also be seen as Kate's desire for assimilation, but the theme is not developed.

Dixon Hartnell

Sandy's brother-in-law Dixon Hartnell is his diametrical opposite in most measures of character and style, with "as many faces to Stern as a totem pole" (176), "like Caliban or God—unknowable" (85). The son of a German immigrant, a Lutheran minister, Dixon was, in Stern's opinion, "as elusive as smoke" (52). Sandy met Dixon Hartnell in the service, and their friendship perhaps turned on their recognition of each other as self-made men: just as Sandy rose as a first generation immigrant, so Dixon came out of a bleak Illinois coal mining town near the Kentucky border. But while Sandy took the conventional and safe route through law school, Dixon embraced the risky, entrepreneurial life of futures trading. (Sandy muses that the first futures traders were Las Vegas bookmakers.) Their differences are so great that Sandy tries to discourage Dixon's marriage to his sister Silvia, to no avail. As Dixon's lawyer, Sandy nags Dixon about his corner-cutting and cavalier disregard of the authorities, again to no avail; it is tempting to see each finding in the other characteristics to admire but not actually practice: Sandy would like to be more daring, unconventional, and spontaneous, but only dares to be so with Sonny

Klonsky; Dixon is envious of Sandy's honor, honesty, and loyalty, but is himself weak and self-indulgent. Dixon's Maison Dixon is hugely successful, rich, and a thorn in the side of the authorities, the antithesis of Sandy's small, very respectable and admired law firm. Brian Dennehy brings Dixon to life in the Mike Robe film of this book.

Silvia Stern

Sandy's sister and Dixon's wife, Silvia, is not fully developed in the novel. She is gracious and still beautiful, a soul mate to Sandy—she speaks to him daily on the phone—and an adored wife to the sexual libertine Dixon, who seems to regard her as a rock of stability in his messy life. Their marriage is childless.

Helen Dudak and Margy Allison

Helen Dudak, a widowed neighbor, and Margy Allison, Dixon's chief operating officer, both Sandy's new lovers, take advantage of his sudden availability and his dawning interest in sexual experimentation. Margy is young and tough, efficient at her job, and very cynical. Helen is older and more vulnerable, attracted to Stern, but fearful of rejection: "She laid out what was on her mind with no more ceremony than a butcher tossing meat onto the scale" (202). Both are very pragmatic in their relationships and in their view of the world, putting another face on female intimacy for Sandy, who has known only the reserved, conventional, and impenetrable Clara.

Sonia Klonsky

Sandy's antagonist in his defense of Dixon, the Assistant United States Attorney Sonia "Sonny" Klonsky, is a fine character (she will share the lead role in *The Laws of Our Fathers*). She and Sandy "meet cute," in movie parlance, sparring fiercely after she sends FBI agents to Sandy's house on the day of Clara's funeral to serve a subpoena on Dixon. Their continuing conflict turns into mutual respect when Sandy comes to understand Sonia's domestic problems and emotional disarray, the humanity behind her prosecutorial persona. For all her "woman-on-the-go composedness," says Turow, "there was something seething, molten, uncontrolled, unknown," about her, "a touching quality . . . [in] a woman past forty, still on the voyages of a teenager" (129). Sonia later admits to a form of hero worship of Sandy when she was a law student. Their emotional connection has the potential to become love were it not for Sandy's fatherly consciousness of the difference between their ages. The *sympatico*, or emotional harmony, between them is deeper than the connection Sandy has with his lovers.

GENRE CONVENTIONS: THE BILDUNGSROMAN MEETS THE FAMILY THERAPY DETECTIVE STORY

A recurrent theme in Turow's works is the domestic price lawyers pay for success: families are neglected and children grow up barely seen by the legal industry parent. In *Pleading Guilty*, Mack Malloy's family has disintegrated, and Malloy points to the exploitation of associates hoping to make partner in large firms when he muses about the long hours lawyers must work. *The Burden of Proof* shows this phenomenon in a smaller firm, for Sandy Stern has turned over family life to a willing Clara, who keeps the home fires burning and raises the children: "He was in his office with his cigars, his books, his phone, his clients, from seven in the morning until nine or ten at night. He came home then to a quiet house. The children were bedded down, gone. Clara waited with a book on her lap in the quiet living room, the aroma of his warming dinner through the house: an image of order, resourcefulness, sufficiency" (64–65).

In this context of the workaholic lawyer, seeing *The Burden of Proof* as a bildungsroman, the German term for a coming-of-age story, makes some sense. Old people don't come of age in a bildungsroman or elsewhere; we might well ask what a man coming of age at 56 has been doing with his life. The answer for Sandy Stern is working, spending 12 to 14 hours per day in office and court and seeing family only on weekends. Stern knows the legal and business world intimately, but his own domestic emotional landscape remains a mystery to him; he is "emotionally landlocked" (96). Clara is repressed and formal, a creature of firm habits and ways, and ultimately "unknowable" (226). Son Peter does battle with his father, and Stern has little in common with daughter Kate. Only Marta, herself somewhat like Sandy, connects with her father.

It is in this way that Stern's story is a bildungsroman, as he learns about the turbulent feelings all around him that have been kept under wraps, and as his investigation uncovers the videotaped sexual high jinks of his neighbor, doctor Nate Cawley, and he learns that other friends and neighbors have kept more than their home fires burning: "In fin de siècle America . . . this was how men and women paid respects. The hell with notes and flowers. Let's get it on!" (243). Stern's sexual initiation came only with

Clara, for he had been too busy working his way through school to go out with women and too shy and reserved even if he had found time. The sexual liberation of the late 1960s passed him by; in fact, his "high-strung, hysterical" mother and soft, dignified wife comprise for Sandy "the familiar range for female behavior" (107). However, with Clara absent, he is discovering the aftermath of the sexual revolution 25 years later. Sandy begins seeing Helen Dudak, and then sleeps with Margy Allison, who he acknowledges understands much about sex and "carnality, that were remote from him" (114). He even has the odd (for a man his age and background) experience of being upbraided by Margy for cheating on a new girlfriend! He is shocked at himself, and pleased, and stunned. As Jonathan Yardley of *Washington Post Book World* confirms, the novel is an "exceptionally subtle, knowing exploration of the myriad ways in which a life can be reborn at any juncture in its course" (1990). Now, "making allowances for his lack of prior experience," Stern is "fifty-six and 'going steady': like some teenager, he was . . . screwing his brains out" (243).

The second genre apparent in *The Burden of Proof* is the detective/investigation story. Sandy Stern's credentials as a true detective in the hard-boiled tradition are suspect, for he is a man of the courthouse, not of the streets. If Stern is a detective, he is soft-boiled, absent all hard edges. Yet Stern fits very neatly within the amateur detective tradition, wherein the individual is pressed by circumstance into an investigative role. He has two mysteries to solve, seemingly completely unrelated cases: Clara's baffling (to Sandy), apparently unmotivated suicide, and Stan Sennett's probe of Dixon Hartnell's futures trading practices. Both Clara and Dixon have kept Stern in the dark, and his task is to uncover the tracks of two secretive persons. As he investigates Clara's past, his queries become more and more intermingled with his other, seemingly unrelated business, his defense of Dixon Hartnell (the unrelated cases merging into one is a classic convention). Sandy's investigation begins as family therapy analysis, a search for what could have led to Clara's suicide. Ironically, as in the classic detective story, the investigator comes to learn as much about himself as about the targets of his queries.

Turow places Stern squarely in the center of the tradition of amateur detectives, who are driven to depend on themselves to ferret out the truth when public officials lack the access, the insider knowledge, to do so. Sometimes, they detect simply out of curiosity but often they have very personal motives for investigating—for example, a need to understand a sequence of events that involves them directly, injury to a loved one, or a threat to themselves or to someone they hold dear. The amateur detective has the advantage over the police of being on the spot interacting with the suspects or the involved parties on a regular and casual basis. At times seeking answers requires some degree of nosiness, as Stern discovers in his queries about Clara's medical condition, and light conversation camouflages probing questions posed to relatives, neighbors, friends, and colleagues. Traditionally, these amateurs are distracted by a number of red herrings that lead them to erroneous and sometimes even embarrassing conclusions, but they persist quietly and firmly until a pattern that makes sense psychologically begins to emerge. The problem of the genre is, of course, the question of how the amateur is to behave when the puzzle is solved and the answers confirmed—whether to bring in the police, face the offender to suggest restitution, or quietly walk away with the satisfaction of finally understanding what really happened.

"Mystery as a genre," said Turow to *Maclean's* reviewer Dennis Kucherawy, "dramatizes and exploits the suspicion we all have about one another: that we don't know each other's deepest secrets and that we may be able to learn them. They may even shock us when we find out what they are" (43). In keeping with this tradition, Stern needs to understand why his wife took her own life and how her death relates to the missing money and the possible federal investigation of stock fraud. His sources of information are the people he has lived with and socialized with, oblivious to the tensions and nefarious activities going on around him. Stern the investigative lawyer uses the tools of all competent investigators. He examines physical evidence, like the bill from Westlab for Clara's medical tests or the medications on the shelf of the Cawley's bathroom cabinet. He questions witnesses, especially Nate Cawley, Clara's doctor, but also Fiona Cawley and his own son, Peter. When Nate proves evasive, Sandy resorts to trickery with the Westlab clerk. He is aware of the "usual techniques" of the FBI, such as making a "pretext call" (34) under false pretenses, for example, claiming to owe money, as when the FBI ascertains Dixon's location at the Stern's home before the funeral so the agents can serve him with a subpoena. Stern does much the same with the Westlab clerk, claiming he just wants to pay the lab and doctor's bill so he must have a name, and thus comes up with Nate Cawley. With Margy, who has a much deeper understanding of financial transactions than he does, Stern practices investigative caution, interrogating in the best detective manner: "The informant could be a 'business colleague.' As evenly as he could, Stern added, 'a friend.' A part of him, on guard, watched her for any telltale response; in this sort of matter, no one was ever above suspicion" (110–111). Later, Stern relies on his intuition (and appeals to hers) as they go over Maison Dixon records: " 'Not right,' said Stern resolutely; then later some of the 'jigsawed pieces fit' " (260); "He knew, with a conviction durable as steel, there was more to it than this" (277). His intuition serves him well; he muses as he evaluates the color of the Kindle River, reading the weather and time of year: "That was the value of experience . . . to be able to read the meaning of signs . . . the large impact signaled by small things" (279). Thus, *The Burden of Proof* also, to some degree, draws on the psychological thriller as well, for Sandy's detection depends most heavily on coming to terms with the psychology of his suspects and intuiting their patterns of behavior.

Stern interrogates his various sources, watching their reactions and judging their credibility: "Stern . . . suddenly had it all, everything, clearly in focus. Nate was Clara's doctor" (404). However, Stern's real strength is that of the prototypical detective, whose Sherlock Holmesian skill of ratiocination enables him to weigh the evidence gathered, judge the witnesses interrogated, correctly interpret behavior, and, having considered the options, draw meaningful and accurate conclusions about the pattern that transforms the parts into a meaningful whole. In performing this intellectually challenging task, Stern the man must reevaluate his life and his relationships and reconcile the contradictions and betrayals that call into question past relationships. His is a quest to come to terms with his dead wife, his alienated offspring, and his wily, devious brother-in-law by finding the truth behind their silences and deeds. In this way two genres meet and merge as the amateur detective, in his moment of enlightened understanding of the events and motives that have lain hidden, pieces together meaning—meaning that explains his past and present and directs his future action. The solution to the mystery also represents his maturation, his coming-of-age as he sees himself, his family, and his world with new eyes. Thus, George F. Will rightly affirms in his *Newsweek* article "The Last Word" (1990) that *The Burden of Proof* transcends the mystery genre to produce literature that will last. What begins as detective mystery ends as the human mystery of coming of age, a venerable literary concern.

ALTERNATIVE READING

One of the quotations that precedes the first chapter of *The Burden of Proof* consists of two paragraphs from Sigmund Freud's *The Psychopathology of Everyday Life* (1901; English translation 1914), a passage discussing how a patient's childhood memory disrupts the course of that patient's marriage, with no consciousness on the patient's part of the connection between the events.

Turow's focus on family and the clues of his opening quotation suggest that an excellent critical approach to *The Burden of Proof* is a psychoanalytical reading. Psychoanalysis began with Sigmund Freud's case studies of the psychological conflicts of his Viennese patients in the 1880s and 1890s. As the virtual inventor of a completely new medical field, Freud frequently resorted to familiar literary allusions to illustrate what he took to be timeless human conflicts, such as the Oedipal competition between fathers and sons, and the Electra complex of attraction between fathers and daughters. Freud's interest in the symbolic and metaphorical language of dreams also drew him toward literary tools in his analysis, and both he and his many followers saw their new "science" as having much in common with the interpretive processes of literary study.

One hundred and twenty years after its founding, psychoanalysis takes many forms, but two of Freud's central concerns, the deep impact of childhood experiences and the repression of socially unacceptable conflicts, appear significantly in *The Burden of Proof*. For Freud, the child is father to the man: we become versions of what forms us as small children. All children and adults face conflicts between desires and what they know to be moral and appropriate behavior, and solve the conflicts by denying or "repressing" socially unacceptable memories and wishes, usually with no consciousness of the denial. Both Clara and Sandy Stern are adults formed by childhood trauma, and both cope with adulthood by repressing parts of themselves that would cause conflict if acknowledged. Peter, in turn, is a textbook case of the Oedipal complex at work as he competes with his father for his mother's love.

Clara was raised by a powerful, domineering, distant father: "When I was a girl, I wanted to be just like him. Before I realized that he wouldn't let me" (264). Turow does not give full details about the nature of the relationship, but her reaction, to devote herself to her children, indicates that the lack of emotional connection with her father was more than coolness in the normal range for a young woman of her social class but rather a psychologically powerful formative impulse, an adaptation. Clara's restraint, her secrecy, her deep unhappiness—perhaps even depression at times—lead her to see no way out of her dilemmas except suicide. Although it is not clear what childhood traumas are being repressed, and her problems with Dixon, her health, and her children are real enough, her response is infantile rather than adult, removing herself from the situation rather than working to fix it. Clara's repressed personality forestalls reaching out and taking any action apart from self-negation—her response is narcissistic in that she protects her feelings by shutting them off rather than by considering the damage her act will do to others. (Killing herself solves no problems, and the truth will come out eventually; the consequences will simply become more complex, but she will be spared them. Her suicide note, "Can you forgive me?", addresses this fact of her weakness and lack of courage.) The roots of Clara's personality could only have been uncovered through lengthy analysis; her suicide negates this level of understanding, leaving only Sandy's investigation.

Sandy, too, is a repressed person, but his ultimate reaction is 180 degrees different from Clara's: he takes over her role as nurturer and "fixer." While he may lack Clara's emotional depth with the children, his willingness to engage the world allows the best resolutions under the circumstances of the mess Clara left behind.

Stern grew up with a father who disappointed his wife and family, ending up "an agitated, feckless human being on the verge of one breakdown or another" (204). The deaths of his father and older brother leave Sandy with his mother and younger sister in increasingly anti-Semitic Argentina, a nightmare prospect for a dutiful young man expected to care for his women folk. As with Clara, we have no details about Sandy's childhood and youthful emotional landscape, but it takes little imagination to draw the pictures that would have materialized unbidden in Sandy's mind: newsreels of the liberation of the Holocaust death camps played in Argentina as they did around the world. All around him were escaped Nazis, and Juan Domingo Perón's government was sympathetic to them. Unlike Clara, Sandy takes affirmative action, emigrating with what is left of his family, embracing American ways (not always successfully), and becoming a lawyer, an officer of the court, and a participant in the civic system.

From Stern's perspective, his Argentine ethnic heritage, or at least the hostile parts of it, deserve oblivion. He keeps his Jewish faith as the center of his being but struggles to adapt to the American English idiom, the "rich American argot, savory as any jazzman's," which Stern speaks in his dreams (8). We are told that Stern, like a number of well-educated Argentines, learned British English, which accounts for his prowess in the formal discourse of the courtroom. Apart from chats with Silvia, he exhibits no ethnic nostalgia for the Spanish language or Argentine food or culture. Sandy married American and became American, diving into the melting pot without a look back. Only American slang and social informality elude him.

Many immigrants, most notably Holocaust survivors and war-zone ref-
ugees, repress their early experiences in their embrace of a new culture.
The particular memories they repress are as varied as their unhappy histories, but Freud's point was that repression does not equal erasure. As
with a computer hard disk, where traces of old, erased programs remain
quiescent but can eventually materialize to cause trouble, so repressed
memories emerge and wreak conflict. The deeper the childhood trauma,
the more energy required to repress it; Clara is left unable to cope with
new challenges, given her damaged self. Sandy, in contrast, while keeping
a lid on his past cultural identity, goes on a quest for truth about Clara
with a will and refuses to be put off. His newfound sexual adventurous-
ness contrasts with his uninspired erotic relationship with Clara. Here,
too, Sandy seems to have been repressing some parts of his "natural" self
to keep the peace with his wife, who devoted herself to children and
domesticity. As noted earlier, Clara may be one of those "married women,
mothers . . . too involved in the dense network of their activities . . . to
broadcast . . . sexual interest" (170). She allowed Sandy entrée only into
the parts of her life she wished to reveal: "He had no idea what dark
crabbed corner of madness she had wandered off to" (372).

    Thus, from a psychoanalytic point of view, Sandy Stern acts as therapist
by relentlessly uncovering the truth, not to heal Clara, of course, but to
heal himself and his family by peeling back the protective layers Clara
had constructed. Sandy's own repression of his cultural and personal conflicts and fears from his background remains untouched, but like many
immigrants to America, he has found a way not simply to cope but to
prevail.

    While the Greek literary figure Oedipus killed his father and married
his mother, all unknowingly, in Freud's formulation sons frequently compete indirectly and passively with their fathers by finding some arena
completely foreign to parental competence or, alternatively, by trying to
outdo their father in his own realm. Peter Stern does both, becoming a
doctor, a distinct alternative to law, but then playing defense lawyer for
his brother-in-law John, mimicking Sandy's devious maneuvering while
remaining unable to master it. (Confirming the subconscious nature of
their battle, Sandy remarks that Peter "had never thought of it this way,"
471.)

    The Oedipal battle between Sandy and Peter is ongoing from the latter's
childhood and ends with a "final curtain" (477) when Peter's meddling
is revealed—though Sandy has hopes for his family's future unity. Peter's
actions in undermining Dixon may have been the last straw for Clara,

becoming the proximate cause for her suicide, but she too seems to bear some blame for Peter's disaffection from Sandy, bonding with her son in ways that could only shut out Sandy. This Oedipal tangle offers much room for Freudian analysis.

Worth noting is the contrast between Marta and Kate: Stern's two daughters are dramatically distinct, each reflecting a different parent. Marta even looks a little like Sandy and has his respect for rules, love of law, honesty, and occasional brutal directness. Kate, thought by Clara the brightest of the children, has Clara's orthodox exterior and conventional manner, but hides inner turmoil and emotional fragility. Like Clara, when faced with problems, Kate is inept, considering aborting her much-wished-for child and embracing Peter's hare-brained scheme.

Reading *The Burden of Proof* as a novel about a psychoanalytical failure, Clara, and a psychoanalytical success, Sandy, enables us to evaluate how well their "therapy" succeeded or failed by asking how much we understand about each. The goal of analysis is clarity, but though we might understand why Clara felt she had reached a dead end, we never see the world through her eyes, Sandy's efforts notwithstanding. She remains obscure and distant, a psychological black hole, like that other closed personality, Rusty Sabich, who, despite a first-person narration and a professed openness, remains murky in motive and shadowy in act.

In contrast, the reader is likely to feel he knows everything about Sandy Stern, from his foolish crush on Sonia to his conflicted feelings about his children. He has been an ideal patient, holding nothing back and examining his every quirk. He is rewarded with the hope of a better, healthier future. In the 1992 three-hour television miniseries, Hector Elizondo effectively conveyed the complexity of Sandy Stern and his voyage of discovery as he uncovered harsh truths about his family's past, overcame grief, and moved on to a more balanced life.

5

Pleading Guilty
(1993)

The *Chicago Sun-Times* reviewer calls *Pleading Guilty* "utterly convincing," and Ross Thomas of *Washington Post Book World* finds it both "fascinating" and richly entertaining (X1). *Time* reviewer Paul Gray describes it as an "irresistible," "dark, moral thriller," a study of motivation and compulsions (66). Katrine Ames of *Newsweek*, while not fully satisfied with the novel (calling it "self-consciously bleak"), relishes "Turow's edgy gift for place" (55). Crime author John Mortimer argues that *Pleading Guilty* proves Turow "worthy to be ranked with Dashiell Hammett or Raymond Chandler" (*New York Times Book Review*, 7).

PLOT DEVELOPMENT AND STRUCTURE

Pleading Guilty is a detective fiction novel written in a modernized epistolary style, as if *Pamela*, the eighteenth-century British epistolary classic, met Sam Spade, the classic American hard-boiled detective. In this case, the detective and first-person narrator is McCormack "Mack" Malloy, a former cop turned lawyer, who has been given the task of discreetly discovering the whereabouts of a missing law partner in his firm, star litigator Bert Kamin. Once again the scene is Kindle County. Over a week and a half, Malloy hunts for Kamin, who has been missing for weeks and who is thought to have absconded with $5.6 million designated to settle a class-action suit against the firm's largest client. The epistolary premise is that Malloy employs a Dictaphone® (a voice recorder widely used in the business world) to create tapes (these are the equivalent of the epistle or letter from the earlier genre). The six Dictaphone® tapes whose contents make up the largest portion of the novel constitute Mack's report to the Management Oversight Committee, which has given him the assignment of finding Kamin. Through these transcribed tapes, Malloy guides readers into the underbelly of the top-notch firm that employs him, exposing the moral ambiguity that informs its transactions, the cutthroat alliances that reflect its values, and a corpse and scams that have become the unanticipated by-product of its behind-the-scenes activities. The dated tapes and their subsections, some also dated, cover the 10 days from when Malloy is assigned the case to Groundhog Day, February 2. By tradition, on that day all the partners of Gage and Griswell (G & G) put on tuxedos and repair to the posh Belvedere Club, where they drink wine, hear reports on the state of the firm, and ultimately receive a sealed envelope indicating their portion of the profits. The Groundhog Day surprise is that there will be no profits and perhaps no firm if Malloy fails to find Kamin and persuade him to return the stolen money. The novel ends ironically, with Malloy making his own version of disbursement on Groundhog Day, paying back his coworkers in a way they do not expect.

As noted, Malloy dictates an account of his activities and surmises onto six tapes, which, transcribed, make up the novel. However, the breakdown of the novel into units taped by Malloy does not quite correspond to the way the book is in fact organized into scenes with the different people Malloy encounters in his investigation. The epistolary premise is very useful in a literary way, creating a confessional voice that bares its soul: "I'll never show a word of this [recorded report] to anyone on the Committee" (209). However, Malloy's reason for secrecy is as much his insulting descriptions of the members and his admissions of his own lies as a desire for privacy. Malloy/Turow speculates, "So we all wonder: who am I talking to?" (209). The speculation about audience that follows ("Maybe you're some fifty-year-old Irishman. . . . Or a kid who says this is boring. Or a professor who concludes it is generally vile," 209) is much more Turow than Malloy, and is a backhanded admission that the epistolary frame has slipped, revealing an author behind the scenes controlling his puppet. Why should some Irishman or a kid or a professor be reading Malloy's confidential report to the G & G Management Oversight Committee? It is worth noting, however, that such winks at the audience were a common feature of eighteenth-century novels like Fielding's *Tom Jones* and *Shamela*. This period invented the novel told through letters, and Turow seems to be indulging its slyly comic whims.

Another feature of the eighteenth-century novel is the artful use of chapter heads and subheads, the tag phrases and labels that alert the reader about what to expect. These tags are often ironic, inviting the reader to consider characters and events in a distanced way. Since *Pleading Guilty* has a first-person narration, the irony is supposed to be Malloy's and indeed captures his smart-alecky, wise-guy attitude toward the world, his profession, and his partners—an attitude conservative partners such as Wash find off-putting. For example, tape 1 has four fairly straightforward sections: "My Assignment," "My Reaction," "My Lawyer," and "Bert at Home." The last, however, "His Refrigerator," goes beyond housekeeping to involve a folded body and combines a knowing eighteenth-century smirk with a hard-boiled cinema *noir* shrug of the shoulders: what else do you expect to find in people's private spaces?

As the search/investigation unfolds, the Dictaphone® tapes fade into the background, although Malloy dutifully assures us that in off moments he is taping all we are reading. Supposedly, then, the text of the novel is a transcript at which the reader is getting an inside look. (Should we trust such an unreliable narrator? We know he lies very credibly since he keeps telling us he does.) Part of the difficulty with maintaining the premise of a taped account is how busy Malloy is during his investigatory adventures: he is breaking and entering, being harassed by the detective Pigeyes, drunk, in bed with Brushy, and otherwise occupied. Lugging around a Dictaphone® and finding the leisure to recount what he has done would strain credibility and interrupt the narrative flow. Instead, the 30 "chapters" (does a taped narrative have chapters, a print convention?) set a scene or a series of related scenes. "A Working Life," the chapter, is broken into "The Mind of the Machine," "Washing," and "Introducing the Victim of the Crime," with each unit focusing on a particular character ("Washing" is about a meeting with Wash, George Washington Thale III) or an event ("Introducing the Victim of the Crime" recounts Mack's long back story with Jackson "Jake" Eiger, TransNational's general counsel, from whom the money has presumably been stolen). Turow's plots are always disciplined and minutely organized, and here the general Dictaphone® units simply serve to establish the broad outline of the investigation: the basic exposition in tape 1, background on G & G, Bert Kamin, and Mack Malloy in tape 2, people possibly involved inside and outside the firm in tape 3, closing in on the truth in tape 4, complications and Malloy taking action in tape 5, and resolution in tape 6. The illusion of a taped account is maintained until the very end—Malloy will send the tapes "Federal Excess" to his boss Martin—but events have made them moot anyway, and Malloy admits, "the telling is the only place where I can really reinvent myself" (464).

Of greater significance in understanding how the narrative is constructed are the chapter headings and the scenes that follow them. As with all Turow's works, but especially with a first-person narration, our understanding of events shifts and grows with events. This sounds like a normal consequence of any plot development, but with Turow the point is philosophical, not simply the accretion of plot details. Greater knowledge and understanding is gained as public faces are peeled away and surfaces penetrated, in the case of Malloy's investigation through precise questions, careful investigations of physical evidence, and the exclusion of the impossible, leading to paradigm shifts in perspective and in point of view. As usual with Turow, motive is always complex and multifaceted; is Jake the egotistical simpleton Malloy knows him to be, or has he put a clever plot in train, complete with the exculpatory possibilities Mack enumerates at the end? Is Martin a heroic attorney or a self-serving administrator? Malloy himself is as slippery as quicksilver, seemingly a smart-alec rogue addicted to alcohol and his own corner-cutting ways, but he is also perhaps the real heroic figure of the book, the private investigator of his literary heritage, sorting out the smug and arrogant rich, the privileged people addicted to the superficial rules of their set and class.

Everyone's seeming nature shifts as we move through the chapters, with even a minor character like Toots Nuncio going from a pathetic old pol about to lose his law license to an information source ("Toot's Walls") to a daring manipulator ("Toots Plays for Us") to a powerful fixer ("Waiting for Bert," "Step Two"). Each chapter and scene turns the kaleidoscope a notch, and our understanding changes as a consequence. The plot/ narrative structure has more in common with theatrical or filmic scenes than with the rhythms of the spoken confessional, although Malloy's voice is the common thread holding events together.

THEMATIC ISSUES

The thematic center of this novel is the driving force of human greed overwhelming the ideal of professional integrity, a theme at play in both individuals and large, corporate entities, as the "rules" of proper legal and corporate behavior are broken and self-interest holds sway over human obligations. This breakdown of rules and proprieties because of the will to acquire money causes disintegration at every level, so that Malloy's dysfunctional family and his impulse to seek revenge on coworkers for real or imagined slights or inequities are related themes, connected by willful and self-serving behavior that flouts convention.

Greed versus Professional Integrity

The prevailing tension in *Pleading Guilty* is between greed for money and a sense of integrity and professionalism. The conflict rises to the surface at several points in the book when main character Mack Malloy muses about what motivates the behavior of his colleagues, clients, and acquaintances; the issue never goes away, however, appearing in various guises while underlying most of the characters' motivations: do people simply seek money and power, camouflaging their greed with socially acceptable reasons, or are they primarily motivated by a personal sense of right and wrong and by the standards their professions hold up as correct behavior?

The ironically named BAD, Bar Admissions and Discipline, comes up throughout the novel. Malloy worked for BAD when starting out, helping to punish lawyers who transgress and to assure that the bar exam standards are met. Malloy changes a bar exam score for his old mentor Jake Eiger, an action that leads to Malloy's cushy and profitable job as one of TransNational Airline's hired guns. He also appears before BAD on the behalf of Toots Nuncio, who is about to lose his license to practice because of numerous transgressions but who is saved when G & G colleague Emilia "Brushy" Bruccia manages a lawyerly scam on the BAD attorneys and Mack goes along with the fraud. Toots, himself, is still nakedly ambitious for power and wealth and offers a quid pro quo that Malloy cashes in on later. The novel shows standards of professional behavior to be negotiable, at the very least.

Turow has two main categories of characters: those like Toots Nuncio and Jake Eiger, whose only interest in the law is as a cash cow for wealth and as a route to power, and those like Bert Kamin, who practice law for nonpecuniary motives. Mack, himself, is spoiled by his large salary and is tempted by money but has standards despite his bad behavior with BAD. Besides lawyers, the novel provides a variety of characters tempted by or selling out for money. Gino Dimonte, universally known as Pigeyes, is Mack's old police partner, a cop on the take turned in by Mack at the end of his police career. Ironically, Pigeyes loves the chase more than the profit possible for a bent cop and, apart from his desire for revenge on

Mack, is, for the most part, driven by legitimate law enforcement motives, although he too is still on the take. Bert Kamin's slide into fixing basketball games illustrates how easily even a relatively honest person can end up corrupted. Bert's gambling with "Archie," Vernon Koechell, the actuary turned online bookie, seems mainly for the thrill of the risk rather than for profit. When Bert falls in love with Kam Roberts/Orleans, a referee for important college games, he becomes privy to information about how strictly Orleans might referee a well-known aggressive star player, which player might be injured, and the like. Neither Bert nor Orleans cheats for the money, yet when the profits pour in, neither seems to be held back by professional ethics. Malloy asks about Bert's gambling, "What . . . compelled him? Did he lust to feel favored by chance, or did he want to dare punishment?" (370–371); he concludes that Bert does not do it for the profit per se. Money, however, is always part of the equation.

The main conflict between greed and integrity occurs in the law firm of G & G. Groundhog Day, February 2, when the year's profits are totted up and dispersed, is upcoming, producing a high level of anxiety among the firm's members. "Points," or shares of profits, are turned into real money, but what is really being measured is prestige—status in the firm hierarchy. Malloy's ongoing commentary about the pricey decor of the various partners' offices is another indicator of how status is measured, in fashionable furnishings and desirable views. Martin, as the lead member of the Management Oversight Committee, has exotic and unconventional artwork that, reflecting his authority, goes against the sober norm.

The tension between greed and professionalism—or "rules," as the G & G lawyers think of it—is at its height in the skirmishes between Mack, Brushy, Martin, Carl, Wash, and Jake. The latter seems befuddled, though he is probably guilty. The three partners all have limits they won't transgress, although in each case self-interest plays a part in promoting adherence to the "rules." Only Brushy and Mack betray all expectations, serving their private ends with little regard for their colleagues. In Mack's case, he is following the example of his fireman father, who considers any loose valuables in a fire lost to the owners and up for grabs. Mack's behavior at the end brings to the foreground another theme familiar to all who work in corporate settings, wreaking revenge on coworkers for real and imagined grievances.

Large Law Firms and Greed

Charles Champlin of *Los Angeles Times Book Review* complains that "the story hardly peeps into a courtroom" (11), but that absence of a courtroom confrontation does not mean the story is not about the law and lawyers. *Pleading Guilty* is Turow's only portrait so far of a large, multiservice law firm of the type he has worked for much of his career, Sonnenschein, Carlin, Nath & Rosenthal. (Other law firms in the novels are either small operations, such as Sandy Stern's criminal practice and Robbie Feaver and Mort Dinnerstein's personal injury operation, or they are shown only tangentially, as in O'Grady, Steinberg, Marconi, and Horgan, Arthur Raven's firm in *Reversible Errors*.) Turow is at pains to distance his real partners and experiences from his sometimes biting fictional depiction; a gracious dedication statement to Sonnenschein et al. placed after the title page thanks the firm and its people for support and emphasizes neither has any resemblance to Gage & Griswell. G & G is large, employing 130 lawyers and is formed like a pyramid: a large base of young lawyers hoping for eventual partnership, a tapering midsection staffed by permanent "service" lawyers (such as Mack) who supervise the youthful workers, and a few privileged partners at the apex, who award each other the most "points," or shares. A nonattorney staff of secretaries, paralegals, and administrators manages the routine paperwork.

The administrative design of G & G will be familiar to anyone who has spent time in corporate or academic surroundings. G & G has departments, management oversight groups, hiring committees, and other accoutrements of large organizations. The difference, at least in Turow's version of the large corporate law firm, is the emphasis on money. While most businesses focus on a product line to garner profits, G & G simply produces billable hours, taking the process one step closer to the profit-making goal than a corporation that produces widgets it must sell. Here, the service, measured in billable hours, is the product. Other service industries fit this model, of course, but few services compare to the high-powered offerings of a large law firm. Mack does not show us abuses of G & G's other clients, but there is no question about the relationship with TransNational Airlines, which, as Martin and others know, could get its law work done much more cheaply by farming out jobs to other firms. Only the personal relationships of Jake with TransNational board members keep G & G on the gravy train. Combined with the personal acquisitiveness exhibited in the run-up to Groundhog Day, the picture is not a pretty one: individual attorneys, most of them type-A personalities and workaholics, whine about their "points" even as the firm as a whole takes advantage of a sweetheart deal. In contrast, Mack Malloy's mild greed—more a comfort level with his substantial income, an inertia—and his guilt about not having better professional values seem positively virtuous: for all Mack's fecklessness he is at least not driven by raw cupidity.

Family Dysfunction

Pleading Guilty's other recurrent theme is family dysfunction, especially Mack's. Malloy's wife left him for another woman, and his son, known initially as Lonesome Boy, has turned into Loathsome Boy in his teenage years. Brushy, who has a healthy, open attitude toward sex and relationships, is the exception at G & G, many of whose partners are on second marriages. There is also the suggestion that G & G is a large, dysfunctional family, family being a common metaphor in the corporate world, and that Martin is the father while Bert and Mack play versions of black sheep sons.

As in the other Turow novels, the author provides readers with a precise insider's description of an activity or phenomenon integral to the plot. Here, it is the processes of offshore banking, the financial transactions carried out by local and international banks in small Caribbean nations that guarantee complete secrecy. How this virtual anonymity is achieved and how it serves customers and the nation becomes evident through Malloy's actions in the fictional island country of Pico Luan.

CHARACTER DEVELOPMENT

As a first-person narration, *Pleading Guilty* naturally focuses heavily on the speaker. We meet all the other characters through him and perceive their commitments to the law and to each other in terms of what the narrator tells us about them and about how they behave.

McCormack "Mack" Malloy

Mack Malloy is a big (six-feet, two inches), 49-year-old partner in the Gage and Griswell law firm, a "service lawyer" in his own description who supervises the younger drones who do most of the work. A divorced single parent and recovering alcoholic, Malloy has been called, by many, Turow's "most compelling character" to date. Turow, himself, says Mack is "corruptible and ultimately corrupt" (Macdonald interview, 2004). A former cop who worked in the financial crimes division of the police department, Malloy apparently had a good early career at G & G, bringing in business through his connection with Jake Eiger, the senior division counsel for TransNational Airlines (Malloy worked for Bar Admissions and Discipline [BAD] and changed Jake's bar exam score so he could be licensed.) However, Malloy is slipping. At one time drunk more often than sober, he lost his wife to another woman and is alienated from his teenage son, Lyle. Now sober, he has lost his edge and his will. His share of G & G profits has been cut back, he has been moved to a smaller office, and he has been regularly assigned unpleasant committee work. Jake has been sending him less TransNational business, and Malloy fears for his job.

Malloy has also been damaged by his upbringing in an Irish ghetto in Kindle County, where his sharp-tongued mother and fireman father left him confused, with his mother "off her nut" and raging (78) and his father bringing home valuables from fires on the theory that they would have been lost anyway (the similarity to Mack's reasoning about stealing the missing G & G money is evident). Of all his relatives, only his sister Elaine, dead by the time of the novel, is "a person of iron conviction" (78), someone he misses more than his ex-wife, Nora. When he brings down G & G at the end, he is in his Sampson mode, ready to bring down the Temple, as contrary and stubborn as he says Elaine was.

As the novel progresses, Malloy increasingly struggles to decide who he is. A quote from St. Augustine follows the title page: "Where was my heart to flee for refuge from my heart? Whither was I to fly, where I would not follow? In what place should I not be prey to myself?" (*The Confessions,* Book Four, Chapter VII). This is precisely Malloy's identity problem, since he understands that attempts to flee his empty and dissatisfying life—whether to Pico Luan or to somewhere else with Brushy—will be futile because he will carry himself along as baggage. Even though he despises many of his colleagues, most are secure in their identities as lawyers; for Malloy, lawyers' "rules" often seem like what Sonny Klonsky in *The Laws of Our Fathers* calls *traumhaft*, the notion that all belief systems are "but a dream with no provable justification in morality or science" (79; the philosophy is from Nietzsche). Brushy is disturbed that Malloy lies with such "elan" (405), and he is ever the radical relativist, seeing few final answers: "Caught in our own foxholes, we never see the battlefield scene" (437). Malloy, however, is convinced that "the one guy I wasn't wrong about was me" (437).

Martin Gold

Martin Gold, managing partner of G & G, is the ideal lawyer from Malloy's perspective: "my Chinaman, the man I admire" (67). Unlike his partners on the Management Oversight Committee, he is neither stuffy nor overtly self-serving, tolerating "odd ducks" (5) like Bert and Mack Malloy, filling his office with witty, playful artwork, and sacrificing himself for the firm. Gold handled the 397 Settlement, the huge air crash case brought against TransNational Airlines and defended by G & G. He took calls from 163 different attorneys in order to settle that case, "an effort that seemed . . . [to Malloy] as romantic and ill-considered as the Crusades" (134). Martin's faith is that "the team is greater than the sum of the parts" (69). He "is one of those men who abound in the legal profession whose brains seem to make them a quarter larger than life" (22). Gold is a "Person of Values, a lawyer who does not see the law as just business or sport. He's on one million do-good committees" (201). But he is not "Mother Teresa. Like anybody else who has whizzed along the fast track in the practice of law, he can cut your heart out if need be" (73).

Gold is thus one of Malloy's heroes, and when he is shown to have feet of clay, Malloy takes out his anger on him (although the degree of Gold's culpability depends on whether Gold or Malloy's understanding of Gold's motives is accepted). As one of the illustrative examples of how the law could and should be practiced in a large firm, Gold stands out as mostly admirable, even though brought down by circumstances.

George Washington Thale III and Carl Pagnucci

The other two members of the Management Oversight Committee are much more conventional and less interesting figures. Wash, formally George Washington Thale III, sounds more authoritative than he is; Turow says that Wash "tends to state the obvious in a grave, portentous manner, the self-commissioned voice of wisdom" (5). When Malloy reveals Jake's culpability to him, Wash is unable to deal with it, and especially with the possibility that Gold is also corrupt. He is an aging establishmentarian, happy to say the right thing to clients and to leave the actual work to the younger lawyers. He always seems several steps behind everyone else; Malloy calls him a fool to his face (302).

Carl Pagnucci is a very different type, a "modern" lawyer who left his previous firm because he wanted a larger share of the profits. Pagnucci never says much, but his mind is working all the time, his "usual aura" being "every soul for itself" (208). Pagnucci's creed is "rational self-interest," believing "all social interaction, no matter how complex, can be adjusted by finding a way to put a price on it" (208). Unlike Gold (and even Wash), he exhibits no loyalty to the firm and well before G & G's current troubles has been feeling out Brushy about leaving to form their own firm.

Emilia Bruccia

Emilia "Brushy" Bruccia is "one of G & G's great stars . . . gifted with that wonderful, devious, clever cast of mind by which she can always explain away the opposition's most damaging documents as something not worth using to wrap fish" (32). Her sleight of witnesses in defending Toots Nuccio's law degree before BAD is creatively clever, but she believes in the rules and forms of the law. Although she professes loyalty to G & G, she has listened to Pagnucci's blandishments, and we learn at the end how thoroughly she has served her own private ends. Likewise, with her aggressive and open sexuality, she puts her interests first, as Malloy discovers to his dismay.

Bert Kamin

Bert Kamin is somewhat like Mack Malloy, a lawyer who perhaps would have been happier in another profession, or at least in a smaller firm. A barracuda as a litigator, he is nevertheless unreliable and unpredictable when not in a trial, someone who disappears without explanation to pursue sports enthusiasms or personal desires. He is a perfect patsy for the theft of the $5.6 million, a flaky and erratic type who might have impulsively changed his life.

Peter Neucriss

A lawyer outside the firm—in fact, a lawyer for the hated opposition—Peter Neucriss, the "Prince of Darkness," defines another type, the wildly successful and dramatic personal injury lawyer. Peter Neucriss represents the plaintiff, the families of the deceased, in the TransNational crash for one third of the winnings. As with Robbie Feaver in *Personal Injuries*, the portrait is devastating: "Lying to Peter is not even a venial sin: speaking to a Frenchman in French" (136), and "the law seems to attract more of these types, the utterly self-impressed who regard the bar as the pathway to a frontier where will and ego can go virtually unbounded" (137). What greatly upsets Malloy is that the success of Neucriss (and his type) is a "sort of revolting advertisement of the fallibility of the jury system" (137) because, despite the obvious "ego run wild, some form of character dis-order" (137), he draws only rave reviews from juries.

The Range of Lawyers

The range of lawyers in and around G & G shows just how varied people and the profession can be in a large corporate firm, usually considered a matrix for conformity and orthodoxy. In finding a style he could live with, Malloy has plentiful models to choose from. That he rejects them all is in part a testimony to the rigor of some of the rules that must be followed by all lawyers (rules Malloy rejects) and in part a symptom of Malloy's own desire to descend into oblivion.

GENRE CONVENTIONS

Turow mixes genres in interesting ways in this novel, combining new and old forms to revitalize the legal thriller, with its limited scope of court-room confrontation. Clearly, he draws on some of the conventions of the legal thriller, because he is explicitly writing in that genre and his topic is lawyers and law firms. *Publishers Weekly* reviewer Sybil Steinberg identi-fies *Pleading Guilty* as "a surefooted legal thriller" whose "world-weary" protagonist-narrator provides "a candid account of the behind-the-scenes workings of a powerful law firm" in "an engaging, street-wise narrative full of plain talk and homespun philosophy" (47–48). She concludes, "Tu-row surpasses Grisham hands down" (48). The feeling readers have of participation behind the scenes of a large, active law firm is certainly a significant appeal of the novel, as are the peeks into the negotiations in the TransNational Airlines and Toots Nuncio cases.

The legal procedural often includes the technical detail and sense of process inherent in a police procedural, as it does in this case. Like a police procedural, *Pleading Guilty* delineates the steps involved in investigating a disappearance and a theft and in linking the two. Malloy is comfortable with reprising the police procedures he practiced before law school, rec-ollecting his work in the financial crimes unit and dealing with a couple of former colleagues; in fact, he often seems more enthusiastic about this police work than about his present work for G & G, which consists more and more of "service" committee work.

To these legal fiction and police procedural conventions, Turow adds the conventions of the hard-boiled detective. Therein, a basically honor-able man delves into the corruption and vices of rich, aristocratic or corporate clients—in this case, the members of his own law firm. The contrast between their lifestyles and his adds an economic bite to his criticism of their self-indulgence and waste. (Malloy is constantly commenting on the lush decor of his partners' offices.) The hard-boiled detective is presented with a puzzle—a missing man and missing money—and must follow where the puzzle leads, even if it turns back on the very people who hired him, a classic reversal. His investigation leads him deep into a heart of darkness that tempts him as well. Often he proves a tarnished knight, one who is tainted by the money he is paid (in this case, he is tainted by the money he walks away with).

In a March 14, 1994, review, Verlyn Klinkenborg of *The New Republic* finds the conventions of spy fiction at work here, too—particularly those that developed during the vacuum created by the demise of the Soviet Union and the end of the Cold War. Klinkenborg finds in Turow's novel "the same relentless insistence on the process of discovery, the same murky subterfuge, the same sense of divided loyalties, of fundamental allegiances gone awry, of being caught in a world where black and white have given way to shades of gray" (34). In fact, the spy fiction convention involving a monolithic spy organization that betrays the individual, that sends him into desperate circumstances to ferret out trouble knowing he might be killed and not caring what personal harm comes to him (Malloy complains that Bert might shoot him), fits the moral ambivalence of *Pleading Guilty* more neatly than does the hard-boiled convention of the tarnished knight-detective, for the spy genre creates a kind of satisfaction when the pawn in a complex game brings down the king and walks away with the winnings. Therefore, within the conventions of the spy novel, the amorality of Malloy's final act, which jars with the conventions of the hard-boiled detective, is in fact appropriate and right—the cog in the machinery getting back at the unfeeling mechanism that has used him and that will discard him. The misdirections and misrepresentations of the first-person narrative voice are also in keeping with spy story conventions. Where the hard-boiled detective is blunt, honest, and direct, the spy hero is accustomed to tailoring his story to fit circumstances, and there is the suggestion here of layers of information hidden from the reader and even from the narrator, and the impossibility of ever knowing the full truth of even the simplest act concerning G & G's manipulations.

However, this novel also builds on a much older literary genre, that of the epistolary novel—that is, a novel whose story is told through a series of letters or reports written by one or more fictitious characters. The epistolary form began with the eighteenth-century convention of letters between father and son, with the father providing advice to cool a young man's intemperate behavior, as in Horace Walpole's letters to his son. The first English novel, Samuel Richardson's *Pamela* (1740), was an epistolary novel, consisting of letters from Pamela, a maid servant, about the sexual pursuit of her by the young master of the household in which she was employed and the means by which she protected her virtue from devious and sundry assaults. Other epistolary novels from the same period include Richardson's *Clarissa* (1747–1748), his *Sir Charles Grandison* (1753), Jacques Rousseau's *La Nouvelle Heloise* (1761), Tobias Smollett's *Humphrey Clinker* (1771), Johann Goethe's *The Sorrows of Young Werther* (1774), Fanny Burney's *Eveline* (1778), and Pierre Ambrose Choderlos de Laclos's *Les Liaisons Dangereueses* (1782). In these, the author, nominally the writer of the letters, becomes a fictionalized character within a story told through letters. Likewise, there are two audiences: the character within the story who purportedly will receive the letters and the reading audience. The letters reveal the character of their writers and sometimes the character of their intended recipients. The form gives the reader immediate entry to the social world of the letter writers through "overhearing" a private social interaction. The point of view is by definition subjective, and often little action or quite commonplace action occurs except in the minds of the characters, whose personalities and perspectives are dominant. Hence, the form laid the foundation for the psychological novel. Sir Walter Scott employed the form in his historical novel *Waverley* (1813), and Jane Austen drew on the form to create her more modern narrative voices. Rainer Maria Rilke's epistolary classic *Letters to a Young Poet* consists of a sequence of remarkable letters counseling an aspiring writer. Turow prepares readers for this confessional form in his acknowledgement to *Pleading Guilty* with a quote from *The Confessions* of St. Augustine. Therein, St. Augustine asks where he could go to escape the darkness in his own heart and avoid being "prey" to himself, a question Turow's own confessor, Mack Malloy, must ask himself.

One virtue of the epistolary literary form is that it provides an intimate insider's view of a character's thoughts, supposedly free from an authorial voice. Another virtue is that its very nature suggests dramatic immediacy and anticipated response. A disadvantage, of course, is the narrow point of view of events, especially when there is only one letter writer: his or her limited scope becomes the reader's limited scope. Thus, Bram Stoker's horror story *Dracula* (1897) was told through multiple means—diaries, letters, newspaper clippings, and even transcriptions from a dictation machine—all fabricated, creating the illusion of reality in a fictional account by broadening the epistolary scope. Modern examples of the epistolary literary form include Alice Walker's *The Color Purple* (1982) and Ronald Munson's *Fan Mail* (1993), the latter employing multiple modern forms of communication, including memos, faxes, telephone messages, e-mail, reports, and newspaper clippings. Sometimes the letters hide more than they reveal; sometimes they are a tool or weapon made to serve highly specific ends. Thus, the modern epistolary novel no longer necessarily consists of letters but may instead take the form of diary entries, newspaper clippings, a report pieced together from diary notes, or, as in *Pleading Guilty*, audiotapes supposedly recorded shortly after events occur.

Yet, in drawing on this unusual form, Turow is acting within the mystery tradition, for the epistolary mystery novel was a standard form when the mystery genre began. Letters made up some part of the major stories by nineteenth-century mystery writer Wilkie Collins. C. F. Forester's short mystery story "The Letters in Evidence" is told through letters, as is Dorothy Sayers's novel *The Documents in the Case* (1930), her only non–Peter Wimsey detective novel, supposedly a collection of some 40 letters and two long written statements. Sarah Cauldwell has employed the epistolary form with great success in works like *Thus Was Adonis Murdered* (1981), *The Shortest Way to Hades* (1986), *The Sirens Sang of Murder* (1990), and *The Sibyl in Her Grave* (2000). Her narrative proceeds via letters, with armchair detective Hilary Tamar providing a commentary framework. Clearly, Turow works within the genre even when seemingly far afield, and brings an interesting twist to the thriller by returning it to the conventions of its origins.

The epistolary literary form enables Turow to limit the point of view to that of an insider, someone who is participating in and plotting the action of the story (Malloy sets his own agenda in the investigation). The view is intimate, for the character speaks directly to the audience, as if without an authorial filter, sharing his thoughts, hopes, and schemes. The form provides dramatic immediacy and a tension that comes from the narrator telling what he knows as he knows it and therefore being unable to anticipate future events except as guesswork about potential responses. The problem of the form is, of course, also its advantage: the narrow point of view of events, especially when there is only one letter writer. In this case, Malloy's limited scope becomes the reader's limited scope, and Malloy's wily deceptions and misdirections may be accepted by the audience at face value as fact. Readers who accept his self-justifications share, to some degree, in his charming culpability.

ALTERNATIVE READING: FORMALIST GENRE APPROACHES

In the eyes of literary critics, no reading is innocent. That is, no reader, no matter how fresh, young, untrained—innocent—can approach a literary work without predispositions, assumptions, expectations, leanings, preferences, and the like.

It is easy to see why this is true: we are all taught to read in the general sense of processing words and sentences and arriving at meanings, and this training brings with it whole sets of expectations in play before any reading begins. Told to look up a telephone number in a directory, we search for last names, alphabetized, a first name, and a number. Picking up a manual for a new piece of electronic equipment, we expect "how to" directions couched in imperative forms ("do this; then do that"), definitions of parts, warnings, and trouble-shooting directions. Told that we are about to hear a story, we get ready to be presented with a moral, or perhaps to deduce one if it is not evident.

Fiction is particularly likely to be read in accord with the expectations created by the genre, or form, in which it is written. A genre implies a preexisting understanding between reader and writer about the purpose, rules, and strategies of a work. Science fiction as a genre, for example, leads readers to expect technological marvels, voyages in outer space, alien monsters, visitors from other worlds, utopias, or any of the other features of the science fiction genre. When the science fiction genre is combined with the short story genre, then the result must, to some degree, meet reader expectations about both categories. It must be written in prose, not poetry, and be fairly short—that is, too brief a narrative to be published as a separate volume. Thus, it might range from a single page to perhaps as many as 50 pages, with 10 or 12 more common. It is usually a focused narrative with a limited number of central characters (one or two). These are often engaged in a single action, or the story depends on a single concept. The story may hinge on a twist or turn of understanding or perception, but whatever its intent, it must achieve it quickly. There is no time in the short story for the complexities and digressions of the novel. A romantic short story would retain the short story features and use romance conventions, such as thwarted lovers, separated by blocking characters and suffering private agonies, and so on.

The more we have read in a genre, the more features we have been taught to expect. Some writers, however, produce powerful literary effects by straining against their chosen genre, pushing the envelope by omitting expected features or inventing new ones, or perhaps by putting a twist on well-established conventions. Formalist critics who focus on genre as a means to better understand the intrinsic features of a literary work believe that form and content cannot be meaningfully separated and that what makes a text literary is the interrelation between and interdependence of the two.

Genre criticism has a long history. The philosopher Aristotle spent a good deal of his *Poetics* (written between 360 and 322 B.C.) classifying the Greek literature of his time, and his classification-description of tragedy and comedy is still the starting point for modern drama criticism. Shakespeare makes fun of this very human need to classify plays into rigid categories when he has Polonius praise the ability of some traveling performers to enact multiple dramatic categories: "tragedy, comedy, history, pastoral, pastoral-comical, historical-pastoral, tragical-historical, tragical-comical-historical-pastoral, scene individable, or poem unlimited" (*Hamlet* 2.2.362–365). While the simple classification of works of literature into genre categories is no longer credited as a critical activity, the consideration of genre as a matrix that can be slavishly employed or stretched to convey new ideas is a regular practice of formalists—that is, critics who examine the mechanics of a work of literature. The New Critics (far from new, since they reached their greatest influence in the 1940s and 1950s) were particularly interested in genres such as the pastoral in poetry, and examined how the literary form dictated a certain content. Poststructuralists have "deconstructed" genre conventions to show how what is *not* said or talked about may be more important than what is, allowing, for example, some forms of conventional love poetry to reinforce gender distinctions and ideologies.

Pleading Guilty, as noted in the previous section, employs elements of two main genres: the epistolary novel and the American hard-boiled detective story. Elements of the late-term espionage/spy thriller serve to complicate the figure of the hard-boiled detective, as do evocations of the police procedural. Critics interested in genre, whether traditional, new critics, or recent adherents of poststructuralism, would ask how Turow uses these genres to advance his cause, and perhaps how the expectations of the genres shape the story and characters. For example, as noted earlier, the epistolary novel is associated with its first practitioners in the eighteenth century, and certainly with Jane Austen and her disciples. These writers were mainly social satirists or commentators on manners and mores. The novel-in-letters is also by its nature social in outlook: letters are revelatory of a given social milieu, emphasizing externals such as relationships and events. Although they may be confessional, depending on the relationship of the letter writer and audience, they are entirely of another order of psychological reality from the classic first-person revelations of *Pleading Guilty*'s other overt genre source, the hard-boiled detective novel. Even when written in the third person, these hard-boiled works are usually omniscient in their point of view, with film-like "voiceovers" providing inner thoughts and confessions—things too personal to put out in public. Thus the genre critic must consider the results of this odd mix of genres in *Pleading Guilty*.

Malloy's "confessions" are particularly intriguing when considered as epistles, as communications to a particular audience. As Mack (and Turow) acknowledges, his superiors will never read his report, which is both rude and an admission of various dishonesties. So perhaps his listeners/ readers will be a "fifty-year-old Irishman. . . . Or a [bored] kid . . . Or a professor" concluding it "generally vile" (209). These people, of course, might be among Turow's real readership, and the admission cheekily violates our suspension of disbelief, our willingness to listen to Malloy as if he were a real person, not a collection of marks on a page. This self-consciousness is a direct consequence of the epistolary form, or rather of its violation. Why does Turow have Malloy drop out of character? Writers in the eighteenth century liked to wink at their audience, or perhaps Turow was infected by the flippancy of his creation, Mack Malloy.

A genre critic would focus on this tension between genre traditions—one the semipublic "report" Malloy is supposedly writing, the other his private soliloquies and musings (the latter revealing Malloy as an unreliable narrator, in that he rarely tells the whole truth). Moreover, these two genre traditions, although not necessarily mutually exclusive, frame the conflict between fact and misdirection: What is "factual" about the situation at G & G and the disappearance of millions of dollars? Who in this varied cast of characters can be trusted? Are Martin, Brushy, and Jake, like Mack Malloy, skillful actors deceiving with a convincing public front? Can readers be sure of anyone's interpretation of events?

Malloy also violates our expectations of the hard-boiled hero by betraying his trusts. The classic Raymond Chandleresque detective is a knight errant, hewing to a moral code even when suffering beatings and abuse. Malloy is all too ready to betray his firm, his partners, even his ideals of being a lawyer, the "rules" or code that supposedly unifies the legal tribe. In some ways Malloy seems more comfortable with the routines and fiddles of his financial crimes police investigative past than with his current lawyering. His readiness to sell out his firm, perhaps assuring its demise, suggests the spy novel at the end of the Cold War, when the claims of patriotism and "the firm" (in the sense of spy agency) came to play second fiddle to self-interest. Like a John le Carré or Len Deighton spy, Malloy is distanced from his corporate fellows, who are ready to throw him overboard, and he is ready to trade allegiances. Chandler's hard-boiled detective hero Philip Marlowe would be appalled.

Thus, a genre critic would find the meaning of *Pleading Guilty* in the margins, as it were, in the tension between the genre expectations more than in what Malloy actually says and does, which is so variable and self-contradictory as to be at times seemingly incoherent. The form provides the message, overcoming the moral confusion of the central character.

6

The Laws of Our Fathers (1996)

The Laws of Our Fathers, a main selection of both The Literary Guild and Doubleday Book Club, has received high praise from critics and reviewers: "splendid," "gripping," and "profound," "a bravura performance," "a stunning achievement" (*Los Angeles Times, Chicago Sun-Times, San Francisco Chronicle*, among others). Mary Frances Wilkens of *Booklist* calls Turow's narrative technique "masterful" (31), while *Time* reviewer Paul Gray, in "Up Against the Law," finds the novel "enthralling," because Turow "genuinely cares" about his characters and "the lost possibilities they might somehow redeem" (90). Jeff Giles of *Newsweek* finds Turow an extraordinarily "canny and empathetic observer," "easily crossing lines of race, class and gender," to "convincingly" demonstrate "how few real connections" one makes in a lifetime and "the cold shadows parents can cast" (89). Interviewer Alden Mudge, in "When Characters Slip from the Confines of Plot," asserts that a "broad but unobtrusive intelligence . . . informs the movements of [Turow's] characters and their actions" (www.bookpage.com). Tom De Haven of *Entertainment Weekly* calls the novel "a smart and dispiriting meditation about racism's daily cost, legacy, and corrupting persistence," and praises its "ethical vision and historical range"(104).

Turow told Alden Mudge that he felt he could not write about the 1960s without writing about race, and writing about race led him to violate a fairly well-established taboo against writing in dialect. Making it work became "quite a balancing act." Turow takes pride in the urban dialect some of his characters employ in this novel, because it was "the product of much studied effort—listening to clients; hanging out at Chicago housing projects as the result of a case which took me down there; paying attention to hip-hop music; reading books like *Monster*; and keeping my ears open on public transportation. I worked hard, and I think I got it right" (Macdonald interview, 2004). *New York Times Book Review* critic Teresa Carpenter agrees with his assessment, arguing that when Turow slips into the voices of the Black Saints Disciples gang members, the vitality and realism of the prose is "like a hit of pure oxygen" (10). Although some white readers complained that the first chapter was incomprehensible, Turow explains why he thought it was important to be true to the sounds of the street and the language of the people he depicted:

> That language is a measure of the separation [between the races] . . . was, of course, the point: My main guiding principle was to be fearless. I wasn't going to put up with the idea that blacks have exclusive ownership of their own experience, any more than I would think it wise for a male writer not to write women. (Macdonald interview, 2004)

This "fearlessness" in being true to his characters—their life experiences, their special diction, and their economic, social, and cultural situations—is, in large part, what makes this book an honest look at the distances that separate our citizenry.

PLOT DEVELOPMENT AND STRUCTURE

In *The Laws of Our Fathers*, a drive-by shooting in a drug-plagued Kindle County housing project proves explosive because the victim is the ex-wife of a well-known politician and because their adult son is charged with the crime. The investigation of her murder and the trial that follows reunite an unlikely group of men and women (including the judge) who knew each other in California as youths caught up in the revolutionary protests and crusades of the 1960s. The novel not only demonstrates the disastrous consequences of a single wrong choice but also explores the aftermath of life decisions made by young people finding their way in a period of dramatic changes.

The Laws of Our Fathers is divided into three parts: Accusation, Testimony, and Judgment. Each part is preceded by a quotation from the work of "Michael Frain," a fictional nationally syndicated newspaper columnist who writes meditations about middle-aged baby boomer issues, particularly (as the ironic title of his feature "The Survivor's Guide" indicates) surviving the turbulence of the 1960s. Frain is actually Seth Daniel Weissman, the male lead in the novel, who assumes the name of an anti–Vietnam War activist in a complicated scheme recounted later in the book to allow Weissman to escape the draft and Frain to escape the FBI. Twenty-five years later—the Frain passage at the head of part 1 is dated 1995—Weissman still keeps "Frain" as a pen name for his work as a columnist and writer since he has been known that way since 1970.

Seth Weissman is the most thoughtful and self-aware of the characters in the book, introspective almost to a fault, and to some limited degree an analogue to Turow. Both are serious writers, men led inexorably to their craft even as they practiced other trades, journalism and law. Both were in residence at prestigious California universities around 1970; both professed flower child sympathies. Both have demanding parents and a Jewish heritage that becomes more significant in their middle age, especially to pass on to their children.

The Frain quotations set the theme and tone of the book, a mixture of melancholy and nostalgia at the self-evaluation of middle age, the "awful doomed inquiry of our middle years" (2), as Frain-Weissman terms it. The baby boom generation was not "blinkered" by need like the poor of other generations and cultures and believed that their American birthright is "the pursuit of happiness" (2). In a column, Frain-Weissman reduces this malaise of aging baby boomers to questions asked by the "harpy's voices": "Is this as happy as I will ever be? Do I have the right to just a little more?" (2). The plot and structure of *The Laws of Our Fathers* permit examination of these questions by people in their forties who, full of promise, had met, mixed, and mated 25 years earlier in the San Francisco Bay area, either as students at the fictional Miller Damon Senior University or as residents of the associated student community. (Damon University looks much like the University of California at Berkeley in the late sixties and early seventies. Turow, of course, attended Stanford.)

Part 1, Accusation

Part 1, Accusation, is the shortest part, about 40 pages in the hardback edition, divided into three chapters or sections, each dated and named by the point of view of its main character:

Date	Point of View
September 7, 1995	Hardcore
September 12, 1995	Sonny
September 14, 1995	Seth

The first point of view is the third-person omniscient perspective of Ordell Trent (Hardcore), the leader of a branch of the Black Saints Disciples, a gang that controls IV Tower, a trashed-out Kindle County urban housing project riddled with open drug dealing and violence. As we follow Hardcore walking the courtyard pavement, we move from Turow's literary description—"Dawn. The air is brackish, although this place is miles from water" (3)—to Trent's own idiom, an artfully rendered ghetto dialect that communicates Hardcore's musings about his security: "Because Ordell sees. From here. He got all them tiny gangsters,—the youngest gang members—'peepers,' as they're called, rovin, scopin. Any po-lice, any rent-a-cop, any limp DEA, any them mothers truck into them towers, Hardcore gone know" (5).

Hardcore is called back down to the street from his apartment by Lavinia, known as "Bug," one of his teenage—she is 15—scouts and drug pushers, with the warning that an old white woman in a worn-out Nova has appeared on the street asking for him. The woman identifies herself as June Eddgar, "Nile's mother," saying Nile couldn't come, and then refers to a misunderstanding between Nile and someone else she knows. Hardcore repeatedly tells her to leave, that there is danger, and suddenly a teenager identified as Gorgo appears out of an alley on a mountain bike and shoots June Eddgar with a Tec-9 machine pistol, wounding Lavinia in the knee. Hardcore makes her comfortable and leaves but knows he has been identified by onlookers as meeting with the obviously dead June Eddgar, and he predicts disastrous police attention.

The scene is out of character for Turow, in part because of the departure from his usual elegant prose to convincing black English, in part because of the minute description of housing project decay (the other books typically focus on posh surroundings described in carefully crafted sentences), and in part because of the sudden and horrific violence of the shooting. This novel begins *in medias res,* in the midst of the crime that propels it, again anomalous for Turow's practice. (He usually begins with the results of a crime but not with the action of the crime ongoing).

Hardcore's case is referred to the court of Judge Sonia "Sonny" Klonsky. She has been recruited to this state criminal division court from her former job as a federal prosecutor: readers first met her as Sandy Stern's tormentor and then friend in *The Burden of Proof*. The judicial reform commission decided, after a bribery scandal, that her integrity was above reproach, and she was made a judge. This good reputation for avoiding favoritism is threatened, however, when she recognizes the victim's name in the current case, June Eddgar, as the wife of Loyell Eddgar, once a theology professor at Damon University, where Sonny was studying philosophy in graduate school, accompanied by her boyfriend, Seth Weissman, now known by his pen name of Michael Frain, a name borrowed from another person in their circle. These youthful relationships are tangled inextricably. Seth baby-sat Nile Eddgar for June and Loyell (usually known simply as Eddgar), so Sonny knows all these people from 25 years earlier. (Her clerk, Marietta, says it sounds like a commune, but Sonny answers, accurately, that they were all acquaintances in the same apartment building.)

Thus, Hardcore's case brings together this extended cast of characters, and, although most have not seen each other for a quarter of a century, some complications still remain for Sonny, who, as a new, inexperienced judge, will be vulnerable to accusations of bias if she is not punctiliously forthcoming. Chief Judge Brendan Tuohey, a featured reprobate in *Personal Injuries*, dislikes Sonny's reformist credentials, as Sandy Stern has warned her; Tuohey would be happy to see her fail. Further complications are that Nile Eddgar, a child in 1970 but now an adult in his thirties, is Hardcore's probation officer, so the killing of Nile's mother appears an extremely unlikely coincidence or, perhaps more likely, a contract killing arranged on the behalf of Nile for some obscure motive. Hardcore is thus accused of arranging the hit. Since Loyell Eddgar is now a state senator, the case promises to be a political hot potato, even though he and June divorced years earlier.

Deputy supervisor of homicide Tommy Molto (another familiar Turow prosecutor first encountered in *Presumed Innocent*) tells Sonny that the state will argue that Hardcore simply arranged the murder at the instigation of Nile Eddgar, so the crime is a matricide. Hardcore is temporarily defended by another Kindle County regular, Jackson Aires. Sonny decides she has little choice but to make her connections known in open court and allow the participants to ask her to step down if they wish. Her introductory chapter ends with behavior typical of her current life, as she rushes, late, from the courthouse to pick up her daughter Nikki from daycare, musing about how often her own mother Zora stood her up.

Seth's chapter brings two more of the California counterculturists back together after 25 years. Seth grew up in Kindle County before he moved with his then-girlfriend Sonny to California for her studies at Damon University. A Kindle County childhood friend of Seth's went with them: Hobart Tariq Tuttle, Hobie, a brilliant but pugnacious African American who enrolled in Damon Law School and was accompanied by his girlfriend, Lucy. After the breakup of the loose flower child community, Lucy accompanied Seth to Seattle and eventually married him. They still live in Seattle, where Seth is based as a syndicated columnist, writing, as noted above, "The Survivor's Guide," excerpts from which intersperse *The Laws of Our Fathers*. Seth and Lucy have had two children, Sarah, who attends school at Easton University in Kindle County and keeps an eye on Seth's aged father, and Isaac, killed in a car accident at age seven while Seth was driving.

Nile Eddgar still trusts Seth from his days as his childhood baby-sitter and has called him in Seattle when accused of ordering the hit on his mother. In turn, Seth has called in Hobie, now a successful criminal defense lawyer in Washington, D.C., to defend Nile. Thus, the stage is set for the trial of Ordell Trent, Hardcore, who will testify that Nile Eddgar gave him $10,000 to have his mother killed. The fact that Sonny lived with Seth, who has solicited counsel for Nile, and knows Hobie and all three of the Eddgars creates complex emotional resonances, especially since she and Hobie, as officers of the court, must maintain a formally distant relationship with their former counterculturalist compeers. The crowded stage is set for any number of reflections on the past and regrets and confusions about the present and future, all of which are evoked during the trial, which is the set piece of part 2.

Part 2, Testimony

The long part 2 (381 pages) alternates between Sonny and Seth nine times, with Sonny's section moving forward chronologically from December 4, 1995, to December 13, 1995, and with Seth's section covering the years 1969 to 1970, with seasonal sections (Fall 1969, Winter 1970) that then slow down to concentrate on the spring of 1970, April 1970, and, finally, specific days the first week of May 1970. This alternating pattern drives the plot, contrasts points of view, and builds to a dramatic conclusion of the second part.

Date	Point of View
December 4, 1995	Sonny
1969–1970	Seth
December 5, 1995	Sonny
Fall 1969	Seth
December 6, 1995	Sonny
Winter 1970	Seth
December 7, 1995	Sonny
April 1970	Seth
December 8, 1995	Sonny
May 2, 1970	Seth
December 9, 1995	Sonny
December 11, 1995	Sonny
May 4, 1970	Seth
December 11, 1995	Sonny
May 4, 1970	Seth
December 12, 1995	Sonny
May 5, 1970	Seth
December 13, 1995	Sonny

Sonny begins the second part with reflections on her mother, Zora, a wild, Rosa Luxenburg–like revolutionary whose commitment to ideology over family assured a lonely, insecure childhood for Sonny. Sonny fears her demanding schedule in court is repeating the pattern with her own daughter, Nikki. Leaks to the newspaper have potentially contaminated the jury pool, and Hobie suggests a "bench" trial, one without a jury, with Sonny making the judgment of guilt or innocence. She accepts this potentially risky obligation over having the trial delayed by the jury question. Seth approaches her and they converse amicably, with Seth suggesting that his column on the court case could be titled, *"The Big Chill* Meets Perry Mason" (57). Sonny refuses to socialize with Seth while the trial is on, given Seth's friendship with Hobie and former relationship with Nile.

The prosecution argues that Nile contracted with Hardcore to have Loyell Eddgar killed, but June became the victim by happenstance; Nile's fingerprints on $10,000 in Hardcore's possession, as well as Hardcore's testimony and that of his assistant Lavinia Campbell, "Bug," will prove this.

Seth's sections provide what movie critics call the back story. His experience in the Bay Area university community of Damon is filled with despair. He is not a student—only accompanying Sonny from Kindle

County for her philosophy studies—and he is at loose ends. Sonny, despite suggesting they live together, refuses any talk of love. He has been drafted and faces a year of brutal Vietnam warfare or escape to Canada, presumably never to return. His Holocaust-survivor parents are unable to see his situation except in terms of their own past. However, Campus "Boul" (Boulevard) is a 1960s bazaar of students, hippies, and the counterculture, and, after selling alternative newspapers on the street, Seth begins writing for one, *After Dark,* starting his journalistic career.

Seth finds some measure of comfort in the artificial extended family at Damon: Hobie; Hobie's girlfriend, Lucy St. Martin; Loyell and June Eddgar, whom he comes to know through baby-sitting Nile after his first-grade class; and Michael Frain, a graduate student in physics who works in the Miller Damon Applied Research Center (ARC) doing classified, and probably war-related, work. On Friday, November 14, 1969, the National Student Mobilization Committee scheduled anti-war demonstrations nationwide, and the Damon demonstration near the ARC turns violent, with Loyell Eddgar leading his Maoist One Hundred Flowers party into possible provocations of the police, who attack the protestors. Eddgar's group smashes windows of campus buildings. The incident marks the beginning of the breakup of Seth's "family," since the authorities step up their already active surveillance of the Eddgars. Hobie, normally lost in skepticism and drugs, becomes involved with shadowy Black Panther violence and begins to regard Seth as a racial enemy; Seth discovers June is Michael Frain's lover; and Sonny flirts with participating in her academic advisor Graeme's group sex parties. Worst of all, Seth's draft reporting date is drawing closer. Sonny, too, is in crisis about her philosophy studies and quits her fellowship to waitress while preparing to join the Peace Corps.

A chance remark by Seth that he would like to be kidnapped and relieved of his impossible choice between going to war or into exile leads to a complex, devious plot by the Eddgars to fake Seth's kidnapping. Someone—Seth believes the evidence points to Hobie's involvement—has blown up the Miller Damon ARC in the wake of the violent protests. Hobie has embraced black separatism and rejects Lucy for her whiteness. Since Sonny has moved out, Lucy moves in with Seth on a platonic basis but begins a bond that will lead to her involvement in Seth's "kidnapping," her leaving with him to the Pacific Northwest, and their eventual marriage.

With Sonny gone, Seth is at loose ends, having no real reason to stay in Damon. He continues to baby-sit for Nile, and after the Damon ARC is blown up, he yields to June Eddgar's argument that he must cooperate in a fake kidnapping to raise money from his parents. The cash will free on a bond a suspect in the bombing, Cleveland Marsh, thus protecting Hobie from revelations by this apparent turncoat. Seth's motivation for allowing the kidnapping is complex: a wish to make his notoriously stingy father choose between his money and his son; fear that Hobie has provided bomb parts and will be caught; genuine pity for the dilemma of June, Nile, and even Eddgar, himself, despite the revolutionary's brutal ideology; and the influence of June, who uses her sexuality and confidence to persuade Seth (Seth says insightfully that she was "a human being who, unlike me, had finished the journey to whatever it was she was to become," 232). The Eddgars have some involvement in the ARC bombing, along with Hobie; whatever their culpability, the government will destroy even the innocent Nile in retribution. In effect, Seth, now deprived of Sonny, will lose all the important people in his life if he doesn't agree to shake down his father, and when he is assured that his mother will not suffer too much anguish, he agrees.

June and Seth call his father from a motel, telling him Seth has been kidnapped for ransom and ordering him to open a betting line for Seth at a Las Vegas casino, with a wire transfer of $20,000. Seth will go to Las Vegas, buy the chips, and mail them to a post office box in San Francisco. After Seth says goodbye to Hobie, the Eddgars tell him the FBI has been looking for him as a kidnap victim.

Seth, it is decided, should fly immediately to Las Vegas in the company of Michael Frain, who would pick up Seth's father's wired money using Seth's identification. The plan supposedly protects Seth from the FBI if his parents are the ones who have notified them, while his presence in Las Vegas with Michael in casual circumstances would show Michael as uninvolved in the kidnapping. Because of Michael's affair with June and his hopeless love for her, he will do whatever she says. Seth borrows the money for the flight from Sonny.

In Las Vegas, the FBI picks up Seth, who is pretending to be Michael, while Michael disappears. The FBI says they were informed by Michael's mother where he would be, but since Seth knows Michael's mother is dead, he begins to understand June and Eddgar's betrayal of him: the real Michael's fingerprints are on the bomb parts recovered from the ARC explosion, and if Seth/Michael will submit to fingerprinting, he can be cleared. Since the prints will be Seth's, of course, the real Michael, now having assumed Seth's identity, will be exonerated and can safely disappear. Seth will be stuck with "Michael Frain" as a new identity, but that saves him from draft evasion. The Eddgars have manipulated Seth to allow Michael's escape.

Seth and Lucy drive to Seattle, where they eventually become lovers and he begins his career as journalist "Michael Frain." Seth learns through Hobie that Eddgar had arranged the release of Cleveland Marsh (who had implicated Eddgar in the bombing) in order to have him killed by an "accidental" drug overdose.

The past thus established in these alternating chapters, the trial of Nile for murdering his mother acquires resonances understood only by the members of the Damon tribe present in the Kindle County courtroom. If the past is father to the present, it is not a father known by all his children: only Seth and Hobie know (most) of the story of the ARC bombing and its aftermath, and it is not clear what other schemes the Eddgars had set in train.

The 1995 sections of part 2 follow the courtroom proceedings of the trial of Nile Eddgar and show the tentative efforts of the Damon participants to remain civil to each other; the law requires them to keep their tangled histories at arm's length while their emotions and curiosity pull them toward each other. Hobie dominates the courtroom; his prosecutorial opponent, Tommy Molto, is no match for the deviousness of the defense.

Seth keeps arranging encounters with Sonny, who finally relents and compares notes with him: her marriage to Charlie, a poet, and their daughter, Nikki; the death of his son, Isaac, in a traffic accident with Seth driving; his uncertain marriage to Lucy since that loss; his aged father and daughter, Sarah, both in Kindle County. Seth wangles an invitation to dinner on the weekend, where they discover the old attraction has not been lost, although Sonny insists on distance until the end of the trial. In court, Hardcore presents a credible account of Nile's guilt; tests show the money he claims he received from Nile to have cocaine residue, suggesting it was commingled with his drug-business funds.

After court, Sonny attends a social function where Chief Judge Brendan Tuohey suggests indirectly but forcefully that she rule to free Nile, as a favor to Loyell Eddgar, who is a powerful state legislator. She is so overwrought that she sleeps with Seth and smokes marijuana for the first time since getting her law license. The next major witness is Loyell Eddgar, himself. He testifies that he wanted Hardcore and other gang members to give up crime and organize political action movements in the ghetto. The next day, it comes out that the $10,000 supposedly paid by Nile to Hardcore to arrange the murder may have been a political contribution solicited by Eddgar for Hardcore's organizing of ghetto residents. Hobie forces Eddgar to admit that his self-interest lay in having June dead, because she knew damning information about his past. Nile, free on bond and devastated by his father's testimony, disappears. Sonny grants Hobie's motion for a mistrial, removing herself from this impossible case and allowing all the participants, with the exception of Eddgar, a partial victory.

Part 3, Judgment

Part 3, like part 1, is relatively short (112 pages) and initially alternates between Sonny and Seth before moving on to other characters. The final four sections almost balance the three sections of part 1. During this long coda, some aspects of the truth, but not all, emerge about the case, and Sonny and Seth move tentatively toward each other again. Conflicts from the 1970s are reconciled, if only by the passing of time. Seth's father dies, ending their long torturous relationship. At the visitation or shiva, Lucy, Seth's outgoing wife, has a heart-to-heart with Sonny and tells Seth she wants him to go home to Seattle. Later, Hobie lets Seth know that the money Nile supposedly gave to Hardcore actually was sent to the real Michael Frain (now spelling his name Frane), who has been living in the same small Wisconsin town where June Eddgar lived, so everybody's guesses about the money trail have been wrong.

This section alternates points of view and includes Nile's musings as if his private thoughts were being overheard, revealing that he had been in love with Lavinia and had been smuggling drugs into jail for Hardcore under cover of his job as a probation officer. When Eddgar finds out about Nile's smuggling, he confronts Hardcore, who makes the fateful early morning appointment that June will keep in Eddgar's absence. We also hear Eddgar's and Hardcore's private thoughts, as well as a letter to Seth from Sonny and eulogies for Bernhard Weissman by Seth and Hobie.

The book ends with Seth joining Sonny and promising to adopt Nikki. Part 3 is nostalgic, melancholy, and ruminative, in marked contrast to the violence of part 1 and the courtroom tensions and theatrics of part 2.

THEMATIC ISSUES

With so complex a book, Turow covers a number of themes, including the central theme raised in the title: how do we live under the laws and customs of our fathers since we are indisputably a new, different generation? Related themes are the importance of family, the impulse to form clusters or family-like associations, the binding power of love, and every generation's claim to uniqueness. The novel is replete with father–son and mother–daughter conflicts, battles that involve the legal meaning of "laws" and also the more general sense of "ways," mores, and even pre-scriptions of proper behavior. None of the sons lives easily with his father's "laws," not even Hobie, whose parents are exemplars of moderate good sense; Sonny's conflict over Zora isn't resolved until Sonny is almost 50. Family groups recombine and nonfamily units cluster around father–son surrogates, bound by common interests, loyalty and affection, with each rebellious generation repeating old patterns while thinking itself new and special.

Turow told Alden Mudge that for people of a certain privilege (like himself), the 1960s helped shape "their sense of humanity" and awakened in them a social conscience. Doing *pro bono* work in the late 1980s had a similar shock effect for him personally: "I did not realize how bad, how desperately bad the plight of the black urban poor had become," he told Mudge. "I was incredibly shaken during those visits." The gang-plagued housing projects that were a legacy of the sixties inevitably, then, had to become part of the thematic look back in *The Laws of Our Fathers*.

The Laws of Our Fathers

The human problem in adhering to parental laws is that every generation has a legitimate claim to its own set of unique life experiences, ones different in essence from the environment that brought about parental "laws." Such a claim is particularly persuasive in any era of great change, such as the 1960s in America when young people could be forgiven for thinking that the world had been born anew, that a brave new world was emerging that would be unlike any other: the 1960s saw global revolutionary wars, open rebellions over racial inequality that had been suppressed for 400 years, near-instant communication, and a youth culture that self-consciously promised to transform the world. Many young people felt an almost tribal loyalty to what seemed to be a completely original new way of living.

Nonetheless, as *The Laws of Our Fathers* shows, some essential elements of any given life bend even the most committed revolutionary and the most stubborn individualist back into patterns recognizable in the history of their parents. Middle age, professional and personal failure (or success), marriage, and, in particular, parenthood all make claims that a generation is exceptional seem overblown at best. Sonny was traumatized by Zora's inattention and is determined to give of herself to Nikki in copious measure, but she discovers the demands of the bench on a single mother's time leave her rushing to pick up Nikki at daycare, always late, feeling guilty, and comparing herself to Zora. Seth is confident that he is essentially different from his father, a man of the world as a journalist rather than a professor, someone in control of his destiny rather than an emotionally crippled Holocaust survivor. "I knew there could never be another Holocaust," if the world could be reformed, thinks Seth, believing he would then be free of his father's burden (129).

Yet, Seth, too, loses a young son, suffering irreducible guilt for events so random that they cannot be anticipated. Eddgar reacts against his Southern planter father's racist mistreatment of his African American workers and neighbors, shaping his life as a man of God committed to the poor and helpless, yet finds himself arranging the murder of a black man in order to protect his family and himself. Later in life he ends up in a brutal contest with Hardcore to protect Nile, who in turn has turned all of Eddgar's strictures on their heads to become a drug runner, in part as a means of continuing an affair with Lavinia. Even Hobie, brought up in middle-class comfort by well-educated parents, becomes involved with the Black Panthers and acquires street patois, rebelling late against his parents' benevolent upbringing. The laws of our fathers, whether the legal constraints of segregation in the South, the rigid expectations of Seth's father, or the proper "roles of men" of the Vietnam era—as conformist warriors following aging generals into unthinking combat (90)—continue to control us, if only by fueling rebellion against them. Moreover, some laws run deep in biology and human practice and are as inescapable as gravity.

The Importance of Family

A related theme is the importance of family, the need to come together in groups united by consanguinity and cooperative mutual interest. In 1995, Eddgar and Nile huddle as aged father and feckless son, needing each other's presence even through mutual irritation and disapproval. Most family groups in the novel are even worse failures, with Hobie failing repeatedly at marriage; Eddgar and June divorcing; Seth separating from Sonny in 1970 and failing in marriage with Lucy while Sonny fails with Charlie; and even Nile being unable to sustain a romance.

Yet the characters continue to cluster as extended nonbiological "families" (even Eddgar's One Hundred Flowers radical leftist group is a kind of family, as are Hobie's Black Panther compatriots, always surrounded by women and children). June, Michael, and Nile act as family members, and Seth and Hobie, despite their conflicts, are brothers. Nile, always the needy child, turns to Seth when in trouble, even as an adult in his thirties. Seth and Sonny decide to cobble together a family around Nikki, fueled by Seth's optimism.

A related "family" is the Black Saints Disciples, certainly a dysfunctional group of gang-banging drug pushers but one that clusters together for emotional and practical support. Hardcore is a kind of father to his flock of baby gangsters and even competes with Eddgar to become a surrogate father to Nile. Lavinia, "Bug," may be a drug seller, but she is comfortable with her place in her community and seems to understand that the outside world means her little good. Turow is always sensitive to the plight of the poor and alienated, and here he shows real empathy for and understanding of gang psychology in the African American community, never shrinking from the abhorrent violence and destructive behavior of the ghetto, but also showing how gang membership provides respect, loyalty, support—all family values at their best.

Love

Still another related theme is love, the binding agent of family when common interest is not enough. Sonny is the first to ask a recurrent question, in this case about one of her clerk's romances: "What happens to love?" (18). Her own love for Seth was inadequate to keep her with him when he needed her, yet love returns 25 years later. Seth and Nile and Nile and Michael are tied by parental love much stronger than Nile's biological links. Youthful passion and her guilt bind Michael and June. June and Eddgar have an odd relationship—platonic yet passionate spiritually. Seth and Lucy's love has been damaged by the death of their son Isaac, but Seth's love for his daughter, Sarah, and surrogate child, Nikki, only grows. Love waxes and wanes, yet never disappears; it even ties together such opposites as Seth and Hobie.

The Sixties: Unique or Cyclical?

Seth's "Survivor's Guide" column raises a key question about the stability and endurance of parental laws/strictures, families, and love: was the period of the 1960s unique, as the participants in its joys and debacles always told themselves, or was it just another stormy period in history, with just another new generation self-convinced of its exceptionalism, inventing new laws, family groupings, and types of love, assuming confidently that the world began yesterday? Is it surviving the sixties or surviving youth?

The novel suggests both forces at work, with the undeniably revolutionary aspects of the period being exaggerated and magnified by youthful confidence. Sometimes there really *are* new things under the sun, and the global communication of the 1960s is certainly one of them (the Damon tribe is always listening to the Vietnam news on the radio or watching clips of the war on television). There have been revolutions led by the young of a culture in many periods of history, but never one triggered by near instantaneous news reports of events 5,000 miles away, such as Nixon's invasion of Cambodia in 1970, which led to thousands of protests across America and the fictional bombing of the Damon ARC. It is hard to imagine the events of the Damon part of the novel taking place if the participants had had to read the news in the newspaper; because of electronic communications, the rapid pace of events created a synergy that was convincing about the depth and irreversibility of change, a social shift that really was persuasively new.

We are still in the thrall of these accelerated times, which, thanks to telecommunications, have made their beginnings in the sixties seem leisurely, so it is probably impossible for us to evaluate accurately whether the consequences are truly new or just a superficial twist on every generation's sense of its newness. Turow wisely leaves the last word to Seth's meditations in "The Survivor's Guide": "People my age are hung up on the sixties . . . so naturally I think something special happened. . . . Didn't it? Or was it because I was at that age, between things, when everything was still possible, that time, which in retrospect, doesn't seem to last long?" (44).

CHARACTER DEVELOPMENT

The relationships between characters, over time, are as follows:

CHARACTERS AND RELATIONSHIPS

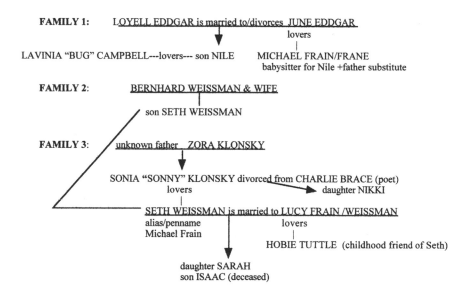

MAJOR CHARACTERS

Turow said that Sonia Klonsky, "Sonny," is among his favorite characters and simply took on a life of her own in *The Laws of Our Fathers* (Macdonald interview, 2004). Promoting her to judge for this book enabled Turow to write his first judge and his first female character from an interior point of view. Seth, too, is powerful, perhaps because he shares some of Turow's real background of enduring enthusiasms, such as a West Coast experience in the 1960s, thoughtful writing and social commentary, and a sympathy for the oppressed. Hobie also, says Turow, began to write himself. The Eddgars are somewhat less immediate but nonetheless compelling in their credibility.

Judge Sonia Klonsky

Despite Turow's opening chapter focus on Hardcore, whose state's evidence gives the impetus to the case at the book's center, and despite Seth Weissman's active role in events, it is appropriate to begin with Sonny, Judge Sonia Klonsky of the criminal division of the Kindle County court, because it is to Sonny's court and Sonny herself that the story continually reverts. She, like Seth, is at the center of the book; although her involvement with some characters from the past has been minimal, she, through Seth, remains their common link.

Sonny has received her judgeship as a result of the judicial scandals examined in *Personal Injuries,* recruited from the local federal prosecutor's office as a figure above reproach. Yet she feels insecure about her position as judge, her role as a mother, and the direction of her life. She is limited in criminal court experience, suspicious that Chief Judge Brendan Tuohey has set her up to fail, underpaid and scrimping given her feckless former husband and the costs of single motherhood, harassed by work schedules versus the time parenting demands, lonely because her age (late forties) and judgeship isolate her, and fearful—as one of Seth's columns on baby boomers puts it—that her present situation is as good as she will ever get. Even her all-female staff teases Sonny unmercifully, albeit affectionately, about her lack of a love life.

Sonny has always felt tentative in her professional and personal life. In accordance with the theme of the book—the laws of our fathers—the root cause of this insecurity can be found in her childhood, as the only daughter of Zora Klonsky, a wild leftist labor organizer whose commitment to politics and organizing left little time for Sonny. Everyone except Sonny thinks Zora is teetering on the edge of insanity, a manic, nonstop talking bundle of nervous energy given to uncontrolled enthusiasms and unpredictable departures.

From this dysfunctional household (no father was present), Sonny learned to cope by withholding trust from people and avoiding commitment to courses of action. When Seth needed her support and company in his escape from the draft to Canada, Sonny decided to join the Peace Corps to fulfill a vague yearning for a meaning to her life. She is unable to sustain a marriage to the weak and selfish Charlie Brace, and only her six-year-old daughter, Nikki, provides Sonny with a semblance of social connections through her preschool and other activities. She is uncertain about men, thinking Tuohey, Hobie, and Seth are able to play her because they see what she can't recognize in herself (391). She has been absent a father figure in her youth and was imbued with Zora's inspired sexual liberation and independence but has no real trust or means of evaluating trustfulness and, as a result, no sense of how to deal with older males. "Half-orphaned, I simply can't do whole," she muses (391).

In her college days Sonny began and dropped four graduate programs, settling on law almost by default. She has a basement full of the detritus of past enthusiasms gone cold: a loom, winemaking equipment, exercise machines. At the start of the trial she is in some ways a stereotypical baby boomer, harried, guilty about work-childcare conflicts, vaguely dissatisfied with her life. A cancer survivor, she worries about Nikki being orphaned. She is ready for Seth to enter her life, her grudging acceptance of his attention notwithstanding. Ironically, once she has committed herself, it is Seth who vacillates, torn by his love for and obligation to Lucy. Sonny is left to make the decisive move, her letter at the end of the book.

As a judge, Sonny is competent and decisive, masking her insecurity by sticking to the rules and evenhandedly reining in prosecutor Tommy Molto and defense attorney Hobie Tuttle. Seth accuses her of multiplying her "rules" to allow rejection of him when he can't keep track of and adhere to them: "it's what you're waiting for anyway. . . . Let's keep everybody six feet below you [on the bench] and safely remote" (391). While there is truth to Seth's observation, it is also true that Sonny seems to be an excellent judge, well liked and respected by all sides in court and by the permanent staff. She finds a way out of the political tangle of the trial that satisfies everyone except Eddgar, who deserves what he gets. Sonny has found her métier: only her personal life requires resolution, which the end of the novel provides.

Seth

If Sonny declines from her 1970s persona of a competent, assured young graduate student at Damon into personal disarray by 1995, Seth improves from a callow, smart-alecky young man at loose ends while waiting to be drafted into a solid and loyal friend. He has achieved professional success, and, while he still has the performer's need to be adored by his audience (first evident in his regular entertainment of his Damon circle), his world-wide readership has distanced his neediness into a craftsman's calculated ploys to manipulate his audience. Although his personal life is in disar-ray—with an emotional separation from Lucy because of the death of their son, Isaac, while Seth was driving—he is fair and honest with Lucy, a good father to Sarah, a supportive surrogate father to Nile and Nikki, a loyal friend to Hobie, and, most importantly, an understanding though persistent lover to Sonny. Seth has grown into the man he could be, and, although he still exhibits the insecure quirks that once irritated Sonny, they are tempered and more than outweighed by his virtues.

Like Sonny, Seth was shaped by his family, especially his father, Bern-hard Weissman, who, unlike Sonny's father, was all too present. A sur-vivor of the Holocaust who lost his family in the camps and has never fully recovered, a distinguished professor in Germany, he provides excel-lent financial advice that delights investors such as defense attorney Jack-son Aires, but he feels no personal confidence or security. Money is simply a shield against a government or culture, which could turn on you without warning, just as in Nazi Germany. Seth, brought up in the relative toler-ance of the Kindle County middle class, is unable to empathize emotion-ally and has trouble understanding even intellectually; he thinks his father is irremediably stingy and jokes about this with college friends. Seth's liberal optimism is in a sense an answer to Bernhard's gloom and Seth's mother's fearfulness: the task of the sixties generation was to eliminate the obvious flaws in society and create a world where no one need be fearful. While Sonny has her mother Zora's liberated outlook about sex, ownership of things, possessiveness about people, and personal freedom, Seth is more staid and conventional, sometimes finding Sonny's ideas shocking and taking comfort in the milder versions of social progress that Eddgar deplores. Seth believes, along with most of his confreres, that mass protests and community action will change society; only the draft and the prospect of being forced into the war machine paralyze him.

Seth's basic decency is evident in his kindness to the youthful Nile, for whom he is more companion and surrogate parent than baby-sitter. As with Sonny and Zora Klonsky, Nile plays second fiddle to his parents' politics. While Seth is often clumsy and awkward with Sonny, who is unable to commit to him emotionally, she is well ahead of Seth in intellectual sophistication. His problem is the callowness of youth rather than a fault of character. Seth's perceptiveness as a writer is evident in the stories he tells the Damon crew, and his talent as a commentator on his generation is also impressive. He is intense, pursuing ideas and feelings and attempting to capture them in words, as all writers do. Sonny feels he is needy, boyishly requiring approval, although some of this need is the insecurity of the storyteller about his audience. For all his youthful bluster and adult verbosity, Seth has humane instincts, and the personal tragedy of the loss of Isaac softens some of his edge with a sadness that provides a window on human suffering in general.

Loyell Eddgar

In contrast to Sonny and Seth, both of whom escape the extremes of their dominating parent, Eddgar is driven into fanaticism by the shameless behavior of his drunken, racist father. A tobacco planter, the elder Eddgar exploited his black workers, treating them little better than the slave-masters they had supposedly been freed from. Loyell Eddgar becomes a minister exalted by Christ's sacrifice for humanity, seeing his own life's work in service to the poor and downtrodden as counterpoising his father's brutality: "It thrilled him to think these men were the heirs, the successors of the beaten, woebegone souls he'd watched chop tobacco during his childhood" (493). When the influence of June and events lead to a loss of faith in traditional Christianity, Eddgar adopts a form of liberation theology, leading the Maoist group One Hundred Flowers in protests that often become violent. A true believer, he has traded a spiritual faith for a secular one, finding in socialist revolution a practical outlet for his still-potent spiritual belief system: " 'What's Eddgar's sacrifice?' [Seth] asked. 'For the revolution?' . . . 'His faith,' [June] said" (320).

Sonny comments that Eddgar has changed when she sees him again in the trial in 1995. Indeed, he is now in his late sixties and has become a state senator and political wheeler-dealer. His beliefs, however, are constant: "he knew just who he was, when he felt both the torment of people warring all their lives against the dim weight of poverty and scorn, and the furious strength of his dedication to them" (493). Eddgar is long divorced from June but still remains in touch with her. He and Nile live together a few days a week, communicating little, and the father still rescues the son from disaster on a regular basis. Whether he has changed as much as Sonny thinks, whether he is different because he is visibly "softer" physically, is questionable. The impact of death, disease, and failure that have moderated Seth, Sonny, Hobie, and others seems to have had much less effect on Eddgar, and when Seth beards him in his den-like home at the end of the novel, Eddgar still has the fanatic's gaze and an absolute confidence in his own rightness. In court, Sonny notes, he still has the "disdainful scowl Zora always had for her enemies, the rebuke of a superior spirit" (368), prompting her to note that the dirtiest secret of political extremists like Zora and Eddgar is that "their passion to change the world derived from the fact they could not change themselves" (368). June in her maturity asks Eddgar if he ever thought about the past, and he responds in the negative: "It was gone, like his childhood, like their marriage, like the many events of everyone's past that meant something when they were happening but would never return" (500). Everyone in the novel but Eddgar broods about how he or she has changed and how the past affects the present and future. Eddgar simply moves on relentlessly, a prisoner of his heritage fixed in his course.

Hobart (Hobie) Tariq Tuttle

Of the major players in 1970 who retain star status in 1995, Hobie is, after Sonny, the most significant. More than the judge, he steers the trial in unanticipated directions. Hobie uses leaks to the press to assure a bench trial, one in which Sonny, rather than a jury, will decide the outcome. Although the plodding Tommy Molto puts up a decent response, Hobie is the stage manager, showing the invalidity of Lavinia's testimony, impeaching Hardcore, and deviously forcing Eddgar to impeach himself.

Hobie is still the childhood friend of Seth, in fact and in psychological makeup. He had made the urban diction his own, and he put "everything his father had wanted him to care about" in "another generation's wrapper" to recreate himself as "a man on his own terms" (323). Caught up in the revolutionary trendiness of the Black Panthers, Hobie finds himself embroiled in the ARC bombing investigation but manages to extricate himself.

Hobie continues having sex with Lucy after she marries Seth, betraying his old friend, but again finds a way to make amends. He has become a well-known Washington, D.C., lawyer, successful in court, but a failure in sustaining a law partnership (he jumps from firm to firm) or a marriage (he moves from spouse to spouse). Before the bench, he is an African American version of Sandy Stern, the wily, elegant courtroom performer of *Presumed Innocent* and *The Burden of Proof*. More theatrical than Sandy and more of a risk taker, he pushes Sonny to her limits but keeps his cards close to his vest, as we learn at the end when his private investigation comes closest to unveiling the logic behind June's murder.

Turow says Hobie is one of his favorite characters and calls him clever (Mudge interview). Originally just part of the mechanics of the novel, Hobie started to take over in this book and became more and more significant as Turow continued to write.

SECONDARY CHARACTERS

As usual with Turow, the novel is peopled with an enormous cast of subsidiary and minor characters, most of them realized well enough to become major characters in their own right. And of course, some might: Turow spins off characters such as Sandy Stern and Gillian Sullivan to play major roles in subsequent books, fleshing out the legal world of Kindle County.

June Eddgar

June Eddgar is a 1960s love story, practicing an open marriage with numerous young men in Damon but loyal for life to Eddgar and Michael. She likes to be the star of her own performance—the "epic events" of the sixties provided "the heat of the spotlight, the rush of applause" (320). Yet she loved Eddgar as "a divine, beautiful thing," the "man . . . to take her to the greater life out there" (501). June at first seems to be little more than her husband's cat's paw, someone to do the dirty work while Eddgar stays safely untouchable. By the end of the book we see her for the major player she has been, plotting with Eddgar, and sometimes seemingly independent of him.

Nile Eddgar

Nile Eddgar is another son victimized by an obsessed father, a damaged child whose adult strategy is to be everything his father is not. Pathetic as a little boy, Nile wets his bed and clings to Michael and Seth for comfort. Eddgar means well but cannot bring himself to do anything but lecture him, while June, like Zora, is distracted by politics and by Eddgar and her lovers. Nile's sexual relationship with the 16-year-old Lavinia is one of the few relationships he has had as an adult. He is still a child in search of a father; as Hardcore tells him when Nile comes under his thrall, "I be you daddy now" (500). Nile ends up with Michael in an odd "family" that allows each to function.

Michael Frain

Michael Frain is a physicist working at the ARC, a radical, June's lover, and Nile's baby-sitter in the apartment complex in which all the Damon characters live. His fingerprint is found on a piece of the bomb that blew up the ARC, but since the Eddgar's have tricked Seth into assuming Michael's identity in the supposed kidnapping, the print doesn't match Seth's fingerprints taken in the Las Vegas FBI offices, creating a new exonerated "Michael Frain" identity for Seth, with which he can escape the draft. The real Michael changes the spelling of his name to "Frane" and lives a low-profile life in a small Wisconsin town, near June, who later remarries another man there. Michael is taciturn but committed. The bombing, whether his idea or the Eddgars', reflects how decent idealistic folk (Hobie is another) were swept up in the passions of the time. (A scientist colleague of Michael's who was unexpectedly in the building was severely injured in the blast; the incident echoes an historical explosion with an unanticipated casualty usually blamed on elements of the 1970s radical group The Weather Underground).

Lucy Frain/Weissman

Lucy Frain/Weissman is portrayed as a stereotypical sixties hippie, full of "groovy"s and mocked openly by Seth and her boyfriend, Hobie. She reveals unexpected courage in driving across the desert alone and at night in Seth's Volkswagen, and she is a fine mother to Sarah and Isaac. The latter's death leaves her as shattered as it does Seth, and their marriage never recovers.

GENRE CONVENTIONS

Turow jokingly said *The Laws of Our Fathers* is Perry Mason meets *The Big Chill,* but this witty characterization is decidedly self-deprecating. Nile's trial is the polar opposite of Perry Mason: not only does no one jump up shouting, "I did it!", but even most participants are unsure about what really happened. Turow's philosophical and literary premises completely reverse those of the television lawyer.

The trial that is the centerpiece of *The Laws of Our Fathers* is classic Turow. Like the courtroom confrontation in the middle section of *Presumed Innocent*, it is a minutely described yet fascinating depiction of how legal procedure is used, manipulated, and abused by all parties to gain advantage. The truth lies somewhere beyond the scope of the trial, itself a finely tuned instrument for teasing out what happened (or at least culpability for what happened), but one inadequate to this complex task.

Like Shakespeare's sonnets—which claim truth is ultimately a literary question, at least as it survives in the minds of readers—Turow's novel suggests only a novelist can provide a semblance of final answers, eavesdropping on the private inner thoughts of characters as he does with Nile, Hardcore, and June at the end of this book in their italicized (interior monologue) sections, peeking into Sonny and Seth's emotional lives by including the letter she sends him, and otherwise invading the privacy of his characters. No court order could do the like: truth, or its nearest approximation, remains a literary phenomenon.

The other genre precursor of *The Laws of Our Fathers* mentioned by Turow, *The Big Chill*, is a reunion story, a gathering touched with nostalgia at memories of more innocent times, of first loves, of youthful idealism and enthusiasm. There are touches of this kind of story in Arthur Miller's classic play *Death of a Salesman* (1949), which repeatedly shifts time periods to allow Willy Loman and his two sons to relive the dreams of their youth that have become impossibilities in adulthood. Miller set the modern American standard for this kind of bittersweet remembrance of things past through flashbacks, and dozens of works of varying quality have mined the reunion genre. *The Big Chill* (1983) is a more recent model of the same type of story of high hopes and failed dreams. In it, as in Turow's tale, adults who once shared the college experience come together for a funeral, but Turow goes far beyond the clichés of popular film to make the lives more nuanced. His characters are the same people they once were but changed as we all are by time. If Turow has any models, it is nineteenth-century European novels, works with large ambitions about illustrating the impact of time and change on human lives set against backgrounds of turmoil and war, works like those of Leo Tolstoy, Honoré de Balzac, and George Meredith. In particular, he takes the tradition of the bildungsroman, the novel of a young man coming of age amid turbulent times, and makes it the story of a generation coming of age.

In this book, the background is the wild, revolutionary days of the 1960s: the stereotypical era of drugs, sex, and rock 'n' roll, of the Black Panthers and the One Hundred Flowers (a literary equivalent of real radical groups ranging from the Weathermen to Students for a Democratic Society to the Young Socialists' Alliance), of conflicts between going to war and going to Canada, a period of such turbulence it effectively exhausted its participants.

The other genre influence is, of course, the murder mystery, which dominates the long central section of the 1995 trial. A woman has been killed in the present, but the motives that produced the murder are murky and are affected by events that lie in the past. The unraveling of relationships, the investigative process to discover the guilty party, the testimony of possibly unreliable witnesses, the courtroom battle between defense and prosecution before a judge who, in the past, was personally involved with the players in her modern day courtroom all reflect murder mystery conventions.

Thus Turow, for all his joking about Perry Mason and popular films, is indeed combining genres, the courtroom confrontation, the nostalgic reunion, the European bildungsroman, and the murder mystery. Turow, however, infuses his hybrid tale with the values and sensibilities of the most serious literature, combining an engaging and sometimes page-turning plot with thoughtful and profound meditations on aging, family, love, loyalty, culpability, success, failure, parenthood, and all the other significant issues of ordinary life, all set against one of the most intriguing historical influences of modern times, the revolutionary period of the 1960s.

ALTERNATIVE READING: A MARXIST POSITION

Given Loyell Eddgar's political orientation and the significant effect his ideology has on everyone in the book, it seems appropriate to explore how a Marxist critic might approach this story. Classical Marxists find the root causes of all human relationships in economic forces, especially among workers and controllers of capital. Private ownership of large enterprises inevitably divorces capital from labor: the actual producers of wealth—the workers—see little of the fruits of their efforts, while capitalists—large business owners—amass profits and attempt to monopolize their control of particular industries. Laborers become alienated from their work, and class divisions between owners and producers of wealth become rigidified. Only an enlightened or socialist government ruled by the proletariat, the laboring class, can redistribute wealth fairly.

Marxist literary critics employ numerous avenues of analysis but often begin by examining the author's ideology and/or class interests and how such leanings shape the worldview provided by the work, or are inherent in it. Of particular interest are how the author depicts class conflicts and whether such conflicts are tied to economic issues. A Marxist might ask what social values are put forward as desirable (values such as self-sacrifice, struggle against injustice, or passivity) and how bourgeois/middle-class life is shown (as desirable, alienating, or destructive). Finally, a Marxist would question a writer's general outlook, whether he or she supports the societal status quo or criticizes it.

Scott Turow would fare poorly from a Marxist perspective on biographical grounds. As a practicing attorney for a high-powered law firm and an artist made wealthy by his writing, he is suspect as a member of the economic and social elite who maintains hegemony, or near absolute power, over the working classes. While lawyers may be progressive or regressive, Turow, as a former prosecutor, would seem to be on the anti-Marxist side. However, he also has done *pro bono* work, successfully defending the appeal of a death row inmate and serving on Illinois Governor Ryan's Capital Punishment Commission, which declared a moratorium on the death penalty. Since Marxists generally view the death penalty as a means by which the ruling classes intimidate and control the proletariat and maintain their hegemony, Turow might seem a subversive working to undermine the establishment from within.

The Laws of Our Fathers would also provide a mixed message from a Marxist perspective. Loyell Eddgar is certainly depicted negatively, despite his evident and sincere commitment to the poor and oppressed. Eddgar, as Sonny observes, is a radical who wishes to change the world because he cannot change himself. The source of Eddgar's commitment is not simply a recognition of its rightness but also a reaction to his father's racism and brutality, perhaps even an Oedipal revolt. While Sonny, Seth, June, and Michael all support progressive values, the two main characters retreat into work in what Marx called the "superstructure"—the establishment position of criminal judge (putting the underclass in prison) and of syndicated columnist (meditating publicly on the status quo rather than trying to change it). June and Michael marginalize themselves for personal reasons.

Ironically, Hardcore, Nile, and the Black Saints Disciples might look better to a Marxist. All subvert the criminal justice system, a machine, as Sonny acknowledges, that makes almost no effort to educate or rehabilitate and that has very little to do with real justice. Hardcore and the Black Saints Disciples have set up an alternative economic system based on providing what the majority community wants—drugs. While Marxists would deplore drug use and the brutal violence of the ghetto, seeing both as means of oppression, they would acknowledge that Hardcore and his colleagues are taking the initiative under near hopeless conditions. Also, a Marxist critic would recognize that Turow's depiction of the Black Saints Disciples is dramatically different from the usual way gang-bangers are represented: they are a family, a brotherhood of comrades, providing loyalty, support, and comfort in appalling circumstances.

Thus, Turow has the intellectual honesty to see the justice system for what it is and to depict much-despised underclass gang members fairly, and with empathy and understanding. However, from a Marxist perspective, Turow is a member of the wrong class, and his novel fails to pursue socialist goals. Turow also casts doubt on the adequacy of materialism as a way of knowing the world—for example, continually suggesting the limitations of legal facts and knowledge as ways of finding truth. His sharp, critical view of society is admirable but leads in non-Marxist directions.

7

Personal Injuries
(1999)

Kathy Slobogin's October 22, 1999, CNN and *Time* interview with Turow quotes an incident that motivated him to explore judicial corruption in *Personal Injuries*. His grandfather told the young Turow about investing his life savings in a gas station, only to learn that the property had been condemned by the city. He told the young Turow that he didn't sue; he just walked away: "A poor man like me? I can't afford to buy a judge." Turow incorporates this real-life story into his second chapter, as United States attorney Stan Sennett tells defense attorney George Mason what made him decide to become a prosecutor. His Uncle Petros, says Sennett, invested 20 years of hard-earned savings in a gas station, only to have the property condemned under a new city plan announced a few days after the closing sale: "It was a flat out, no-good, dirty Kindle County fraud. And every drachma the guy had was gone" (14). Sennett quotes Petros in the same words Turow's grandfather had used, "A poor man like me? I can't afford to buy a judge," and adds, "he realized that anybody who knew in advance what the Center City Plan provided couldn't be beaten in the Kindle County Superior Courthouse" (14). That injustice decided Sennett to become a prosecutor, "to make sure the Petroses of the universe stopped getting screwed" (14).

In keeping with this anecdote, *Personal Injuries* depicts the widespread

Kindle County court practice of kickbacks and bribes, particularly in potentially high-priced personal injury cases, practices that made the *Kirkus
Review* call Kindle County the Yoknapatawpha of American law (997). The
story is based broadly on Turow's personal experiences with the 1980s
Chicago sting operation known as Operation Greylord. However, interviewer Kate Slobogin, in "Pros and Cons: A Profile of Scott Turow," reports that, "while Operation Greylord might have provided inspiration
for the story, the characters are strictly [Turow's] own creation," and, in
fact, Turow has "kept his characters strictly fictional since his first book,
One L" (October 22, 1999). During Greylord, the FBI and Justice Department joined forces to investigate judicial corruption in Cook County, resulting in the conviction of 15 local judges and 49 lawyers (Slobogin
interview). As assistant U.S. attorney, Turow helped send one notorious
judge to prison for 18 years. Turow told a December 6, 1999, *Maclean's*
reviewer that his experience as an assistant prosecutor in that anti-
corruption drive taught him that at the root of judicial corruption was not
only the expected "greed and ambition" but also the unexpected and "po-
tent forces of loyalty, love, and friendship" (41). In fact, *Personal Injuries*
balances justice with mercy, showing the human side of the guilty and the
train of circumstances that led them to their downfall.

Ironically, then, given the origins of the idea for this story, Turow has
his central narrative voice, defense lawyer George Mason, tempering, re-
sisting, and judging negatively the extremes to which the prosecutor—
metaphorically with the sword of justice in his hand—is willing to go.
Where the prosecution sees absolutes of good and evil, the defense lawyer
sees shades of gray, with some offenders beyond redemption, others acting out of mixed and understandably human motives, and still others on
the edge of the malfeasance—not truly drawn into it, just never forced to
acknowledge it or to take responsibility for acts of dubious morality. Perhaps as a result of Turow's dual vision as former prosecutor and present
defense lawyer, his greatest achievement in the book is the creation of an
unquestionably corrupt and culpable practitioner of such malfeasance, yet
one readers not only come to understand but even sympathize with. Turow's main character, Robbie Feaver, is a pathological liar, an inveterate
womanizer, a cheater in life and court, and much much more; a complex
figure of many faces, he is, at the same time, endearingly human and
pitiable and, at times, even worthy of respect.

The lifting of the prohibition against advertising has made attorneys
familiar figures in the media. The number and sleaziness of television ads
for personal injury lawyers claiming to be the new best friend of anyone

ready to sue in accidents of every sort—no matter the circumstances—
have given personal injury lawyers as a group a very negative reputation.
This reputation is in contrast to the reputation of defense lawyers, who,
despite their vigorous defense of the malevolent, the loathsome, and even
the clearly guilty, stand for the necessary opposition in the criminal justice
adversarial system: they assure the fairness and justice of our legal system
and are often admired for their spirited defenses. When individual defense lawyers act outside legal limits to defend a client, blurring the lines
between advocacy and criminality, they are condemned individually and
do not necessarily taint the entire group of defense attorneys. However,
a corrupt personal injury lawyer, working in civil rather than criminal
court, more often taints the specialty as a whole. The reasons relate to the
amount of money in question (sometimes millions of dollars) and the fact
that loss of liberty and the disgrace of jail are not at stake but reputations
and solvency may be. Moreover, the issues raised in personal injury cases
are not questions of justice owed to the community but instead involve
awkward negotiations about the money owed the unlucky individual
who has lost a wife, an eye, an arm, a foot, or even a toe. Dickering in
court over "worth" tarnishes justice with the grubbiness of commerce and
leads to the appellation "ambulance chasers," a derogatory descriptor that
even lawyers like Robbie Feaver, who acquires his cases in only slightly
more dignified ways, would like to escape.

PLOT DEVELOPMENT AND STRUCTURE

Ann Bruns of www.bookreporter.com says *Personal Injuries* keeps readers in suspense from chapter to chapter, speculating about who is manipulating whom as the plot "twists and spins in dramatic new directions."
The November 1999 *Publishers Weekly* reviewer calls the plot "adroit and
inventive." In contrast, *Newsweek* reviewer Jeff Giles, in "The Sting: Scott
Turow Goes Undercover," denigrates the novel as "far from visceral or
thrilling," arguing that "the plot ignites only in the last hundred pages or
so, like an airplane taking off just before it runs out of runway" (66). The
truth, in fact, lies somewhere in between, for Turow is as interested in
character as in plot and is meticulous in his development of the complexity of his characters, yet his ending pulls all the characters and threads
together in explosive moments that make his novel more of a "thriller"
than a character study, like *The Laws of Our Fathers*, which began with
violence but ended with contemplation.

Plot Strands

The plot of *Personal Injuries* has a number of strands in play. There is, of course, the overriding FBI sting operation headed by the tough, unbending, aggressive U.S. attorney Stan Sennett. The ambitious Sennett seeks incontrovertible evidence that some Kindle County judges are dishonest and on the take. Initially, his case rests on his instinct that the remarkable successes enjoyed by certain personal injury lawyers before particular judges indicate malfeasance, and Sennett is completely committed to developing hard evidentiary proof. Robbie Feaver, a multimillion-dollar personal injury lawyer whose unreported sources of income (a slush fund he controls) have led the Internal Revenue Service to prosecute for tax evasion at Sennett's instigation, has the choice of a long-term jail sentence in a federal penitentiary or a reduced sentence for cooperating with the federal authorities. Feaver, who admits to having offered bribes as part of an established system of paybacks for judicial rulings in his clients' favor, becomes central to this sting operation. He agrees to serve as a confidential informant (a "c.i." in FBI jargon) and is assigned to Sennett and his Justice Department-FBI sting operation, Project Petros, named for Sennett's uncle, who was bankrupted by Kindle County corruption.

Sennett's sting recalls the famed Washington, D.C., ABSCAM operation of 1978–1980, run by the FBI against congressmen and other government employees. As a government witness, Feaver must wear a wire, a recording device, and make tapes that will help convict friends and enemies alike throughout the city's judicial system. Sennett's goal in using Feaver is to get the goods on judges who have been paid for favorable verdicts out of Feaver's slush fund. Feaver has already named names and cases, but, given his criminal conviction, his testimony unsupported by other evidence will have little, if any, credibility. The prosecution needs evidentiary trails that can stand up in court. Sennett's main target is the wily presiding judge of the common law claims divisions, Brendan Tuohey, a tough Irishman who is reputedly an organized crime leader and yet who is coming up for promotion into an even more powerful position, where the possibilities for exploitation of the system are even greater. However, Tuohey trusts no one and has made sure that all exchanges of information and cash occur through intermediaries, with contrived justifications for money changing hands that insulate most of the judges from prosecution.

Faced with suspicion, closed ranks, silence about their activities (even to an insider like Feaver), and an intricate system of financial exchanges that make it impossible to prove lines of contact, Sennett turns in part to ABSCAM-type high technology surveillance equipment and sophisticated investigatory methods to gather evidence, including the audio recording devices Robbie agrees to wear, television monitoring of cash exchanges, pursuit vehicles equipped to turn on remote recording equipment, teams trained to recover marked bills when the suspects spend them, and even a government-owned garbage truck regularly collecting trash from a suspect's back alley to examine it for discarded evidence. Furthermore, Sennett becomes more and more willing to engage in entrapment, sending Feaver in to try to bribe officials who have no history of accepting bribes and using tapes of a sexual liaison with Feaver to try to blackmail a female judge into a confession. The irony, of course, is that the representatives of justice, in their desperation to convict, bend the law and ride roughshod over individuals whose only crimes are bad taste in friends.

Another strand in the complex plot is the relationship between Feaver and FBI undercover agent Evon Miller, an avowed lesbian assigned to stick close to Feaver and keep him honest by providing a daily visual reminder that the government is watching his every move. Miller works hard at keeping an emotional and psychological distance from so unsavory a character and at being impervious to his charm, but then, against her better judgment and for all the right reasons, she comes to empathize with him, to understand his plight, and to feel an obligation to protect him and his dying wife. Another plot thread has to do with Feaver's gentle, loving relationship with his once beautiful, now wasted, suffering wife and his attempts to help her retain her dignity while prolonging her life. Other plot directions deal with Feaver's sexual (and protective) relationships with other women and his dealings with the participants in the bribery scheme (fellow lawyers, judges, and court officials) and with his law partner, whom he tries to represent as innocent and guileless. Feaver's relationship with his lawyer and the steps his lawyer takes to protect his client and to call into question the overly zealous actions of the prosecution is another, highly significant plot strand that provides a very different view of the sting operation than that of the FBI and the U.S. attorney. Throughout, Feaver is putting on the performance of his life (he calls it a "play"), deciding whom to give up and whom to protect, struggling to stay out of jail until his wife is past needing him, and twisting and turning within the confines of the law to find a way to walk away from a prosecutor who is so obsessed with winning indictments that he loses sight of justice and legal restraints.

Structure

The overall structure of the novel follows the chronological progress of the sting operation. Turow divides the 46 chapters into his typical three sections, with the first ("The Beginning") and last ("Afterwards") acting as bookends for the interior sections, titled "January 1993," "February," "March," "April," "May," and "June." The novel begins with Sennett conceiving the operation as a way to produce evidence and Feaver being put into play the second week in September 1992, moves through to the spring of 1993, and zeroes in on the sting at the height of operations in March, April, May, and June. It ends with a four-page chapter titled "Afterwards," delivered by defense attorney George Mason, summing up the limited results of the government's investment of so much time, energy, and public money. The movement is from a close-up conception of the sting, through its ongoing processes until its final wrap-up, and then the aftermath as the point of view pulls back with a distant eye and examines careers made and careers ended by the operation, deaths of key players and new lives begun:

The Beginning, chapters 1–4: the groundwork for the sting laid, the mechanism established, the battle lines drawn

January 1993, chapters 5–9: the sting put in play, the fake suit filed, the targets identified, the strategy and role tested

February, chapters 10–14: motives for malfeasance explored, Feaver's virtues and commitments established, Miller's past revealed, federal budget limitations set, first bribe taken

March, chapters 15–18: three judges under surveillance elude sting

April, chapters 19–24: UCORC ruling; sting complications

May, chapters 25–32: further complications and setbacks; extemporized solutions

June, chapters 33–46: climax; violent resolutions

Afterwards

The "Beginning" and "January 1993" chapters establish the status quo ante, as a lawyer might say of the original situation; then middle chapters explore the five crucial months of the sting; and the novel ends with a brief description of the final changes wrought. This arrangement duplicates the pace and rhythm of the investigation, paralleling form and content.

"The Beginning" lays the groundwork for all that follows. It starts with Feaver hooked and lured into Sennett's scheme, then hiring George Mason as his lawyer on Sennett's recommendation. In chapter 2 Mason and Sennett meet, and Sennett lays out his case against Feaver. On his lawyer's advice, Feaver responds in chapter 3, describing the personal history that led to his involvement with Brendan Tuohey and asserting that his partner knew nothing of what was going on. Chapter 4 reports the final deal: (1) Feaver losing his law license and pleading to one count of defrauding the public by bribing various judges so the government can make Feaver's testimony credible to a jury; (2) the government departing from federal sentencing guidelines to dismiss the time to be served in the penitentiary but tempering probation with a $250,000 fine; and (3) Feaver agreeing to take part in a fake personal injury case, bribe officials in the usual way, and wear a wire while doing so. The problem for Sennett is that under this deal Feaver will be an acknowledged felon and could no longer legally practice law, but Justice Department officials in Washington, D.C., agree that the sting can go forward if Feaver has an FBI watchdog observing him at all times. This chapter also personalizes Feaver's lawyer and marks the path he will take to protect his client from Sennett's uncompromising self-righteous indignation. In the seeds of this beginning lie the destruction and victories to come.

"January 1993" records the setting up of the government task force on the eighth floor of the LeSueur Building, where Mason and Feaver both have offices. The office is a front, with an FBI agent named Jim McManis, who is pretending to start a business, providing the excuse for Feaver and Mason to drop in, supposedly to conduct routine court business with McManis. Feaver goes through a show of interviewing and hiring FBI undercover agent Evon Miller and parades her around as his new secretary/mistress. Chapter 6 focuses on the four judges the operation will try to convict: Sherm Crowthers, formerly one of the best defense lawyers in the city, Silvio Malatesta, Gillian Sullivan, and Barnett Skolnick—all of whom make around $90,000 a year and see their kickbacks as making up for low salaries compared to the lawyers arguing before them, who are making millions. The fake lawsuit is filed, and Evon is introduced to Feaver's world, beginning with his mother, who resides in a rest home, and then his fraternity of male friends. As a lesbian, Evon finds Feaver's spontaneous womanizing off-putting and incomprehensible. Chapter 7 sees the government surveillance equipment being set up and put into use, with Feaver wired for action and nudging Walter Munsch, Judge Malatesta's clerk, into incriminating himself on the tape. Feaver slips into his role with ease, but Evon has to work hard at her part, and her lesbian identity is difficult to repress. Chapter 8 introduces Mort Dinnerstein, Feaver's childhood friend and law partner of 20 years, whose noninvolve-

ment Feaver continues to assert. Sennett pressures Mason to cooperate
with the prosecution, forcing Mason into a defensive position, and the
lines of battle for the upcoming contest are drawn. Chapter 9 focuses on
Feaver and Evon's sparring, as he seeks to charm secrets out of her, and
she resists to the point of actually wrestling him to the ground, a scene
interrupted by Feaver's staff and interpreted as a sexual tussle. The section
ends with more about Evon's narrow, lonely life, and the attractions of
escaping into another reality through her FBI assignment.

"February" moves into the action, beginning with an exploration of the
good motives that led Silvio Malatesta to call on old neighborhood connections to assure him a judgeship and ending with the first step in his
entrapment: his law clerk Walter Munsch accepting Feaver's bribe after
Feaver's virtuoso performance has guided the encounter to its hoped-for
end. The fact that Malatesta's backers threatened him with a beaker of
muriatic acid in the face if he ruled incorrectly provides some understandable reasons why a good man would slip. Likewise, scenes of Feaver's
terminally ill wife Lorraine's (Rainey's) inability to control her flow of
saliva, feed herself, or even swallow goes a long way toward explaining
Feaver's desire to stay out of prison. Feaver's teasing of his blind first
cousin Leo even as he slips him a hundred dollar bill and his sensitive
dealings with a grieving family upon the death of a mother of three further
speak to the daily kindnesses that distinguish him from any stereotypical
lawyer on the take. Further, his evolving relationship with Miller as he
questions her about her Olympic performance in field hockey and as she
probes the degree of his involvement with clients shows a genial, personal
side to this man of many faces. This section also reveals the budgetary
and manpower considerations that necessitate keeping the fake case out
of court. The last two chapters focus on Brendan Tuohey and his right-
hand man, Rollo Kosic, on neighborhood stories of the war experiences
that forged their loyalties and encounters that suggest the primal menace,
and even potential for violence associated with crossing them. Feaver has
good reason to fear their retribution.

In "March," Sennett, under federal restraints, moves in on three judges,
beginning with Barnett Skolnick, whose smarter brother Knuckles got him
his position on the bench and for 26 years has guided his rulings. At the
crucial point in Feaver's "play" with Skolnick (when the judge actually
accepts the bribe), the car surveillance camera and recording equipment
break down and all Sennett has is the judge initially refusing the bribe.
Malatesta (whom Feaver records in a law school men's room) responds
in a code that seems clear-cut to Sennett, but others realize a defense

lawyer could make it sound like a straightforward discussion of a case. Then, unbeknownst to Feaver, Sennett has wired even his private moments and captures Judge Magda Medzyk on tape having sex with Feaver, an action Sennett defines as bribery, with the sex a benefit intended to influence a public official. At this stage in the sting operation, both Jim McManis and Evon Miller begin to part company with Sennett, whom Miller derides as a "powermonger" and whose high-handed methods McManis deplores.

In "April," everyone is putting on a show for everyone else. The authentic Attorney General Janet Reno overrides a Uniformed Crime Oversight Review Committee (UCORC) ruling against FBI agents lying under oath and under a false identity, with the result that the sting against Judge Sherman Crowthers can go forward, but even with Mason helping McManis play lawyer, it is clear that Crowthers is toying with them. The illusion created by the contrived cases is almost too credible. Mason must improvise false tales to satisfy a student who wants to do a case study of one of the sting cases and Mort, who wants to collect earnings, neither knowing the cases are fake. The last two chapters of this section describe the maneuvering to reel in Judge Malatesta, creating a fake emergency but only catching the devious clerk Walter Munsch. The judge's canny ploys to elude their traps suggest that he is on to them, perhaps because someone recognizes Evon Miller from a one-night stand years before. Feaver and Miller put on a show to convince Munsch this is a case of mistaken identity and that Miller is just a bubble-headed secretary and mistress.

"May" provides a number of shocking revelations and setbacks, with Feaver first feeling betrayed, then Sennett and Miller. The relationship between Miller and Feaver is tested: Miller is shocked that an insignificant moment from her past has come back to haunt her and Feaver is angry at what he takes as her lie about her sexual orientation. The outcome is an outpouring of confidences that clarify the tangled and painful progression of her sexual awakening and her present ambiguous loneliness. McManis tries to take her off the case for her own protection, but she bravely opts to see it through. In chapter 26 Feaver purposely makes Judge Crowthers respond by shortchanging his middleman, so when the judge complains of too small a payoff, the sting is made. However, this victory is undercut by Rainey's accelerating deterioration in chapter 27 and in chapter 28 by Sennett's discovery that Feaver failed to pass his final law school course (on legal ethics!) and thus to take the bar exam, negating Feaver's immunity. He is not legally a lawyer, and every case he ever worked on could be contested. With the penitentiary threatening his client, Mason makes a deal to keep the sting on track and to protect Feaver from a lengthy jail sentence, but the price is Feaver wearing a wire on his friend Magda Medzyk. Feaver tries to refuse but is forced to act in chapter 30, a betrayal Feaver considers the worst thing he has ever done. However, Magda proves courageous and in the final chapter independently denounces Feaver's actions to Sennett, thereby saving herself from prosecution. The month ends with a break-in at Miller's apartment by corrupt cops seeking confirmation of her FBI identity and finding it in a birthday card with her real name on it and with Feaver using the situation to approach Tuohey about the "mole" he has discovered (i.e., Miller). In other words, despite incredible setbacks, the sting operation muddles on, jerry-rigged and spontaneous.

"June" marks the final stages of the sting, with Feaver and Sennett taking on Tuohey and being outguessed and outplayed at every turn. After Feaver meets Tuohey in a restaurant and gets nowhere, Tuohey probes Mason for clues about what Feaver is up to and why he failed to follow through on Tuohey's recommendation of a defense lawyer. Feaver tries to record Tuohey's henchman Rollo Kosic, but Kosic identifies some of the 15 FBI undercover agents shadowing them. Feaver publicly fires Miller to show Tuohey good faith. Later, Miller, in her role as FBI agent, threatens Feaver openly with a subpoena to give him an excuse to go back to Kosic for advice. Tuohey wants Feaver to take the hit for all of them and keep silent, and Feaver realizes his life is in danger. A planned encounter on a closed golf course turns out to be a Tuohey trick to expose Feaver as an FBI dupe. At this point, Sennett realizes how effectively Tuohey has anticipated his moves and outsmarted him. Thus, chapter 39 sees Sennett rounding up everyone he has evidence on before Tuohey can further damage his cases; bringing in a befuddled and ailing Skolnick; being turned away from a volatile Judge Crowthers's door at gunpoint, picking up Rollo Kosic; and also bringing in a number of other corrupt officials, including lawyers and judges. Tuohey again anticipates their moves, slipping the story of a courthouse mole to a newspaper reporter to publicly spread word of what is happening to his friends and supporters. When Kosic shoots himself, Tuohey can blame all on Kosic.

In chapter 42 Feaver faces Tuohey, but he is shocked more by Tuohey's story of Mort's betraying him to Tuohey than by Tuohey's threatening gestures. By chapter 43 it is clear that Sennett has been double-dealing, manipulating Mort and others to his own ends, so much so that Mort's lawyer, Sandy Stern, calls Sennett treacherous. Furthermore, this treachery sets Feaver up to be killed, for Sennett believes that Feaver's death will give him Tuohey. There are no loyalties here, and, in his obsession with getting Tuohey, Sennett has become as cold-blooded and even murderous as his supposed nemesis. When Mort and Feaver weep together over this betrayal, Feaver resolves to keep from Sennett the unauthorized tape Feaver had made of his encounter with Tuohey, and Mason and Miller choose to help him in this decision. The grand jury room sees the final working out of Sennett's contrivances, with 13 or more subpoenas brought but also with Walter Munsch fulfilling Tuohey's will, taking out Feaver with a golf club.

The short "Afterwards" shifts time and perspective as Mason pulls back from events to summarize the results: 6 judges, 4 lawyers, and 12 deputy sheriffs and court clerks convicted; Brendan Tuohey promoted to the highest judicial level only to die in an accident after his retirement; Feaver's unauthorized tape withheld as long as possible, then suppressed by a judge; and Evon Miller gone west with a female lover. The final scene is of Miller fulfilling Feaver's promise to help Rainey die before she leaves town.

THEMATIC ISSUES

In the main, Turow's thematic issues grow out of his civic concerns, including the cost of not prosecuting corruption in the legal system, the financial costs and personal sacrifices necessary in any major sting operation, the nature and reliability of forensic epistemology, and the moral appropriateness of prosecution strategies. Related is the competition that drives representatives of the judicial system and the conflict between the perspectives, values, and approaches of prosecution and defense. Other themes concern loyalty, love, gender relations, the far-reaching effects of long-term, debilitating illness, and the general frailty of humans. While many reviewers argue that this is a story of betrayal, it is more a story of loyalty to friends and family and the struggle to remain loyal when beset by adversity.

The Civic Issues

Social Costs of Unchecked Corruption

The themes of *Personal Injuries* begin with civic issues, in particular the social costs of allowing corruption to remain unchecked. Having served as a prosecutor (an assistant U.S. attorney in Chicago), Turow clearly understands the zeal that motivates government agents to incarcerate corrupt judges, lawyers, and court clerks who have hijacked the legal system from the public and who have made bribery and malfeasance so deeply ingrained in the justice system that one old judge in the story no longer even thinks of himself as doing anything wrong. Like Feaver, he is part of the larger, ongoing "play," his role spelled out by his colleagues and associates. When he finally understands that being a judge does not place him above the law, that he has been caught red-handed in a bribery scheme, and that he faces an inescapable prison sentence, he suffers a sudden, painful angina attack. When justice goes to the highest bidder, even honest jurists are tainted, argues Turow, as is the case of Judge Magda Merdzyk, who thinks her sexual affair with Feaver will not affect her judgment of cases involving him as plaintiff, so she does not recuse herself. She is vaguely aware of corruption in others but cannot bring herself to take any action about it herself. Thus, *Personal Injuries* dramatizes the need for aggressive policing of the courts, since the courts cannot or will not police themselves. The Petros investigation takes its name from Sennett's uncle, who could "not afford to buy a judge" after being cheated out of his life savings, and this fictional story is based on a similar tale recounted by Turow's grandfather. The point is, of course, that judicial corruption destroys all possibility of fairness and even of true democracy if the law can be trumped by money.

Human and Financial Investigatory Costs

The novel also dramatizes the gigantic costs, both human and financial, of any large-scale investigation such as the one Sennett conducts—the pitfalls encountered and the hidden sacrifices. FBI undercover operatives, unseen and unappreciated, give up months and years of their lives to uncomfortable, lonely work. In an interview with James Buckley, recalling an agent who, in real life, infiltrated a Milwaukee crime family for over a year, Turow describes the lives of undercover operatives as "tough" and "dangerous" (www.bookpage.com). Motivated by a deep-seated desire to expose those whose criminality undercuts the public weal, these nameless men and women, at great personal cost invisible to the public, sacrifice time and energy in pursuit of justice.

Forensic Epistemology

Another theme might be called forensic epistemology, that is, the problematic question of how we demonstrate what we know to be true (the essential issue addressed by epistemology) before a court of law as proof (the forensic issue). The prosecution has at its command a wide array of prosecutorial weaponry—some high tech (like the FoxBIte, a digital recording device half the size of a pack of cigarettes), some simply disciplined detective work (such as surveillance of the movement of bribe money from hand to hand), or information readily available (such as calls made to a public telephone booth). Forging a legally credible evidentiary chain involves enormous labor, with the prosecution team at each step in the planning process seeking to anticipate how a defense attorney will challenge its completeness. For example, random conversations in a nightclub picked up by a recording device could allow the defense to deny that the defendant was present at the recording site and to insist that he or she was only a casual passerby.

Appropriateness of Prosecutorial Strategies

Turow is less concerned with the efficacy of methods employed to expose and punish judicial corruption than with their appropriateness. Central to Turow's argument are those occasional times when the justice system goes overboard, as does its representative, Stan Sennett, when he becomes frustrated at not being able to establish known facts in ways that will survive aggressive defenses and skeptical juries. The theme is twofold: the difficulty the prosecution has finding bulletproof evidence—a difficulty that should evoke reader respect for their genuine successes—but also, less sympathetically, the extremes to which the prosecution might go to entrap citizens and feel self-righteous about doing so.

Competition and Ambition

This difficulty with legal proof fuels much of the competitiveness depicted in the novel, with Sennett regarding chief judge Brendan Tuohey "as a kind of uncatchable Moby Dick to be harpooned at all cost, with Robbie courting disaster by bribing judges to gain an edge, with Brendan and his minions arrogantly baiting Robbie when he comes under suspicion" (Beachum 13:296). Related is the novel's commentary on ambition, since each character twists principles and maintains a sense of an uncorrupted self in order to excel in the highly competitive upper-level criminal justice profession. The theme of ambition involves the compromises and even corruptions bright people are willing to entertain. Even Evon, once competitive as an athlete but now somewhat resigned to her life as an FBI agent in Des Moines, Iowa, leaps at the chance to live undercover for a year to get her competitive juices flowing again. No character survives unscathed by ambition, either their own or that of the people around them; Feaver and Sennett are worthy antagonists since each sees the means as far less important than the ends. Thus, the themes Turow raises go far beyond questions of corrupt officials and corrupted systems to also explore the nature of investigations, the personal goals behind the public facades, and the inherent conflict between prosecution and defense.

Prosecution versus Defense

The conflicts between the Justice Department–FBI prosecutorial team and the defense pits Old Testament justice—enforcement of the letter of the law—against New Testament forgiveness and mercy, although Turow expresses these viewpoints in modern, secular terms. The corruption investigation enables Turow to demonstrate the day-to-day operations of courtroom attorneys, to depict the moral quandaries faced by decent attorneys and by clients gripped by intractable legal and social forces, and to show the visible elements of the legal system as iceberg tips compared to the subsurface machinations behind the scenes.

Stan Sennett sums up the unbending demands of justice unmitigated by mercy. When he appears on Robbie Feaver's doorstep one evening with three IRS agents and evidence of a slush fund for paying off judges, he knows that he has irresistible leverage over Feaver because Feaver's wife, Rainey, is slowly dying from Lou Gehrig's disease and because Feaver's mother is institutionalized with a stroke. Sennett plays on Feaver's devotion to both these loved ones and his determination to personally care for them to the very end. Feaver will do anything to avoid separation from his wife and mother, including wearing a wire on his co-conspirators. Although Sennett occasionally shows human feelings during the investigation, his ruthless exploitation of every advantage he can grab undercuts these softer touches. Carrying the flag of justice and reciting inspirational speeches to his troops of undercover FBI agents as they set out to clean up Kindle County, he is an unbending man of extremes who cannot or will not see the gray areas that make up most of life. Accused of scraping bottom while reaching the stars (315), Sennett, a self-made man who has risen by his own willpower from modest circumstances to a position of respect and authority, is both egotistical and ambitious. His sense of justice is abstract and inextricably bound up with his self-image.

George Mason and Robbie Feaver are set in direct contrast to Sennett; they see human beings as frail and vulnerable and seek compromise as the means to solve every impasse. Mason describes defense attorneys as living in a murky world of concession, always dealing for reduced penalties and searching for excuses and rationalizations as exculpatory arguments: "We are all servants of selfish appetites," repeating "all of us" several times (100). As a personal injury lawyer, Feaver champions the weak and injured against the goliath insurance companies; there is no justice in his eyes, only payment for pain and injury. Sennett's abstract principle that life can be kept in balance by punishing the guilty means nothing to Feaver, who would say we are all guilty to some degree, and can only ask that our losses be compensated for. In sum, Turow's primary theme contrasts justice and mercy, with prosecutor Stan Sennett carrying the standard of justice and with Robbie Feaver, defense attorney George Mason, and FBI special agent Evon Miller standing for mercy.

Loyalty, Love, and Gender Relations

Running parallel to considerations of mercy and justice is Turow's concern with gender relationships, loyalty, and love, tested in varied ways: put under strain by a high-pressure investigation, by a debilitating disease, and by a conservative upbringing at odds with personal discoveries about the self. Feaver's relationships with his wife, Rainey, with his watchdog, Evon, and with his sometime lover, Magda, reveal different facets of gender relationships. With Magda, Feaver can take pure animal satisfaction in providing a sexual outlet and a moment of genuine affection and passion for an intelligent and kindly woman who has been repressed by her mother and upbringing. They don't talk together; they just act, with great intimacy and affection. With Evon, Feaver experiences curiosity about a gender pattern he has never understood—lesbianism—and, in seeking to gain advantage with someone who has control over his present and his future, to find out what makes her tick, he calls into question the premises by which she has led her life and creates a compelling human bond that death cannot break. With Rainey, he feels love and passion, obligation and helplessness; she is like all the victims of circumstances and fate that he defends daily in the courts, but unlike them, she is someone he has loved and betrayed and continued to love. He is willing to risk everything to keep her comfortable in the last days of her life, even ultimately to give up his own freedom. These personal connections cannot help but make readers see and understand Feaver in ways quite different from Sennett's image of him. To Sennett, he is a felon to be used and manipulated to entrap other felons; to readers, he is a flawed human being with great strengths and virtues that match, and to some degree mitigate, his great weaknesses and vices. The proof lies in his effect on Evon, who begins with Sennett's view of Feaver and ends with Mason and Rainey's view—of a sad man with a good heart who has gotten caught up in a corrupt business and, not seeing how to extricate himself, has gone with the flow, to assure his clients the successes he and they need, to guarantee Rainey the care she needs, and to enjoy the game, the roles, the "play" in a cruel and rather meaningless, existential world.

Far-reaching Effects of Long-term, Debilitating Illness

As a counter to the rigid, predictable motivations assumed by the prosecution, Turow asserts the human drives that have, in part, compelled Feaver's criminality. Most powerfully presented throughout the novel are the effects of long-term, debilitating illness on families and family members: the emotional and psychological toll taken by watching someone one has loved slowly and inexorably succumb to an incurable disease (in this case, amyotrophic lateral sclerosis [ALS], popularly known as Lou Gehrig's disease). Then, after the personal and monetary sacrifices come the difficult life and death decisions that must be made. Turow was perhaps drawn to this theme in part because of his personal knowledge of the suffering of fellow author and creative writing teacher Philip Simmons, an associate professor of English at Lake Forest College in Illinois. Turow reviewed Simmons's moving *Learning To Fall* (1997), a study in the art of living while in the midst of dying, as "gentle, beautifully realized and completely inspirational. A wonderful meditation on fallibility in a world of grace" (Macdonald interview, 2004).

An early reference to Stephen Hawking provides a familiar icon of the tragedy of this disease: intelligence and emotion trapped in a decaying body that makes one appear agonizingly less and less human. While under FBI investigation and acting against his will to entrap his colleagues and associates, Feaver must cope with his wife Rainey's slow but irreversible decline, realizing that at some point, she will no longer be able to even breathe on her own, as every muscle in her body goes out of service. Her struggle to retain her humanity as she literally wastes away and loses those physical characteristics that enable her to interact with others (facial expressions, speech) vividly communicates the awful human costs of this disease and lends a pathos unrelated to her husband's criminality.

Long before the novel begins, Rainey had lost her ability to walk, but as the novel progresses, so do the debilitating effects of her disease, as her muscles go slack and she cannot move her limbs even when reclining. Family decisions are first about wheelchairs and other ambulatory devices; then about beds with lifts, pulleys, and mechanical support attachments; next about computerized voice synthesizers; followed by a system of eye blinks for communication. An inability to swallow necessitates a percutaneous endoscopic gastrostomy for feeding a liquid diet directly into the stomach. When the muscles that move the chest begin to go, the decision is about using an artificial respirator to take over her breathing. Ironically, the modern engineering, electronics, and equipment that ease the life of a chronic patient also trap criminals with their own words. Robbie goes from high-tech equipment at home that comforts Rainey to equally cutting-edge technology developed by the FBI to permit the sting to work.

The nightmare is that throughout this process of physical disintegration, thinking and feeling capacities remain unchanged. Thus, Rainey, lying helpless in bed, still feels jealousy when her husband brings a good-looking female assistant along when he drops in to check on her, and she cries with him in chapter 35 about their never having had children. When their patients or loved ones are trapped in ruined bodies, unable finally to communicate except by means of computerized voice synthesizers or eye blinks, ALS family and caregivers suffer a special form of emotional torture: their responsibility to deal with how long their loved ones wish to be kept alive by artificial means. The reality is that 90 percent of ALS patients choose not to be put on ventilators after their lungs can no longer draw air; the effort to live on is just too great to be endured. Over the course of this long novel, Turow brings readers to feel Rainey's pain and isolation, as Evon Miller does. Inevitably, a humanized Rainey, patiently enduring this nightmare existence, totally dependent on the goodwill of others and struggling to retain some semblance of individualized personality and femininity, leads readers to ask how long this suffering (with death the inescapable end) should be prolonged. Her 48 hours without an ability to communicate until the new laser-controlled tracking device following eye movements is in place captures the terror and isolation that awaits her as her body winds down. Rainey's final decision to have Evon end her life poignantly captures the rightness of arguments for the terminally ill being allowed to choose a dignified death over progressively worsening suffering and excruciatingly prolonged wasting away.

It is evident throughout the novel that Feaver's million-dollar cases are what have enabled Rainey to live on with far less suffering than other ALS patients. The wealth of his practice, tainted though it may be, has financed around-the-clock professional care, medicines, painkillers, and equipment that ease her pain and enable her to endure physically. Turow never preaches, but readers cannot help but wonder about the fate of other sufferers of this disease if Rainey—who has every technological and medical aid money can buy—is in such agony. How much worse must it be for poor or middle-class sufferers, without the expensive painkillers or the mechanisms for maintaining movement and communication, to say nothing of full-time nursing care? Turow makes visible and heart-felt the harrowing daily suffering of ALS victims and their families in hopes of raising the consciousness of his readers about ALS, a condition little understood in its cruel depredation of the body. His acknowledgment thanks his many informants (including ALS patients) about this "Cruelest Disease" (403) and provides Web sites and support group information.

Turow also expands his theme of humankind battling disease in his depiction of the personal injuries of other characters throughout the novel. For example, Mort, Feaver's partner, as a former polio victim, has a remaining limp as a daily reminder that the tertiary effects of that disease could recur at any point in his middle years and not only weaken him, but perhaps return him to the paralyzed state he overcame in his youth. Mort had been in an iron lung for months before the paralysis receded, and a leg brace made him the butt of childhood teasing. Feaver's once attractive mother, who abandoned Feaver when he was 16, has had a stroke and, as a result, suffers hemiplegic paralysis; she later dies from a second stroke. Other personal injuries include Miller's memories of her father's fatal bypass surgery and her grandmother paralyzed from disk surgery gone bad as well as the son of a court reporter's case of encephalitis ("Like a body on a bier, the boy floated toward the gates of death and lingered there for days," 132). When taken into custody, Judge Skolnick suffers an angina attack when he realizes the seriousness of the charges. Finally, there is Walter Munsch's pancreatic cancer and his realization that he can only die once and therefore might as well die as he lived, providing cover for Brendan Tuohey by killing Feaver.

Thus, Turow combines the best of both sides of the courtroom: the high ideals and lofty demands of prosecutorial justice tempered with the wisdom and understanding of the defense, the recognition of human frailty and of the gray areas of human existence that lead courts to temper justice with mercy. His image of ALS, a disease that debilitates and destroys, parallels the hidden perils that with time become more and more evident until they finally end Feaver's life.

CHARACTER DEVELOPMENT

The Library Journal 2002 reviewer of the Joe Mantegna audio version of *Personal Injuries* says of Turow's characters that what one sees on the surface is not the reality one comes to know by the end of the book, for Turow is "among the best in the business at pulling the rug out from under [reader] expectations." To this perception Ann Bruns of www.book reporter.com adds, "Turow skillfully slides his characters under a literary microscope and as they come into focus, we see the breakdown of definitive heroes and villains into numerous shades of gray." In "The Case of a Lawyer and His Judicial Sting," *New York Times Book Review* critic Michiko Kakutani agrees, asserting that Turow has "set new standards for the genre, most notably in the depth and subtlety of his characterizations" (6). Likewise, the *Chicago Tribune* reviewer declares Turow "the closest we have to a Balzac of the *fin de siècle* professional class," particularly in his sense of the human comedy ("laced with tragedy") and in the nature and variety of his characters: "rogues in the know, dragged by greed and self-promotion into moral swamps, matched up against moralists who also have their price." Indeed, *Personal Injuries* has the complexity of character development that one expects in the nineteenth-century novel: characters are developed over time as products of their society and culture.

Robert Feaver

Robert Feaver, "Robbie," makes the novel work. *Newsweek* reviewer Jeff Giles calls him a "windbag" and a "cheezy womanizer" (66)—both true, though a bit harsh, for he is more than the sum of his parts, as other reviewers confirm. Kakutani says Feaver may be Turow's "most inspired creation yet" (6). The August 2, 1999, *Publishers Weekly* review calls him "a character of almost Shakespearean contradictions," a charmer who nonetheless shows "superhuman reserves of love and patience to his dying wife at home" (69). In turn, the November *Publishers Weekly* reviewer calls him "Turow's richest and most compelling character to date" (47). In an interview with James Buckley, Turow describes the complicated personal relationships he developed as a prosecutor, experiences that inspired his characterization of Robbie: "You hate their guts when you see them [the objects of a sting operation] for what they are, but you can also become beguiled by them in a certain way. At the end of the day, you get mixed feelings about standing up and saying, 'Send him to the penitentiary'" (www.bookpage.com). Probably as a consequence of Turow's own mixed feelings about men he helped "sting" and prosecute, Feaver is indeed the most interesting, most complex character in the novel, a psychological type and yet much more. An almost stereotypical ambulance chaser, Robbie seems to make the injustices dealt to prospective clients his own cause, weeping on cue in emergency rooms, holding hands with the bereaved, and seeming to casual observers a family member or a close personal friend of those in anguish. Yet he is a shameless self-promoter who shades the truth as a matter of practice and who relies on his training in Method acting to attract clients and win in court. His whole life is an act, so when government prosecutors force him to participate in their sting operation, he moves into the role of double agent setting others up for a fall with aplomb. Nonetheless, when the dimwitted Judge Skolnick is caught, Feaver finds himself beset by the "warring impulses of self-congratulations and [self-]loathing" (183).

Feaver's wife, Rainey, warns Miller that he lies about everything, while Miller herself accuses him of having no core beliefs, of treating everything as a "play," a game, psychologically or emotionally manipulating people and situations to personal advantage. Miller, still a believer in moral absolutes despite her distance from the formal religiosity of her upbringing, is appalled by Feaver's relativism but is unable to counter his arguments and is emotionally swayed by the elemental attraction to him most people feel. She also sees that, despite his lack of an ethical belief system, he does good along the way—although sometimes somewhat randomly (for instance, calling out the car window to a city worker about how good she looks today, not to seduce her, just to make her feel good about herself). At first Miller regards Feaver as a near psychopath, unable to empathize with others, but she comes to see the reverse, that Feaver is empathetic to a fault—he sees no contradiction between feeling for others and pursuing his own interests. He simply tries to avoid harming others, but Sennett's ultimatum has put Robbie in an impossible position. He is truly the novel's greatest achievement, an unforgettable marriage of contradictory elements, a character almost existential in his ability to operate without illusions. Miller is constantly surprised at his unanticipated depths, his spontaneity, his ability to think fast on his feet and reinvent himself. In an amusing scene, an unemotional FBI man hugs Robbie, calling him the best confidential informant he has ever worked with (364).

Feaver tells Evon, "It's just The Play. It's like life, you know? There's really no point, except getting your jollies, and even that doesn't add up to anything in the end. You think any of this makes sense when you stand back from it? You think God made an ordered universe? That's the laugh with the law. We like to pretend it makes life more reasonable. Hardly" (49). Explaining his wife's disease and his personal injury cases, he asks, "Why her? Why now?" and responds to his own query:

> One minute you're a cheerful salesman on the highway, the next minute you're a meatball in a wheelchair. It's The Play. Ball hits a stone on the infield, hops over your glove, and you lose the World Series. You go home and cry. It's really chaos and darkness out there, and when we pretend it's not, it's just The Play. We're all onstage. Saying our lines. Playing at whoever we're trying to be at the moment. A lawyer. A spouse. Even though we know in the back of our heads that life is a lot more random and messed-up than we can stand to say to ourselves. (49)

Later, however, he modifies his position slightly when he explains to Miller his ability to call forth real tears at the bereavement of strangers whose personal injury case he wants to assume, emphasizing that the sentiment is genuine. As a consummate actor, he can call forth tears on command by imagining the real pain his clients endure. "Get real," he tells Miller: "I can't bear to come back to these people and say, I lost, you lost, fuck hope, it's only pain, and it's only going to get worse." That's why he needs the play, and they need the play, he argues. When his lack of a law degree is exposed, he tells the angry Miller that the only role he doesn't know how to play is himself.

Evon Miller

A former Olympic-level field hockey athlete, FBI weapons specialist and undercover agent Evon Miller (her real name is DeDe Kurzweil) reflects her roots. Her conservative Mormon community and her rigid FBI training have provided her an unforgiving moral code, a self-convinced sense of right and wrong. Like Sennett, she is a straight arrow, for whom the lines of proper behavior are clearly demarcated. She is initially somewhat literal minded about moral issues, a view in keeping with the FBI's own strict outlook: "She believed every word about mission and duty. She lived it and liked it and liked herself for doing a good job right" (234). Miller seems tough, but Turow shows us her vulnerable side. Her doubts about her sexual identity and her discomfort at her sister's keeping her children from knowing about Evon's unconventional sex life confirm her deep personal insecurities. She also seems impervious to Robbie's repertoire of charms but deep down is attracted to him. She is dedicated to her job, but partly because it offers her an escape from the drab reality of her routine existence. She has no childhood friends and envies Feaver's close and enduring friendship with Mort. She is deflected from her initial work assignment by becoming personally involved in the life of Feaver and those who depend on him. Increasingly affected by Feaver's open humanity and his legitimate love for family, friends, and even clients—though she continues to condemn his macho womanizing and his lies—she begins to see in his behavior and affection a value system worth emulating. Because Miller's assignment requires her to walk in Feaver's shoes moment by moment, her point of view comes to guide reader responses far more than does that of narrator George Mason. By the end of the book, her disdain for Sennett and her loyalty to Feaver shape our conception of who wins the battle between justice and mercy. (We might compare Sonia Klonsky's similar final disdain for Sennett in *The Burden of Proof* and her growing warmth for her courtroom opponent, Sandy Stern.)

Miller, too, leads us to better understand the odd relationship between Robbie and Rainey. He is the world's worst husband—an unrepentant womanizer who sees every skirt as a challenge—yet he refuses to abandon his stricken, helpless wife, whom he loves with a deep, undiluted passion, her condition notwithstanding. Miller's first encounters with Robbie evoke from her a conventional feminist critique (he is a sleazy womanizer, a macho showoff, bragging to his male associates how much of a stud he is). However, as she learns more of Feaver's depths and meets Rainey, her reactions grow more complex. Feaver, of course, initially sees Miller as a prospective conquest, but his own openness and frankness encourage her to fully admit her lesbian sexual orientation for the first time, though perhaps as a defense against the intimacy between them that threatens her sense of identity and control. Of the Miller–Feaver relationship, *New York Times Book Review* critic Gary Krist writes that watching these two main characters "gradually probing the multiple veils, curtains, and trapdoors of each other's personalities, penetrating a little deeper each time," provides "the kind of reading pleasure that only the best novelists" can produce (7).

Over time, and only gradually, Miller and Feaver develop a complex friendship, incorporating her disapproval of his lies and corner cutting, yet allowing legitimate respect for his unlikely strengths of character. For example, he is utterly devoted to his partner and childhood friend Morty Dinnerstein, to a blind cousin (whom he drops in on regularly and whom he teases in a friendly, confidence-building way), and to any number of other people he has encountered in his practice. He is courageous, adopting the role of confidential informant without regard for his physical safety, although he is well aware of the hazards. The contrast between Feaver and Miller is clear from their response to Brendan Tuohey: Feaver realistically doubts the FBI will ever get anything on Tuohey, while Miller believes the FBI can do anything. At the end, Feaver proves right, and Miller realizes the validity of his perceptions, just as she comes to realize that, despite his being wily and incorrigible, he is driven by two motives—love and loyalty—and, with him as her friend, she can rest assured that were she to stumble, he would come to her assistance, just as he had helped Rainey kick an earlier cocaine habit and as he had protected Mort all his life. He accepts her confession of lesbianism, responding that they have in common their liking of girls, and musing on a truth readers begin to recognize in Miller: she is always undercover.

Her continuing encounters with Feaver and her observations of the many ethical complexities involved in the Petros Project sting lead Evon to a new identity by the end of the novel: working undercover wipes out past identity to begin with, and rather than return to her unfulfilling life as a Des Moines FBI special agent, she consciously becomes someone quite different—more mature, more well rounded, more humanized, with a stronger set of values, tested against human realities, that enable her to see the right action to take for Rainey's sake, although it might not be the legally approved action. By helping Rainey through her final agonies, Miller has stepped into Feaver's morally relativistic world; by accepting herself as gay and eventually finding a female lover, she breaks with the rigid roles her family and even her loving sister had imposed on her. She is changed by Feaver, as is everyone in the book.

Stan Sennett

In her bookreporter.com 2004 review, Ann Bruns describes Stan Sennett as an idealist, but one "intolerant of any minor indiscretion or bending of the law." *Library Journal* 2002, in turn, calls him "humorless, brilliant, driven," while Tom De Haven in his October 8, 1999, *Entertainment Weekly* review describes Sennett as zero tolerant, like Clinton prosecutor Ken Starr "without the spooky fixed smile and carton of coffee" (64). Turow finds Sennett's goals good but his methods questionable and his inability to accommodate the fine differences in people a significant human failure (Buckley interview, www.bookpage.com). An intolerant crusader with the legal clout to coerce others to do his will, Stan Sennett drives himself to be more forceful and more ruthless than others at all that he does, even at jogging. He begins as Feaver's antagonist, but once Feaver is hooked and desperate to avoid jail time, they become wary coworkers striving for a common goal: to gather reliable evidence on the bribed judges. However, as he reminds others, Feaver is, from his perspective, simply "a Trojan horse with a body recorder" (152). Sennett's motivation, however, is not simply his sense of justice but also his desire for personal glory, an ambition fueled by Stan's relatively modest background and his sense of entitlement: Why should others be cut some slack when he never enjoyed much leeway?

Nonetheless, Sennett is not a villain here. He is fanatical about his job, but he is also very good at it. He feels that he is up against ruthless men, with no limits on their bad behavior, and he is right about some of them, especially Brendan Tuohey. When his associates begin to doubt the accuracy of their informant, he sees right through Malatesta's court moves, recognizing the deviousness of his "snow job for the record" (85) and understanding the clever double meaning in the phrasing Malatesta uses to thank Feaver for his bribe.

George Mason

George Mason is the main narrative voice throughout the novel and the spokesman for the defense. From the start he tells his audience, "This is a lawyer's story, the kind attorneys like to hear and tell. About a case. About a client" (3). He has always been both friend and antagonist to Sennett, with the two in steady competition, first as classmates in law school, then while serving different rulers in their legal careers: Sennett the uncompromising strictures of the prosecutor, Mason the messy mistress of compromise in defense of the accused. Mason's quasi-aristocratic Virginia upbringing (he is a distant relative of the Revolutionary War's George Mason) is worlds apart from Sennett's far more modest beginnings. Because of his origins, Mason feels a certain *noblesse oblige*, a sense of obligation to serve a common good and to tolerate ambiguity. Mason's father had been a racial "agitator" working for integration in the late 1950s, so Mason is personally saddened by the fall of African Americans like Judge Sherman Crowthers, who served as models of progress and racial justice. Mason's final triumph over Sennett is a victory of ambiguity over true belief.

Mason is a fine choice as a narrator of events because, as Feaver's lawyer, he must be privy to the ins and outs of the case; as a friend of Sennett, he can provide multiple perspectives. As a voice of reason, he can be judgmental. He recognizes that, by betraying him, Sennett has betrayed himself and, in the name of fighting evil, has been tempted to evil himself. Mason falters somewhat as a credible narrator when he shifts into Evon Miller's imagined point of view and hypothesizes about scenes he never saw; yet these hypothetical conjectures reconstructing events outside his vision and inferring the thoughts and motives of others are some of the best perceptions in the book. In the main he gives the sense of being a fly on the wall, the silent observer who fades into the woodwork but understands the implications of the deeds that pass before him. Events and character details Turow has him report provide readers insights beyond Mason's rather limited observation, that all the participants serve selfish appetites.

Brendan Tuohey and Crew

Turow includes dozens of other memorable characters. Tuohey begins as a stock figure, the Irish cop turned political judge and ward boss— tough, mean, and politically savvy, dependent on street politics and street loyalties to retain his position and thus unforgiving of those who might betray him. He is the canny target, silent and perspicacious, trusting no one and giving nothing away, a wily, arrogant double-dealer with multiple layers of protection between him and the dirty business he practices. Feaver tells Miller that Brendan kneels to no man (187) and that underneath the charm, poise, and genuine humor, he is a terrible human being. Typical is his decision to get the husband of a woman he lusts after a good job 350 miles away so he can make her his mistress. He is well drawn, but mainly from the outside, because few have access to his inner being.

Barnett Skolnick

More vivid are some of Tuohey's fellow judges on the take, especially the pathetic Barnett Skolnick, so dim-witted his politically connected brother "Knuckles" put him on the bench because he didn't have the sense to practice law. Twenty-five years later he is no smarter, trying to return a bribe because he feels he didn't earn it. When he is finally pulled in, even FBI agent McManis pities him and fears he will die of fright if Sennett continues his relentless badgering (344).

Sherman Crowthers

Angry, aggressive, cynical, and yet even more sympathetic is the bluff Sherman Crowthers, a six-foot-six-inch African American who has climbed from a poor black neighborhood to the bench through force of will and personality and who believes that gives him the right to be as corrupt as all the whites in power who once kept him down. As a defense lawyer, he was best remembered for pointing a loaded gun at a police pathologist during cross-examination. As in *Presumed Innocent*, Turow has an articulate understanding of the forces that impinge upon black jurists and the double standard that condemns the recently enfranchised for doing what their predecessors have done for generations. Crowthers is a tragic figure and resists until he can resist no longer, and even then he goes down with dignity, on his own terms.

Walter Munsch

Even a minor figure like Judge Malatesta's clerk Walter Munsch comes to life through brief, memorable vignettes. He is dour and deliberate, using verbal indirection to protect the judge as a buffer and yet benefiting himself in his position as go-between. He extorts a set of golf clubs from Feaver during a battle of wits in which Feaver is trying indirectly to get Munsch to, in effect, give up the judge. Ironically and appropriately, at the end, when his world has fallen apart thanks to Feaver, he uses a golf club, presumably from this ill-gotten set, to kill Feaver for his betrayal.

Jim McManis

FBI agent Jim McManis acts as the plaintiff in the fake court case that is the key to Sennett's sting operation. He plays the part of a "middle-aged expendable cut adrift in another of the ruthless corporate downsizings familiar to recession America" (34). In court, his nervousness and his intense pursuit of fairness for his side, even after the judge has ruled the way Sennett wanted him to, makes the fake case seem real. Later, he consults with Miller about the over-the-top ruthlessness of Sennett's methods and thus provides a neutral observer's confirmation of the rightness of Miller's disapproval.

GENRE CONVENTIONS

Personal Injuries, like Turow's other novels, belongs to the broad general category of mystery/thriller. That is, it is a form of suspense story involving an investigation into criminal activities. As such, it meets the popular culture mystery formula, peeling away layers of events to arrive at discovery, including one murder and at least two near murders, and closing with several dramatic, shocking twists. In subject matter (the business of the law and the procedures that representatives of the law use to develop prosecution cases or defense arguments), it belongs to the subcategory of legal procedural. However, unlike many novels in this subcategory, it is not set in the courtroom, although its characters move in and around the courts and are headed toward a confrontation in a mock trial. Instead, its main action occurs in the offices of lawyers and judges and in the reception areas of those who guard the privacy and set the schedules of these court officials. Just as mystery novels may include maps of the crime scene or of the village in which events occur, so *Personal Injuries* includes a map of Kindle County and its key locations. In fact, the *Beacham's Encyclopedia of Popular Fiction* entry on *Personal Injuries* describes Kindle County as "a place no better than it should be," a place "full of fascinating details that suggest a real place, somehow very familiar, but also distant"; moreover, this imaginary county enables Turow to bring together rich and poor, black and white, native and outsider, and to set them in action in credible ways, demonstrating "a literary perfect pitch, an ear for speech, and a wicked insight into human nature at work in modern urban settings" (13:293).

Turow, however, rarely sticks to basic genre formulae, and his writing style, with its highly metaphorical descriptions, shifts of perception, and overall lapidary style, is consistently at a much higher quality level than that usually found in popular fiction. As a result, asserts Michiko Kakutani in "The Case of a Lawyer and His Judicial Sting," Turow's audience experiences "the kind of reading pleasure that only the best novelists . . . can provide" (6). Tom De Haven, in "Brief Encounters: Scott Turow Presents the Best Book of His Career," complains about how "depressingly formulaic and melodramatic" most legal fiction has become lately and praises Turow for writing "a riveting, impeccably crafted legal thriller" that is "highly charged," smart, and funny as well (64).

Turow's prose style in this book is elegant, his sentences carefully wrought models of clarity and precision, yet sometimes demanding, lawyerly, and literary. His dialogue—of which there is a fair amount, more than in his earlier works—is completely credible: characters speak appropriately for their educational level, social class, race, and background; they sound just as we think they should. Even his minor characters (and there are many in a novel about so complex an operation) are sharply drawn individuals, unique and distinct, with no cardboard creations filling a plot need. In addition to plot function, each has a personality and a history that is his or her own, as in Walter Munsch's back story as a soldier in World War II. Turow's frequent metaphors and similes are witty and precise, the products of a disciplined, orderly mind. At times they reflect the way the law operates by correspondence and precedent, as when Judge Malatesta sums up both sides of a legal argument through comparable cases or situations. He contrasts Jim McManis's argument that a person should not be permitted to drink himself senseless and then blame others for resultant mishaps with Robbie Feaver's counterclaim that balcony railings must be high enough and strong enough to prevent a fall, no matter the reason for the fall (whether the victim is tripped, stumbles over his own feet, or falls down drunk). "In Mr. Feaver's view," sums up Malatesta, "a railing is like a lawn mower or a pharmaceutical drug, where the manufacturer is strictly liable for any injuries resulting from use of the product" (84). The use of analogy to express precedents in this way directly reflects lawyers' courtroom argumentation. Another example illustrates Turow's powerful literary use of metaphor to capture a difficult truth. Feaver sums up Rainey's dreadful and irreversible condition painfully but perfectly when he describes her as a Yahrzeit candle Jews light to commemorate a death in the family: "That's Rainey. That's what she is now, just a long sad candle melting, burning down to this soft puddle of stuff which will finally drown the light. That's Rainey" (93).

Narrative voice is very important in the mystery genre, determining what facts the readers can credibly be given and their significance to themes and plot events. Turow's narrative voice is carefully crafted; the point of view of George Mason dominates, providing a rebuff to the firm convictions of the prosecutor. At times, however, the narrative hits snags, with Mason, for example, telling readers what he imagines happened between Evon and Robbie or between other characters when there is no way he could have been present. Mason explains these lapses by telling the reader he later learned of these events from Evon Miller. In fact, "surmises," "conjectures," and "inferences" may be "the only avenue to the whole truth that the law—and a story—always demand" (27), but direct testimony convinces better than hearsay, and different narrative perspectives might have helped Turow get to the "truth" of his story more easily. At times, however, as in the "March" section, readers clearly hear the voice of Robbie Feaver in all his glory, as he wittily and good humoredly plays his audience, acting as an intimate, gossipy entertainer showing off for Evon Miller or for "the guys." His comments are edged with irony, as in chapter 15 when he asks how the dim-witted Judge Skolnick ever passed his bar exam, knowing that he himself never even took his bar exam, or when he recounts an outrageous Skolnick tale. Therein, the judge calls the defense and prosecution attorneys to the bench and whispers to them that the bribes they both paid him were the same amount, so he has to decide the case "straight," that is, on its merits. Their bribes negate each other, but Judge Skolnick is so clueless he feels he has to inform them of the fact.

During the course of the novel, Robbie Feaver buys a legal thriller, *Mitigating Circumstances* (1993), for his wife since she enjoys "law guys" stories (234). The author, Nancy Taylor Rosenberg, also appears as the given name of the imaginary child Robbie and his wife dream up. Thus, Turow not only works in the genre, but also lends his support to fellow writers new to the genre.

ALTERNATIVE READING: A STRUCTURALIST PERSPECTIVE

In the early 1900s a Swiss philologist and teacher, Ferdinand de Saussure (1857–1913), revolutionized the study of linguistics by asserting that language has built into it highly systematized rules and structures of its own. The theories and assumptions, techniques and methodologies of Saussure led to a critical approach popular in the 1960s called structuralism. Presupposing that the structures of language and the structures of literature have much in common, structuralism offers a more scientific approach to literary analysis, and structuralists find meaning in the system or structure that relates the various components to the whole. Rather than focusing on what happens within a single work, they examine patterns used repeatedly in a number of works, the system of rules by which texts relate to each other, so that structural analysis places individual works within a structural system recognizable as a literary pattern. Structuralists seek to demystify literary texts by ignoring the reader's personal responses, the literary period or historical background, and even the author's stated intentions, concentrating instead on the systems of codes that convey textual meaning—how a code functions intertextually and how the rules of literature create meaning. Social anthropologist Claude Lévi-Strauss, for example, identified in world mythologies recurring themes that transcended cultures and time periods, themes that involved a binary opposition between characters, values, and behavior. Social theorist Roland Barthes, likewise, by analogy with language patterns, found binary opposition a means to decode meaning. The Russian structural narratologist Vladimir Propp identified 31 fixed elements, or functions, that occur in a predictable sequence in stories; others like Bulgarian Tzvetan Todorov and Frenchman Gerard Genette explored the syntax of narrative and provided a metalanguage to describe *how* a text creates meaning. In the 1970s American Jonathan Culler called for a return to the assumptions and principles of Saussure.

Structuralists would find *Personal Injuries* employing familiar structural patterns of binary opposites. The novel, in effect, modernizes and updates the medieval morality play, with a good angel and a bad angel battling for the soul of a representative Everyman. Stan Sennett seems to stand for absolute justice, right, and retribution; George Mason represents the opposing voice of excuses, escape from culpability, and permissiveness; and Robbie Feaver is Everyman, pulled in different directions by his good and bad angels. The binary opposition between good and evil seems appropriate for the genre of legal thriller because the law itself sets up unforgiving binary oppositions. The accused is never declared partly guilty: there is no middle ground, only guilt or innocence.

However, a closer look at the patterns of the text suggests not just one pattern of opposition, but several competing patterns. The iconology of good versus evil falls apart upon closer examination, because Feaver is not the sinner deciding not to sin; he has already committed his offenses and been caught. He has been proven guilty and sentenced to prison time, so the only question seems to be how he can make up for what he has done—by serving that sentence or by helping the government prove the guilt of co-conspirators. Feaver's restitution in the form of trapping other sinners will determine how much he will be punished (with Mason protecting his client from Sennett's excesses). Thus, although at first glance the alternating voices of prosecution and defense pulling Feaver in opposite directions recall a familiar historical pattern—that of the morality play—and set up contraries in keeping with the legal perception of guilt and innocence, the details don't exactly fit. Robbie Feaver is not a modern Everyman torn between good and evil; his soul has already been fought over. He broke the law and, as the novel begins, is already in Sennett's strong grip, his punishment in progress. The historical literary pattern his life fits best is that of the turning wheel of fortune, which carried him to the top of his field and is now bringing him down.

However, competing binary oppositions draw the reader in a different direction, with rigidity set against flexibility and oversimplification set against complexity. In these oppositions, the pattern of good and evil, guilt and innocence is reversed. Sennett and the prosecutorial stance he takes are rigid in contrast to the greater flexibility of Mason and the defense; likewise, Sennett oversimplifies motives and acts and in doing so misses the complexity of individual situations. Thereby, Turow provides an interesting, modern twist on a mythic structure, bringing to it the ambiguities that have led modern man to question the rigid morality of the past and to advocate moral relativism. In this case, the soul that is fought over is that of Evon Miller, for she is the one in the novel who must make a judgment about right and wrong. The competing "angels" are Sennett (backed by the FBI forces and FBI training he represents) and Feaver (backed by Mason, defense arguments, family, and friends). This modern morality play reverses the iconographic expectations: Sennett stands for a black-white vision of reality, while Feaver stands for the gray shades that are the human mix of good and bad. Although Sennett wields the righteous sword of justice, he is the bad angel, the representative of narrow-minded absolutism that ignores the human element and denies the need to temper justice with mercy. The nominally bad angel, Feaver, in turn, takes on the cause of virtue, standing for common humanity, human love and loyalty, forgiveness, and acknowledgment of the mistakes we all make.

The battle rages throughout the book, with Evon initially firmly on the side of Sennett and absolute justice. Her FBI training and her feminism make her see Feaver as unquestionably evil, a scummy, corrupt, lying male chauvinist, who has shamelessly broken the law throughout his career, who feels no regret for his deeds, and who deserves the punishment that will be meted out to him. However, as she follows his day-to-day affairs, she begins to see those realities that Sennett would deny, the human situations that send good people for the best of motives down the wrong track, the kindnesses Feaver shows, the odd mix of cold-hearted lawyer and genuine anguish in the face of his clients' pains and sorrows. He clearly benefits ordinary people when he supports them against large companies with corporate finances. Evon's conversion to Feaver's side is a conversion of the heart, not of the brain. The loneliness and self-isolation that she practiced as an agent had shut her off from the complexity of human relationships and allowed her to reduce justice to a rigid system (like Sennett's), one of logical cause-effect patterns, with humankind divided neatly into those who observe the law and those who break the law, the sheep and the goats, the good and the bad. Being thrust into the lives of others and caught up in their sufferings provides her a different perspective on morality, as does her realization that she, too, is not above error, that a meaningless one-night stand she had had years before could

ruin a case and possibly cost lives when her cover is blown. Turow describes that moment of self-discovery metaphorically: "Her mind was like
a ship stuck in ice. The engine revved but the prow couldn't break
through" (305).

At the end of the novel, her choice between Sennett's world view and
Feaver's is quite clear, for she acts on her new-found wisdom, breaking
the law to act humanely, to assist the isolated, dehumanized, and suffering
Rainey end her life before her body so collapses that she can no longer
communicate her wishes to others. George Mason says that Miller "always
experiences a special clarity in urgent moments" (199), and with Feaver's
death she sees clear-sightedly the nightmare that Rainey will have to endure as she becomes a ward of the state with no one to speak for her or
her wishes, left to vegetate and die slowly, isolated in her own consciousness and unable to communicate. By Sennett's rules (and what previously
were her own), when she assists Rainey's suicide, she has committed murder; by Feaver's and Rainey's rules, she has acted out of love and fellow
feeling to comfort someone who depends totally on her mercy for release
from the unbearable. Where she had condemned Feaver's lies—for lying
is wrong—she now engages in a lying pattern imitative of Feaver's own
to reassure Rainey and to comfort her in her final moments.

Thus, Turow begins with a venerable and quickly recognized structural
formula of the righteous prosecutor confronting the shady defense and
transforms it from the rigid world view it stood for—a morality lesson
based on a black and white vision of the world and of truth, with good
on one side and evil on the other and man in the middle choosing between
the alternatives—to a modern tale of the difficulty of determining guilt
and innocence, right and wrong and with the choice not between the rigid
polar opposites of absolutes but between shades and gradations, between
inhumanity and humanity. Miller rejects the absolutes for the human, and
in doing so confirms the value of Feaver's approach to his fellow beings;
she does not forgive him all, but she learns from him significant lessons
about shared guilt, shared culpability, shared responsibility, the obligation
to deal mercifully and to recognize that it is in the gray areas that we test
the worth of our legal system and our own self-worth.

8

Reversible Errors
(2002)

Reversible Errors continues *The Laws of Our Fathers'* exploration of love affairs taking place between characters in the midst of a trial. *The Laws of Our Fathers* focused on a judge trying to keep an even keel when reunited with an early lover and confronted by the whole tribe of 1960s counterculturalists who had witnessed their love and shared West Coast flower-child turmoil. *Reversible Errors* also tells two tales, following two couples, near-middle-aged men and women, again recapturing youthful passion, but mismatched in their work and legal aspirations and experiencing disconnects that affect their personal relationships.

The term *reversible error* is defined in the legal sense in the pages following the dedication as a mistake made by a trial court so significant that an appeals court must set aside the judgment, leading to dismissal of the charge, a retrial, or some other solution. Turow's titles almost always pun on the literal meaning of a legal term and its ordinary sense when applied to the characters in the book; here the ironic general point is that there can be no reversal of a death penalty once carried out. The "error" in the broad sense of wrongly convicting the accused, Rommy Gandolph, is barely rectified in time by a legal reversible error, the disqualification of a judge. Thirty-three days from execution, only information triggered by a chance remark avoids the "irreversible" error of an execution taking place. The title also puns on the errors made by the characters in their personal lives. In classic Turow fashion, the legal term of the title has resonance well outside courtroom precincts, here suggesting that lonely middle-aged people might try to change the course of their lives, reversing the bad decisions of their youth. Which of our life errors are reversible and which are not? The answer is difficult for the two couples.

Although some critics, like *Entertainment Weekly*'s Bruce Fetts in "Case Dismissed" (109), found the story boring, the prose "purple," and the characters not "compelling," or, as *New York Times* critic Michiko Kakutani complained in "Nerdy Workaholic Lawyer," "disappointing" (E7), they are clearly in the minority. Instead, the majority of reviewers, critics, and scholars find the novel "surprising," "enlightening," "entertaining," and even "masterly," as did Bill Robinson, in *Mostly Fiction* (www.mostly fiction.com). *Washington Post Book World* reviewer Jonathan Yardley calls the novel "one of Turow's best" and Turow himself "the champ" of all lawyer-storytellers (October 27, 2002, 2). Even Kakutani finds the hero "highly sympathetic if unlikely," "complex and conflicted," and the story itself providing "an intimate sense of the incestuous and highly competitive world" Turow's characters inhabit (E7). William W. Starr, of *Knight Ridder/Tribune News Service* (November 13, 2002, K4537) and the *Kirkus Reviews* critic (August 1, 2002, 1073) both conclude that the book is a "deeply satisfying" experience overall, with "sharp" characterizations and a clear plot. Tom Nolan of the *Wall Street Journal* simply says "superb" (D6).

Reversible Errors has been produced as a CBS television miniseries of the same title, starring William H. Macy, Felicity Huffman, Monica Potter, and Tom Selleck and shown May 23 and 25, 2004. Mike Row, who directed *The Burden of Proof*, also directed this highly successful rendition of Turow's book.

PLOT DEVELOPMENT AND STRUCTURE

The general plot idea comes directly from the case studies Turow had examined while performing his duties for Illinois Governor George Ryan's Commission on Capital Punishment. The action centers on death row inmate Rommy Gandolph's final appeal. During the month-long countdown to execution, Gandolph, despite his original confession, insists on his innocence and enlists the once highly skeptical court-appointed attorney, Kindle County corporate lawyer Arthur Raven, in a fervent crusade to prevent his execution. Rommy had been convicted of a particularly heinous crime: three people were shot to death and placed in a restaurant freezer, the female victim, an airline clerk, apparently sexually violated after death.

The novel is divided into three parts:

Part 1, Investigation, chapters 1–13

Part 2, Proceedings, chapters 14–24

Part 3, Decisions, chapters 25–42

Each chapter is headed by a date and tag, beginning with chapter 1, April 20, 2001, "Attorney and Client," and ending with chapter 42, August 30, 2001, "Release." These "present-time" period initial and final chapters act as brackets, recording the start of the "recent" period that begins 33 days before Rommy's scheduled execution and marking his release into a fresh start as a media celebrity manipulated by his new Afrocentric attorneys. In between we flash back to the past and forward to the "present" (Raven's final appeal as he struggles against a determined and self-convinced district attorney and the original detective who hid crucial evidence, browbeat Rommy into confessing, and remains stubbornly sure that the verdict was correct). The most important element in the plot, however, is not a single attorney or investigator but rather Turow's depiction of the law, not as blind justice, but instead as a collective—the product of the personal relationships of a large number of public servants (some talented, others hacks) who can be fallible, foolish, hardheaded, corruptible as individuals, with personal motives that often outweigh their obligations to abstract justice. Human beings are fallible, and that fact guarantees that human systems will also be fallible. Sometimes ambitious prosecutors and smart police officers make mistakes, particularly in cases involving the poor and the vulnerable. The life of a slightly retarded, not very pleasant loser rests in their hands, and they are the state, they are "justice," and they are wrong.

After Arthur Raven and Rommy Gandolph are introduced in "Attorney and Client," the following chapters systematically bring the other major players on stage. Chapter 2, "The Detective" (1991), focuses on detective Larry Starczek and prosecutor Muriel Wynn in a hotel room when they hear of the murder of Good Gus. Chapter 3, "The Former Judge," jumps to 2001 and parallels and contrasts the earlier lovers by having Gillian Sullivan meet Arthur, who, in a most unpromising start to a romance, questions her about her possible judicial misbehavior while she was trying Rommy. Chapter 4, "The Prosecutor," goes back to Muriel at the Paradise restaurant crime scene in 1991, and chapter 5, "Running Leads," shifts to

Larry at his investigative work in the same period. The next chapter recounts Erno Ersai's letter to Gillian, "Gillian's Letter," in 2001. Chapter 7, "The Jail" (1991), has Larry interviewing Collins Farwell. In chapter 8, "Squirrel" (1991), we see Larry neatening up the evidence against Rommy, making it appear that he was arrested with a victim's locket in his possession. We jump forward to 2001 with chapter 9, "Inside," as Gillian meets Erno in the prison hospital to discuss his letter to her and to introduce Arthur to him. In chapter 10, "The Confession," we are back to 1991, when Rommy tells all to Larry. "Kind," in 2001, brings Arthur and Gillian together emotionally as they are forced into each other's company on the prison visit. "Breaking the News," chapter 12, covers Rommy's written confession in 1991, his interview with Muriel, and her visit to Paradise to tell John his father's murderer has been captured; Muriel also breaks the news to Larry that she is marrying Talmadge, and then has one last sexual fling with him. Part 1, "Investigation," ends with chapter 13, "Normal," as Arthur and Gillian conclude their prison visit in 2001.

Seeing the shifts graphically helps one visualize the dramatic alternation in time:

Chapter	Date	Chapter	Date
1	2001	8	1991
2	1991	9	2001
3	2001	10	1991
4	1991	11	2001
5	1991	12	1991
6	2001	13	2001
7	1991		

As noted in the biography chapter, Turow reports that word processing on a computer changed his composition of narrative, allowing him to move set pieces of material around into new chronological order in lengthy experimentation with time shifts and variant ways of unfolding a plot. The shifts in this book seem a clear example of the end result of this process, intermingling past and present to show their relationship and to highlight comparisons and contrasts that would fade into the background were 1991 and 2001 recounted with strict chronology. The alternation also leaves it "up to the reader . . . to construct the story's linear progression," says *Library Journal* critic Nancy McNicol (94), creating a demanding involvement with readers, who cannot simply sit back and turn pages.

The shifts from 1991 to 2001 reveal the process of investigation initially conducted by the forces of the prosecution but finally taken on by the defense in the last stages of the appeal process. The time shifts make the point about the enormous effort that has gone into the prosecution and defense of Rommy over the decade: some participants have moved into middle age; Gillian has fallen from her high position, served a jail term, and begun rehabilitation, all while Rommy languished as a Yellow Man (the color of the condemned prisoners' jumpsuits) on death row. Even so, the marginally retarded Rommy isn't quite sure how long he has been in jail. Although silent, the question is nevertheless posed in the back of the reader's mind: is the death penalty worth this time and effort?

A second effect of this alternation between past and future is to show how even a detective's detective like Larry Starczek and a born prosecutor like Muriel Wynn can be completely wrong. It is not that the prosecution is necessarily corrupt or dishonest, although Larry's stubborn refusal to accommodate emerging facts is on the edge of prosecutable malfeasance (he temporarily suppresses evidence, "losing" the forensic report on the gun by tearing it up before finally confessing to Muriel). Often, Turow says, as with Muriel, wrongful prosecution comes from people trying very hard to do their jobs. The larger problem is epistemological, the philosophical question of how we know what happens. In Turow's view, our knowledge is always incomplete, our understanding blinkered by our roles and prejudices, so even the rigorous discipline of the law provides only approximations of the final truth. The conflict between Muriel and Larry is an object lesson in this idea and shows alternatives open to the prosecution when evidence falls short: she is fiercely partisan but still follows the rules of the courts, while Larry neatens up what happened to shape a stronger case, modeling the street justice of the police and investigatory elements of the justice system. A villain like Erno can and does manipulate these tendencies to his own ends, leaving truth by the wayside, in some cases permanently.

Part 2, "Proceedings," speeds up the action as the countdown to Rommy's execution makes every day crucial. In contrast to the decade-long period, "Investigation," which ends with the May 22, 2001, visit to the prison by Gillian and Arthur that in turn starts the final appeals process, all of the events of part 2 take place in June 2001, most of them on the 12th and 13th: Muriel prepares to engage Arthur's attack on the case against Rommy, Erno testifies, Erno is cross-examined, and, in the last chapter, victim Luisa Remardi's friend and colleague Genevieve Carriere is deposed. We learn more about the parallel love affairs: we get some of

Muriel and Larry's back story but mostly see Gillian and Arthur, and we meet Arthur's sister Susan. The fortunes of the prosecution and defense cases shift dramatically, as each adapts to the strategies of the other. The love affairs, too, never run smoothly, with Gillian constantly exhibiting doubts about her future with Arthur and Larry upbraiding Muriel for passing him over (he claims at one point his despair led him to have Dr. Kevorkian on speed-dial).

Part 3, "Decision," is almost as fast-paced, covering the period from June 28 until Rommy's release on August 30. The ups and downs of the opposed parties become even more dramatic and are summed up in the title of chapter 24, "He Did It," quoting Arthur, who suddenly decides his client is guilty after hearing of his threats against Luisa in Genevieve Carriere's deposition. But the evidence finally speaks louder than Genevieve's deposition, and Larry's grudging admission of Erno's fingerprint on the murder weapon leads to yet another deposition, that of his nephew Collins, which brings out the whole story.

Again, as in part 1, Turow's point in the alternating points of view and dramatic shifts of fortune is the fragility of the chains of logic that bind evidence and testimony into conclusions about guilt or innocence. Rommy's confession—in the public mind and in Larry's view the most damning evidence—is barely material; the depositions of Erno, Genevieve, and Collins all suggest different conclusions, some of them contradictory. The forensic evidence is clearly factual, but without a context it can lead in different directions. With Erno, an evil Wizard of Oz stage-managing interpretations, the kaleidoscope keeps changing how things fit together, and even at the end, we cannot be sure in any absolute sense, for example, if Collins has minimized his involvement in the murders. There is a general conclusion about guilt and innocence, but some points remain murky or irretrievable, and the process toward this consummation—while seemingly on the surface governed by the weighty machinery of the law—has in fact been affected at every turn by personal relationships, chance remarks, serendipity, and just plain luck. Would Arthur have kept on as relentlessly without Gillian, whom he is trying to impress, at his side? What if Larry had held back the fingerprint evidence permanently? Would the outcome be the same if Jackson Aires, Collins's attorney, had not dropped the fact of Gillian's drug use to Muriel in a casual parking lot conversation?

No one knows how these happenings affected the outcome, and Turow's point is that, as in daily life, chance plays a major role. How can this fact be reconciled with the death penalty, a situation in which errors cannot be reversed? The machinery of capital punishment is too unreliable to be trusted with such fateful decisions.

CHARACTER DEVELOPMENT

As outlined above, *Reversible Errors* alternates between two time periods and two couples involved in Rommy Gandolph's case. Muriel Wynn, an assistant prosecutor, and Larry Starczek, a homicide detective, represent the prosecution side. Arthur Raven, a civil lawyer assigned a *pro bono* defense of the convicted murderer's appeal, and Gillian Sullivan, a former judge who heard the case but was disgraced in the stings of judges that end *Personal Injuries,* represent the defense side. The convicted murderer, who is nearing execution, is Rommy "Squirrel" Gandolph, a petty criminal with a low IQ who was found guilty of shooting a popular Kindle County restaurateur, Augustus "Good Gus" Leonidis, and two apparent customers unfortunate enough to have been in his Paradise eatery late one night. The 1991 murder, subsequent investigation, and trial figured importantly in the lives of Larry and Muriel as detective-investigator and prosecutor of Rommy; Gillian Sullivan was the judge who sentenced him. Arthur Raven (although he had been a prosecution colleague of Muriel's early on and appeared as an attorney before Gillian) becomes involved late, in 2002, as Rommy's death penalty appeal process is winding down and Raven is assigned the *pro bono* defense. The triumphs and defeats of the prosecution and defense become interwoven with the complicated relationships of Muriel and Larry, each of whom is at one point or another married to someone else, and Arthur and Gillian, who find passion and love long after they had given up hope of personal happiness. For all of the major characters, revisiting the past means coming to terms with past wrongs.

Muriel Wynn

Muriel Wynn was born to be a prosecutor: "Collins could frame [his story] however he wanted to—as a sinner repenting, as one of the earth's wounded and ill-used. At the end of the day, [Muriel would] stuff it back into the right little boxes of the law" (495). Turow portrays successful prosecutors (and even unsuccessful ones like Tommy Molto of *Presumed Innocent, The Laws of Our Fathers,* and this novel) as distinct personality types, possibly best defined by the Stan Sennett of *Personal Injuries.* Like Stan, Muriel is self-made, a product of the working class who has grown up with uncompromising moral judgments about right and wrong: "the pathway from anger led to resolve. Stand up. Fight back. Those were her father's mottos in dealing with arrogant powers" (478)—and clearly she has made them her own. In fact, Turow describes the way Muriel "relished the aspect of the advocate's role that required her to rip through everyone's poses" (60). In this world good and evil can be clearly delineated, and neither Stan nor Muriel is even marginally hesitant to punish miscreants, who get little sympathy from either. In *Personal Injuries*, Stan sits behind a massive desk in an intimidatingly large office; Muriel has a similarly impressive desk in spacious quarters (though more modest, given the difference between federal and county budgets). Her personality type and background make it unlikely she would exercise self-doubt, even when the evidence might justify it: "Muriel . . . believed in punishment. Her mother, the teacher, was the touchy-feely type, turn the other cheek, but Muriel had always agreed with her father" (56).

Muriel, however, is more interesting than Stan Sennett, not simply because she is Turow's first female prosecutor in the canon, but because her character has more complexity and nuance than does the decidedly one-note Stan. Muriel, in Larry's view, "could be savage about everyone but herself" (520), but it would be a mistake to see her as a simple hypocrite or egotist. As Larry complains frequently, she is constantly calculating advantage and never does anything that fails to advance her self-interests to some degree. She makes quick and creative decisions and sees her opponents with a brutal and devastating clarity. She is capable of underhanded personal intimidation, for example, when she lets Arthur know that she will make his new girlfriend Gillian an issue if Arthur attacks Muriel for prosecutorial misconduct. She commits adultery almost casually, at least in Larry's eyes, indulging sensation and her wishes with no apparent thought about the future. Her willingness to destroy Gillian at the end of the novel is a brilliant tactical solution to potential professional embarrassment for her and Larry, but it is also a brutal act against the crushed and vulnerable Gillian. As Turow writes about another character in another book, "Like anybody . . . who has whizzed along the fast track in the practice of law, he can cut your heart out if need be" (*Pleading Guilty*, 73), a line that describes Muriel quite precisely.

Yet Muriel has also found religion in her middle age and is apparently, to Larry's agnostic irritation, sincere in her devotions. After her own fashion, she is loyal to her husband, Talmadge Lorman, and treasures her role as a stepmother to his child. Most importantly, she is true to her own compass heading and, although Larry feels she simply does what suits her, Muriel has rules she will not violate: "[Repentance by criminals] never bothered Muriel though," writes Turow, "God could sort it out. That was why She was God. Muriel's job was assigning responsibility here on earth" (495). Turow describes her as "barely five feet and one hundred pounds," but notes, "she hit like a heavyweight" (473). Furthermore, he points out, "She meant what she said. But she'd never fully remove self-interest from her calculations" (525). Half of the police, we are told, love her for her uncompromising toughness, and half hate her for her political nature. When Larry admits to tidying up the evidence against Rommy by recovering a locket another policeman has stolen from Rommy, and by claiming that Larry found it in the suspect's pocket, Muriel isn't really bothered, but she refuses to let him go too far: "Larry, hiding fingerprints on the murder weapon isn't the same thing as tightening up the case" (485). Muriel always bounces back from reversals: Larry "could see her good sense, like a life jacket beginning to bring her back to the surface" (485). Despite her calculating nature, she adheres to principles: "The election [for the prosecuting attorney position she so desires] is the least of it. There's still the law. There are rules. And fairness. Christ, Larry, it's ten years later and listening to you right now, I wonder myself about what actually happened" (486).

Muriel always seems to know what to do, especially with regard to the law; it is one of the reasons Larry is attracted to her. Her feelings about her actions, on the other hand, are much less clear to her, something Larry finds frustrating to the extreme, for he always knows how he feels. While Muriel "swam through the murk of her feelings" (480) about their res-cuing their affair, for Larry complex emotional landscapes can be reduced to a clear-cut either-or abstraction: "If I knew what I thought, one way or the other, Muriel, I'd have come around and told you" (480). Larry simply needs to sort his feelings out and then he knows what to do. For Muriel everything is ultimately contingent, including her marriage to Talmadge Lorman, her position as the potential prosecuting attorney, and her com-mitment to seeing Rommy executed. She is willing to calculate and finesse her roles and position, shading and balancing them to get as much as she can from each, while Larry is an absolutist, demanding all or nothing from her. In their early years as lovers, this was not always so. Larry and Muriel were in law night school together, both pursuing new identities. However, while Muriel persisted, Larry traded the ultimate certainties of the law—in compliance with which all the shades of gray must be turned into ver-dicts, decisions, definite final judgments—for the rough justice of the street. There cops tolerate ambiguity and complexity but report it upward to the courts in neat packages of charges and complaints, as Larry tells Muriel, "The prosecutor never knows everything. You don't want to know everything. . . . You don't go to the butcher and ask for his sausage recipe. It's sausage and you know it's sausage. There's nothing in it that'll kill you" (484).

Turow says that although some people were very taken by her performance, Monica Potter, who played Muriel in the miniseries, was not necessarily his idea of Muriel. Linda Tarrentino's toughness might have made a closer fit, but the realities of Hollywood marketing necessitated a brief nude scene, so the actress had to be conventionally beautiful. Turow says, "I wrote about a woman who was sexy by will, not because of what God had given her, someone not particularly good looking" but strong and intelligent (Macdonald interview, 2004).

Larry Starczek

If Muriel was born to be a prosecutor, Larry is a quintessential cop, and this disconnect between the two worlds continually troubles the Muriel–Larry relationship. He repeatedly makes evident this disjunction in the philosophies that underlie their unequal roles, saying bitterly, "I'm just a cop" (486) or making a similarly wounded comment. The tension between their professional outlooks and attitudes spills over into their personal relationship, which in turn complicates their roles in the justice system, though tellingly, their romance never completely derails their professional obligation. They are very well matched as detective and prosecutor and are romantic and sexual soul mates—other partners can't compare: "They went to the center, to that timeless essential place where pleasure becomes our whole purpose on earth . . . they had each other's button, and as her eyes briefly opened, she gave him a grin of perfect celestial delight" (517). Yet they can never commit to each other publicly. Larry, like many cops, has a troubled and distant marriage, a relationship secondary to the thrills of life on the street—where he can go "dancing along on his nerve endings, a feeling reprised from game time when he played high school ball" (483)—and now also secondary to his recaptured emotional life with Muriel. His feelings otherwise normally center on his two sons and his side business of buying and renovating old houses, a middle-aged enthusiasm that brings out, to his surprise, the aesthetic impulse in him (through gardening for curb appeal and the design decisions renovation entails).

Larry's role in *Reversible Errors* is subservient to Muriel's both in the hierarchy of the justice system and personally (the truth about why he withholds from her the discovery of unsuspected fingerprints on the murder weapon was "he'd just been sick of letting Muriel make all the rules" [483]). Fearless on the street, Larry realizes "the person in the world who scared him most" (483) was Muriel. His own lack of calculation and insistence on commitment leaves him at a disadvantage before Muriel's virtually automatic analysis of the calculus of each event: Larry had "never been certain how firmly Muriel stood on principle. She meant what she said. But she'd never fully remove self-interest from her calculations" (524–525).

Actor Tom Selleck, who played Larry in the CBS miniseries version of the novel, describes Larry as "very good at what he does," a "flawed" human being, "not good at relationships," but a "very good cop" (Walker, 7). The *New York Times* repeatedly criticized Tom Selleck's performance as Larry, but Turow felt he was "superb" in the role: "His performance was extremely nuanced. It was clear from the time he got to the set that he knew exactly what he was doing, playing against type. His body language and face captured what was going on inside. He was so anguished. I thought Tom was great" (Macdonald interview, 2004).

Arthur Raven and Gillian Sullivan

The other couple in the novel, Arthur Raven and Gillian Sullivan, also face a disastrous end to their relationship, a consequence of Muriel's shift of the blame for the failure of the case against Rommy through her vilification of Gillian. Ironically, perhaps because Arthur and Gillian are both cases of arrested development, they ultimately value each other more than do Muriel and Larry, and they preserve a chance at staying together.

Gillian, like Muriel, is self-made, overcoming the influence of a large dysfunctional family to become an academic star in the law. Returning to Kindle County, she quickly was named to the bench, only to be caught up in the sting of corrupt judges, recorded in *Personal Injuries.* Gillian's downfall was not greed, however (taking money for fixing cases was so common that she simply went along with the majority when pressured to do so). Rather, a casual sexual relationship with Toby Eliás, an assistant in the attorney general's office, led to a heroin habit, apparently as a lark initially, as two tightly wrapped souls broke free in private, flouting the law and their professional obligation to avoid being compromised. Gillian's smoking of heroin remained secret despite her conviction for bribery; the common assumption was that she had fallen from grace because

of an alcohol problem, a misapprehension Gillian allows to remain un-
disputed until she is outed by Muriel.

In fact, Gillian's drug use appears to be a result of her dysfunctional
upbringing and the desiccated emotional and social life that upbringing
led to. Gillian, beautiful as a fashion model and blessed with unerring
taste in clothes, is thought of as an ice queen in the courthouse, as Larry
says when he learns she "tooted" or smoked heroin rather than injecting
it, "can't get a needle into an iceberg" (521). Where Muriel had indulged
her hot-blooded sexuality with Larry and her first husband, Gillian kept
her fires banked and found relief through the oblivion of her chosen
narcotic.

As a judge hooked on smoking heroin, Gillian drifted through trials
interspersed with her drug use, at first using discreetly, since she could
dip into drugs brought into her court, but finally buying them on the
street. Given her social isolation, she could hide her habit because her
behavior was read as alcohol abuse—a more acceptable, since legal, failing. When her superior, Brendan Tuohey of *Personal Injuries,* gets word of
her real addiction, he sends his henchman Rollo Kosic to force her into
their common personal-injury bribery scheme. Prison actually prompted
Gillian's social and emotional development, as she advised fellow inmates
on their appeals and was forced to confront her real identity without the
bulwarks of her scholastic career, judicial privilege, and drug use. Prison
forced Gillian to face life as Gillian, rather than as an actor in a pre-scripted
role. She has undergone prison 12-step anti-addiction programs and re-
sides with Duffy Muldower, her "sponsor" or guide in her recovery
program.

As she and Arthur become closer, Gillian resists romance in her desultory way, in part because of Arthur himself—he is physically unattractive (the hairiest man she has ever known) and is so self-deprecating that
his negative view of himself becomes a self-fulfilling prophecy—and in
part because she recognizes her reputation will harm his career. She fore-
sees no happy ending to their affair but is swept along by Arthur's relentless pursuit of her, his kindness, and his solidity.

Arthur Raven is another fine Turow character. Turow calls him perhaps
"the most heroic of my 'heroes,'" most of whom are "corruptible and
failing" (Macdonald interview, 2004). Like his avian namesake, he is anything but gaudy—unmarried at 38 (he had a "brief, hurtful marriage" in
law school [6]) and a recent full partner in his law firm, O'Grady, Steinberg, Marconi, and Horgan, but suffering from the "droop and pallor of
middle age since his teens" (6). Arthur's sole indulgence is his German

luxury car, but even this appurtenance of wealth and power gives him no chance with his beautiful young associate Pamela Towns, who is helping him with the *pro bono* case. Although formerly a deputy prosecutor who once worked with Muriel Wynn, Arthur does not care for the criminal bar, finding the less messy conflicts of the civil cases he handles for his well-connected firm more to his liking. (The Horgan in the firm's name is Raymond Horgan of *Presumed Innocent,* who became a rainmaker for the wealthy corporate law firm when he lost the prosecuting attorney election.) Rommy Gandolph's impending execution brings him to interview Gillian, the presiding judge in the original trial, about her rumored abuse of alcohol while on the bench. As both the case and the affair unfold, Arthur is transformed internally, finding a new life both professionally and personally. By the end of the book, both Gillian and the reader appreciate Arthur's virtues. Although still small, stooped, and pallid, he has the virtue of relentlessly keeping on with his task, of a hopeful positive attitude toward his case, and with Gillian, of decency and kindness. His panic when he realizes that his death-row client is innocent is evidence of the seriousness of his commitments: "Justice, indeed, the whole principle of law . . . now depended on him. He was the main variable: his work, his wits, his ability to wage and win civil society's most momentous battle" (171). He suddenly understands that the lost look in Rommy's eyes is "terror" and that "if something goes wrong here," he will feel as if "somebody sucked the light out of the universe" (207). Of William Macy as Arthur Raven, Turow observes that: "Macy was very good, even though that wasn't my image of him at all. Though very attractive in person, Bill is about as unattractive as Hollywood will ever allow for a hero. But he was very effective. I also thought his wife [Felicity Huffman playing Gillian] was lights out" (Macdonald interview, 2004).

Rommy Gandolph and Others

The other characters in the book, although sharply delineated, are there for their role in the drama and (unlike the main characters) change little over the course of the novel. Rommy Gandolph is a persuasively drawn small-time crook and loser, a ready patsy given the circumstantial evidence against him and his confession, forced by Larry not with a beating but by psychological pressure and Rommy's shame at soiling his pants.

Erno Ersai is a convincing con man who fools even the most cynical of experts, Larry and Muriel. His nephew Collins Farwell is a credible born-again believer, anxious to make what amends he can but also a life-long misrepresenter of who he really is. We come to know Luisa Remardi, the female murder victim, through the testimony of her friend Genevieve Carriere, her coworker at TransNational airlines. Arthur Raven's sister Susan is a schizophrenic whose behavior is strange while she often is also oddly sweet and appealing, giving a sense of real mental illness rare in fiction.

A host of other characters people the book in typical Turow fashion, almost all sketched with details that make them seem based on reality rather than fictional constructs. *Contemporary Authors, New Revision Series,* sums up, "Turow captures the full range of damaged souls that inhabit the legal system, as well as the interdepartmental rivalries: the angry, underappreciated cops on the front lines, the ambitious prosecutors, the ever-more-important DNA and gun technicians, the remote judges, the unspoken undertow of race" (vol. 111). Reviewer Ann Bruns (www.bookreporter.com) succinctly sums up the essence of these characterizations: Turow "never succumbs to the temptation of fellow authors by simply fictionalizing the sensational for his own intent," but instead crafts "a magnificent exposé" that "finally brings each character to the edge of their own moral abyss" and the haunting truth that "when one human being crosses paths with another, both lives are dramatically altered—for better or worse—forever."

THEMATIC ISSUES

The Death Penalty

All the characters and situations in *Reversible Errors* revolve around the issue of capital punishment. The Rommy Gandolph case brings them together and to a greater or lesser degree affects their private lives as well. The great divide between prosecutors and defense attorneys becomes all the more profound given the consequences to the defendant. However, while *Reversible Errors* is ultimately an anti–death penalty book, if only in its repeated insistence that no one would know of the miscarriage of justice had not chance occurrences such as Erno Ersai's cancer conspired to release Rommy, the novel is vastly different in its arguments against state-sanctioned execution from other books in the genre (see the following section on Genre Conventions). Rommy, although pathetic, is never made sympathetic. He is so slow and uncomprehending (his IQ is in the 70s) that he thinks he can claim money from the family of the woman he is accused of murdering because she had shorted him in their stolen tickets scam. His misapprehension shows Rommy has no understanding of how the world works. Pamela, Arthur Raven's associate, is never sure whether Rommy's flirtations with her and offers of marriage are playful or are meant literally. Beyond a kind of animal cunning, Rommy has no evident reasoning skills and is never shown as likeable.

Turow, then, ignores, clearly by choice, the emotional argument against the death penalty that humanizes the culprit, showing him as human as the rest of us, setting in its place a kind of epistemological argument: we can never know what truly happened, even in a case with a confession, a motive, and physical evidence of guilt. Witnesses shade the truth or lie outright; confessions may be coerced; different multiple motives may underlie apparent good reasons for murder; physical evidence alone lacks a context. In Turow's home state of Illinois, two years before *Reversible Errors*, Governor Ryan's moratorium on capital punishment was based on the shocking discovery that DNA evidence showed many death row inmates in his state were innocent, a discovery that weighed heavily in his commission's agreement about the moratorium.

A second argument against the death penalty comes from Gillian Sullivan, who, although she imposed a capital punishment sentence on Rommy, believes enforcing the death penalty to be "too much trouble" (42). She apparently means that the enormous costs and labor involved distract the justice system from its central tasks, diverting resources that might reduce crime; clearly, the long wait before the sentence is carried out makes any benefits in deterrence (or future crime prevention) dubious. While relatives of victims may feel in some "remote segment of their consciousness—the primeval part that was scared of the dark and loud noises" (538)—that when a killer is executed their "lost loved one would come back to life" (538), Turow finds retribution no answer, calling it the "pathetic logic of revenge . . . [trading] life for life" (538). This is the logic "learned in the playpen, and of the sacrificial altar" (538), but this atavistic calculus, the hope for "an awful equilibrium being restored to the world" (538) changes little, even among victims' families. Even Muriel cannot "remember why inflicting more harm would make life on earth better for anyone" (538). Her final word to John Leonidis, the son of "Good Gus," is that in "death cases. . . . You try to make rules, and somehow none of them stick, or even make sense" (540). Ironically, Muriel, the fierce advocate of retribution, seems at this point to have almost come over to Gillian's attitude: the death penalty is "too much trouble" (42).

Turow followed *Reversible Errors* with *Ultimate Punishment: A Lawyer's Reflections on Dealing with the Death Penalty* (2003), a nonfiction meditation on his personal experiences with the issue. It stands as a kind of parallel to *Reversible Errors*, touching many similar points and issues and coming to conclusions not much different from Gillian Sullivan's. Never an anti–death penalty absolutist, Turow felt no moral objections to executions, especially as a way to provide a measure of justice to victims' families, to "restore the world" for them (*US Catholic*, 2004, 6). Nonetheless, although the deep human need for revenge should be taken seriously, retribution leaves the world at large unchanged and possibly makes it worse.

Turow came to this position, one very similar to the conclusions at which *Reversible Errors* arrives, after defending Alejandro Hernandez, who had been convicted of the rape and murder of a young girl on the strength of a single sentence spoken in English during a conversation in Spanish. Turow said he "became virtually unhinged" because he could not believe that such a blatant injustice could happen in America (McCarthy, 64). Participation in Governor Ryan's Commission on Capital Punishment resulted in Turow, like Arthur Raven, visiting Tamms Prison, Illinois' maximum security facility, to see if Hannibal Lecter–like criminals could be kept securely imprisoned. In the final analysis, he is a death penalty opponent but still understands the deep emotional and social needs for retribution that make the issue contentious.

Professional versus Personal

Reversible Errors also examines the theme of conflict between professional work roles in the legal system and satisfactory love relationships and personal lives. Larry Starczek, Muriel Wynn, Arthur Raven, and Gillian Sullivan all find their public identities interfere with a normal love life, whether it is Larry's addiction to the emotional charge of a cop's street life, Muriel's calculation that Talmadge can help her career while Larry could hurt it, Arthur's painfully lawyerly way with all his relationships, or Gillian's uninvolved judicial distance with everyone and her very real fear of ruining Arthur's reputation. These characters would not suffer this way if they were bus drivers or accountants, but then, they are personalities drawn to their professions to satisfy deep emotional needs. The law, suggests Turow, is a harsh mistress, consuming all one's life; unlike less dramatic ways of making a living, it attracts certain psychological types and then reshapes them further in the distinct roles the profession offers.

Possibility of Change

Another theme in *Reversible Errors* is the possibility of change. Rommy, with his low IQ, is doomed to play the same victim role all his sad life, but Erno Ersai and his nephew Collins Farwell both reshape themselves in unpredictable ways; they almost literally become different people. For all their intelligence, Muriel and Larry keep playing the same destructive games with each other, but Gillian and Arthur find love, passion, and potentially even happiness when all possibilities had seemed to have passed them by. Thus, Turow's hopeful outlook seems to be that even apparently hopeless miscreants can transform themselves morally, while alienated sad sacks approaching middle age can find soul mates. As Collins Farwell's attorney Jackson Aires says, never give up on a human being, even a hoodlum: "Can't be any reason to what we're doing here, if we're gonna give up on people" (515).

GENRE CONVENTIONS

In an October 31, 2002, *USA Today* review "Turow Thrills with Timely 'Errors,'" Dierdre Donahue asserts that calling Turow "the author of legal thrillers is as diminishing as calling P. D. James a mystery writer," for both "employ murder and the law to explore life's largest and most perplexing questions about morality, justice and revenge" (www.usatoday.com). *Kirkus Reviews* agrees, observing that *Reversible Errors* includes none of the standard thriller fare, "no car chases, explosions, threats against the detective, movie-star locations, or gourmet meals," and is instead "about deeply human people who just happen to be victims, schemers, counselors-at-law, or all three at once" (1073). While it is true that Turow goes well beyond the bounds of the legal thriller, *Reversible Errors* is more in the genre of death penalty protest works than merely legal thriller in the first place. As such, it belongs in the company of George Orwell's persuasive short description "A Hanging," Truman Capote's powerful and shocking fictionalized account of two murderers *In Cold Blood,* Sister Helen Prejean's book and film *Dead Man Walking,* and the Clint Eastwood/ Stephen Schiff countdown-to-execution film *True Crime.* (See chapter 2 on Literary Heritage for more about each.)

Such works as these reflect a specialized area of the legal procedural that has concentrated in particular on the countdown to execution. In general, these works are time driven, with the clock ticking away as old witnesses are reinterviewed, new witnesses are sought, and every opportunity is taken to prevent a miscarriage of justice. Usually, they follow a straightforward chronology, a linear progression Turow leaves to the reader to construct as he skillfully moves between past and present (see Nancy McNicol, *Library Journal*, 94). Writers of death row novels may concentrate on the character of the inmate to suggest a faulty genetic inheritance (low IQ; crack baby), family culture (abusive parents), and social conditions (ghetto values; street gangs; poverty) that lead to crime and that, to some degree, absolve the criminal of full responsibility; often their appeal is to upper-middle-class guilt about successfully escaping social upheaval. However, Turow does not go in this direction. Other death row novels assert that humans have no right to take the life of another; that matters of life and death rest in the hands of the deity and therefore, no matter the crime, the state is criminal to do what it forbids others to do. Turow avoids such moral appeals. Still others concentrate on knocking down the more utilitarian arguments often used for capital punishment, for instance, that it provides revenge for the family that has lost a loved one and discourages others from committing a similar crime. Turow is sympathetic with the emotional force of the revenge argument but believes it changes nothing; he does not think executions decades after the crime deter new crimes.

Turow does, however, follow some of the genre conventions. These include a revisiting of the crime and of the original trial, examining past records, interviewing the members of the investigative team, looking at the events surrounding and leading up to the crime, the forensics in the case, and the original judge in the case. As is typical of these works, the discovery of saving evidence goes down to the wire and ends up as an indictment of the legal system—its failures based on fallible humanity—and the suggestion that a system designed to see humans in black and white terms misses the gray areas into which so much human behavior falls.

ALTERNATIVE READING

The emphasis in *Reversible Errors* on the unreliability of a confession, the dubious validity of the testimony of people involved, and out-of-context forensic evidence lends itself to a poststructuralist/deconstructionist interpretation. Whereas the structuralist movement in anthropology and later in literary criticism stressed analysis of paired opposites or bipolar oppositions (light versus dark, good versus evil, as discussed in the Alternative Reading of *Personal Injuries*), poststructuralism casts doubt on the legitimacy of the neat oppositions created by language and logical categorization. Deconstruction, a particular critical approach within the general poststructuralist movement, sets out to undo the carefully "constructed" interpretations of conventional criticism.

Poststructuralism argues that reality comes in shades of gray and that even apparently definitive labels distort rather than clarify. The biological either-or of male–female, for example, seems to end the discussion, yet there is clear evidence that each sex includes the biological tendencies and social attitudes of its supposed opposite and that the rough categories may obscure as much as they define. Even in nature, hermaphroditic categories are common enough to cast doubt on female–male opposition; in human culture, the "social construction" of gender, the influence of the expectations created by culture, goes far toward creating the categories of sexual classification. In all situations, a poststructuralist questions the legitimacy of the neat sorting processes encouraged by words and classification: when we decide to put something in one box or another, we may have to ignore characteristics that would undermine our decision making.

The law, of course, flies in the face of poststructuralist thought. Legal categories include guilty and innocent, culpable and nonculpable, responsible and nonresponsible, and the like. Only the Scots allow a verdict of "not proven." The great social task of the law is to deny the poststructuralist insight that nature is often not reducible to either-ors, and to insist that final decisions can be reached for the good of the community. The other great assumption of the law is that the truth can be established and defined, brought to the foreground out of the confusion of actual events by the discipline of legal reasoning, forensic methodology, and the rules of evidence.

The plot of *Reversible Errors* works to show the inadequacy of the courts and the law in determining the truth in death penalty cases. In capital cases, error cannot be reversed once the sentence has been carried out. *Reversible Errors,* however, barely escapes such a miscarriage of justice, only by 33 days and some chance events. The categories of guilty and innocent do not fit Rommy adequately. Although innocent of the murders, he is nevertheless involved in ways that make him seem guilty and lead in part to the confession that convinces Larry Starczek: Rommy's consciousness of guilt for the ticket scam and for threatening Luisa with murder lead him to distort his role and perhaps to confess.

The impossibility of ever knowing absolute guilt or innocence (was Collins Farwell a horrified bystander when his uncle Erno did the shooting, or did he take part more actively?) casts doubt on the death penalty as a legitimate punishment, for the truth lies somewhere in between the either-or categories of guilty or innocent. What really happened remains an ineffable truth, unavailable to human beings who so ardently desire definitive answers. We are left with "the mirage that truth often becomes in the courtroom" (*New York Times* on the Web, November 22, 1999).

9

Conclusion: The Staying Power of Turow's Canon

Scott Turow has indisputably had a significant impact on American popular fiction. Before *Presumed Innocent,* the legal thriller was a crude instrument, no more than a page-turner meant to entertain and while away the boredom of travel or waiting rooms. Ambitious works like James Gould Cozzens' *By Love Possessed* (1957) inhabited a special niche in widely read fiction, but it was Turow who virtually invented the genre of the serious legal thriller. Critical reaction and sales have been in rare accord: both professional readers and the public have been enthusiastic consumers of his works.

In his early fifties, after producing six substantial novels that have garnered great praise, Turow can look forward to a long period of further exploration of the legal landscape. In the past decade and a half, he has put under the microscope a deputy prosecuting attorney for Kindle County *(Presumed Innocent)*; a defense attorney in private practice *(The Burden of Proof)*; a cop/lawyer/private investigator working for a large law firm *(Pleading Guilty)*; a criminal court judge and a defense attorney *(The Laws of Our Fathers)*; a personal injury specialist, a federal prosecutor, a defense attorney, and an FBI undercover agent *(Personal Injuries)*; a prosecuting attorney, a detective, a defense attorney in a capital case, and a former judge in disgrace *(Reversible Errors)*; and various corrupt judges

along the way *(The Laws of Our Fathers, Personal Injuries)*. The legal field
provides other roles and numberless dramatic situations for a novelist just
hitting his stride, one who steadily produces a book every three years, to
further anatomize the courtroom and legal life.

At this rough midpoint in his writing career, then, how does Turow
rank among his peers/competitors? More significantly, will his works
have the staying power that is the mark of true literature? Answering the
latter question necessitates answering the broader question of what makes
popular fiction endure as literature, as the best of its kind has done, with
Dickens's works the best-known example of popular success and canon-
ical lasting power. Some academicians notwithstanding, the enthusiasm
of many readers does not automatically indicate a deficiency of literary
quality (nor does it assure quality, of course); sometimes, the democratic
readership polls can be absolutely on target. The problem comes with
evaluating popular works apart from the fads and conventional wisdoms
of the moment, the feeling that a writer is on some stylistic cutting edge
or other, or that the writer has a finger on the pulse of the time. All such
judgments can seem ludicrous a short time later.

The queen of modern British detective fiction, P. D. James, puts the issue
of literary quality in clear and elegant terms in a commendation of mystery writer Frances Fyfield: "There are crime writers whom we think of
as primarily novelists. They provide not only the expected satisfactions
of the genre—excitement, tension, mystery, and horror—but the psychological subtlety, intelligence, and excellent writing which are the hallmark
of first-class fiction" (back cover blurb for *Blind Date*). The words could
have easily been written about Turow, but James's criteria for "first-class
fiction" (whose practice she has long mastered) are helpful general mark-
ers of literary excellence. If for "psychological subtlety" we read "well-
rounded, convincing characters," for "intelligence" we read "significant
themes," and for "excellent writing" we understand just that—care, orig-
inality, and beauty in the crafting of sentences and paragraphs—then we
have reasonable and specific benchmarks for quality.

WHAT MAKES POPULAR FICTION ENDURE
AS LITERATURE?

Thousands of novels are published in the United States annually, some
to considerable acclaim, only to drop out of sight with startling rapidity.
Author's Digest, printed in 20 volumes in 1908 by the Author's Press,
promised to provide readers commentary on the most significant authors

of the time and the most famous names in fiction. While the importance of authors like Jane Austen and Honoré de Balzac remain, others have disappeared into oblivion. Who remembers Irving Bacheller, Wolcott Blestier, John Banim, Amelia Edith Barr, Arlo Bates, Frances Courtenay Baylor, Cuthbert Bede, Henry Ward Beecher, or Aphra Behn? A few literary specialists might read William Beckford's *Vathek: An Arabian Tale*, if they could find a copy, but the difficulty is that a majority of authors from the *Author's Digest* list are no longer in print. Only 10 of the American authors listed as significant in 1908 remain remotely familiar: Louisa May Alcott, George Washington Cable, James Fenimore Cooper, Joel Chandler Harris, Nathaniel Hawthorne, Oliver Wendell Holmes, Frank Norris, Edgar Allen Poe, Harriet Beecher Stowe, and Edith Wharton. Others such as Mary Elizabeth Doge, Nathan Haskell Dole, the literary brothers Edward and George Cary Eggleston, Fanny Fern, Paul Leicester Ford, Jessie Fothergill, Howard Frederic, among so many more, evoke no recognition at all. Moreover, of the well over 400 pages of famous names in fiction in *Author's Digest*, only a handful would be recognized today by the average English major. (The omissions—where are Mark Twain and Herman Melville?—only reinforce the point that enduring quality can be hard to anticipate.)

Nor are large numbers of books sold the key to long-term survival that big numbers are in the biological world; as a strategy for permanent impact, producing millions of copies and perhaps a movie option often leads to a blank stare among readers and bookstore clerks a generation later. Books read with enthusiasm in the 1960s and 1970s have already disappeared from print. James McClure, for example, whose Kramer-Dondi mysteries (like *Steam Pig,* London, 1971) have been called directly responsible for helping end apartheid in South Africa, are no longer available, even from online vendors. Now, paperback books are disposable artifacts, made of cheap, acid-based paper and with fragile bindings: they are meant to be used, not kept. Most novels in paper disappear rapidly, their physical makeup like their impact on the culture, a mere bump in the road. Even in the past, when books were made to last with high-quality paper and sewn bindings, most copies failed to survive unless some notoriety gave them worth as a physical commodity. Original eighteenth- and nineteenth-century novels, for example, may still be found in used bookstores, but only in small fractions of their original print runs.

If the marketplace alone is a poor final judge of quality, then long-term survival depends even less on critics and reviewers, whose power is usually limited to spurring short-term sales. The "buzz" a book creates is usually no more than a passing thing, a spur to purchase kept alive by book tours and interviews. What gives a work of fiction long legs, the endurance of a long-distance runner?

Committed Readers

For a work to survive requires, appropriately enough in a democratic society, the votes of committed readers, whether a passionate few or an extended tribe of enthusiasts. Such readers make requests of booksellers and libraries, pressuring publishers to fund multiple editions, reissues, and reprints, keeping a novel alive while its many competitors are re-maindered, lost, forgotten, or turned into pulp. If some of these readers are academics, the novels may find their way into syllabi and high school and college reading lists, introducing them to new generations of fresh readers and evoking the critical commentaries that turn up in libraries to pump up a writer's reputation past the publishing cycles of newspaper and magazine reviews. Although not a guarantee of respectability, such critical commentary—in academic articles, overviews of a given genre, guides and summaries—gives an author or work a chance at long-term survival by creating new readers. Happily, it is the pleasure of serious readers and their enthusiastic recommendations that will keep a book repeatedly read and "alive."

A Familiar Fictive Landscape

What provides such pleasure to readers, and how will Turow's works fare in the long run? Page-turners seem not to last without other literary elements to enrich them. Topicality is another issue in the durability of popular fiction. Turow's novels provide a satisfaction different in nature from the works of the writer who is often named along with Turow as the definitive lawyer-writer, John Grisham. Grisham's books are indeed page-turners, providing readers the thrill of immediate engagement, the need to know what happens next. In contrast, although Turow's stories can be gripping in the page-turner sense, they more typically engage us with a character—Rusty, Robbie, Sonny—and a created universe, a world we sometimes are reluctant to leave when we reach the last page. This kind of bittersweet emotional connection with an author's world, almost a nostalgia for an entirely make-believe society, is a familiar feeling among readers of serious fiction, particularly of the nineteenth century but also of a large number of more recent works. John Ronald Tolkien, for example, created a fantasy world of hobbits and sorcerers that can seem more real to young people than their own world, and the Frank Herbert Dune series' huge following has led to a film and a television miniseries. Likewise, mystery writer Margaret Cole, over a series of novels, brings to life the inhabitants of the Wind River Arapaho Reservation and the Wind River Mission, creating a contemporary image of Native American society, much as Tony Hillerman did with his Navajo books about policemen Joe Leaphorn and Jim Chee.

In Turow's books, Kindle County becomes a landscape inhabited by figures we come to know over the course of the canon, characters we recognize initially as types but who can come to seem as real as people in our own communities playing similar roles. Such fictive community-building has little connection with page-turning in the thriller sense; the bond between reader and text is essentially different, and the pleasure given is unlike the roller coaster of the classic promotional cliché and more like a return visit to a half-forgotten town: we experience shocks of recognition, confusion about dimly recollected figures, déja vu, the engaging feeling of making sense of puzzles, the joy of a new acquaintance in old circumstances.

Kindle County as a setting is, in fact, one of Turow's best achievements and offers him continuing possibilities for extending his canon without repeating himself. As noted in chapter 1 (The Life of Scott Turow), *Presumed Innocent* was initially meant to be set in Boston, but the locale became more like Turow's hometown of Chicago.

Particular locations carry with them associations and stereotypes, so that a personal injury lawyer like Robbie Feaver in New York would inevitably be seen as a New York lawyer, not as a general American type. Likewise, a story about the death penalty set in California would carry with it all the baggage of California death penalty debates. A real setting can strain credibility, lead to judgments of characters and action based on "reality," get in the way of authorial needs and goals, and reduce the universal to the provincial. Kindle County seems "real" but has allowed and will allow, if Turow continues to write about it, a Yoknapatawpha north, one with legal values rather than rural ones.

Topical Themes Made Universal

What features of Turow's works, besides their sales and critical praise, suggest the longevity of literature? As discussed in chapter 1, Turow, as the inventor of the genre, was ahead of his time in anticipating the current fascination with legal drama. Turow's works are topical by definition. If interest in legal thrillers fades, perhaps because of an oversupply, will

Turow's novels endure? If literature is the popular fiction of the past that is considered worth preserving and rereading, will Turow's work achieve this status?

Even the most certain, pontifical blessings of critics of contemporary authors as producers of literature have been wrong as often as not. Obviously, to some degree, Turow's popularity bodes well for his long-term reputation since the "votes" of millions of readers count in the final analysis: can so many readers be wrong? Students of popular writing have puzzled over the issues of topicality and popularity and the uneasy relationship the academic establishment has with popular, or "mass," culture. Most thoughtful commentators agree that the exciting plots of page-turners are often associated with "entertainment" and not much else; literary quality requires (but is not guaranteed by) serious themes, complex characterization, and excellence of writing style.

Turow's themes certainly qualify as serious. His overarching topic is how their environments shape people, a staple concern of the nineteenth-century novel as written in Europe, Russia, and the United States. Like the American realist Theodore Dreiser, Turow is fascinated by people trapped into preordained roles, especially by parents and family. Stan Sennett's relentless and merciless pursuit of wrongdoing, for example, is in large part triggered by the example of Sennett's Greek uncle, a decent, hard-working immigrant who invests his life savings in a gas station that, it turns out, will soon be appropriated by the government, a scam the powers that be are well aware of. Sennett understands that American democratic capitalism depends on civic honesty, trust, and the credibility of government as the referee that provides oversight; if city hall or the state house is corruptible, and if judges are for hire to the highest bidder, the whole system is at risk. In Turow, there is always a tension between the law as a business—a firm being an amoral collection of hired guns available to any side that can pay—and the law as a repository of civic virtues that serve the common good. A scathing passage in *Pleading Guilty* asserts that Carl Pugnucci "believes all social interactions, no matter how complex, can be adjusted by . . . [putting] a price on [them]. . . . But what kind of ethical social system takes as its fundamental precepts the words 'I', 'me' and 'mine'? Our two-year-olds start like that and we spend the next twenty years trying to teach them there's more than that to life" (208). If the marketplace can buy government that suits its goals, few other groups besides lawyers can put a brake on its excesses, even personal injury lawyers like Robbie Feaver. The possibility of the lawyer as Atticus Finch of *To Kill a Mockingbird* lies behind Turow's concern with corruption, both public and private. Lawyers are the rare professionals left who can hang up a shingle and serve the common weal in single-attorney offices. The single or small group practice still remains a reality, and often still tilts at windmills, especially in protecting the environment. The "rules" that govern lawyers can be empty codes of conduct to be circumvented the way Mack Malloy manipulates BAD in *Pleading Guilty*, but they can also be the firmly held principles that guide a Sandy Stern throughout Turow's canon, rules to which even ambitious prosecutors like Muriel Wynn of *Reversible Errors* adhere. The idealistic lawyer as the defender of the weak and the common interest is among the most important of modern themes.

Turow's other common themes are also very serious: loyalty and betrayal of trust, father–son and mother–daughter relationships, family influence on the young, the difficulty of maintaining a normal family life while practicing law, the effects of professional success and failure, the process of aging. Having such weighty themes, of course, is no guarantee of literary quality: how the themes are handled is vital. In a way, such a judgment about theme comes down to the most venerable of literary questions: Does the writer have anything to tell us? As the classical Roman writer Horace had it, is the work both *dulce* (sweet) and *utile* (useful/ educational)? Such judgments are unfashionable in the early twenty-first century, but seem inevitable, and clearly underlie current judgments about important twentieth-century writers. William Faulkner is still considered a first-rate author, a source of wisdom about the South and racial conflict. Ernest Hemingway has suffered a decline in reputation largely because his position on gender issues has become suspect. Accomplished storyteller Howard Fast was shunned because of his Marxist sympathies and outlook. Turow's works are replete with acute observations about the legal profession, modern society, and the law. How these observations will be evaluated in the future is unknowable, but he is well positioned to be regarded as are classic nineteenth-century authors—such as Theodore Dreiser and Steven Crane—as a spokesman for his time, capturing its essential conflicts and concerns, but in ways that continue to have immediacy because of their universality.

Memorable, Well-rounded, True-to-Life Characters

Another important marker of literary worth is the creation of memorable characters. Popular writing is often dismissed as entertainment, or worse, because of "flat" characters, figures who are one-dimensional and not well-rounded. The charge involves mimesis, how well a literary piece represents, or "copies," real life. Literature, the argument goes, provides a sense of trueness to life, of credibility and validity that is absent in popular writing that manipulates to entertain. (Such validity is enhanced by themes that seem to address "real world" issues.)

Memorable characters convince us that we could really know them, or someone very like them, in our lives. They bridge our day-to-day life and what we know to be fictional and imaginary, suspending our disbelief to give a construct of words and images an odd kind of life, as if apart from the artistic work in which they appear. Mark Twain's Tom Sawyer and Huckleberry Finn, Charles Dickens's Mr. Micawber and Ebenezer Scrooge, and Shakespeare's Hamlet and Polonius are all types we use as touchstones to define real people we meet, but they also lurk in the memory along with our recollections of real people we know. Turow has his share of such characters. Can anyone, having once read *Personal Injuries*, see an ad for a certain kind of personal injury lawyer and not think of Robbie Feaver? Stan Sennett and Muriel Wynn are the very definition of the relentless prosecutor, recognizable on the front pages of any big-city newspaper. Mack Malloy and Sandy Stern evoke opposite ends of the moral spectrum when lawyerly ethics are at issue; most of us have encountered real attorneys who remind us of one or the other.

A Literary Style

Finally, literature can be distinguished from popular writing by its medium, both as narrative in the broader sense and as style at the level of paragraphs and sentences. While a transparency of narrative technique and prose style can often be a virtue—what we see the first time is what we get, a user-friendly approach, as computer jargon puts it—it can also be an empty shell once its message is conveyed, a simple vehicle good for bare-bones delivery but nothing else. Does the prose stand repetition? Can we learn something from the subtleties of the narrative on the second (or third or fourth) read? Jane Austen and Ernest Hemingway, an unlikely couple, share a seeming simplicity of narrative voice and sentence style that hides layers of meaning and sometimes wicked evaluations of the speakers involved. Readers return to both repeatedly, finding something new each time. The rubric "literature" comes not from clever plots, great themes and ideas, fine characterizations—although all are present at times—but from narrative and stylistic excellence. (Hemingway is reputed to have revised his sentences as many as 30 times to achieve his great "transparent simplicity.")

Turow is an architect of devious narrative. His philosophical take on the law is that what you get is never simply what you see, and his medium parallels and reinforces this message. The mystery element of most of the novels remains ambiguous at the end—we might think we know who killed Carolyn Polhemus and why in *Presumed Innocent,* but what Rusty knew and when and to what degree he has manipulated his wife, his lawyer, and us as readers are teasingly left beyond our view. The narrative, too, typically shifts point of view and time period, with the chronological shifts often showing just how blind the legal system can be at the time of the crime, or how lost events can become in retrospect. Inferences, both legal and commonsense, fill in gaps in the story, but the ultimate truth remains untold.

Turow's prose style is adventurous and unquestionably literary. His sentences are as carefully structured as his narrative and are embedded with images that extend reader understanding with the vividness of their correspondences. Turow has resisted the twentieth-century "plain style" of Hemingway, opting instead for a richer, more baroque prose that combines tough-minded precision with a richness, even an occasional lushness, that F. Scott Fitzgerald would be comfortable with. In *Presumed Innocent* a tangle of metaphors teases out the subtleties of relationships and motives. Rusty Sabich's polished narrative style and philosophical voice reveal surprising twists of character as the story builds slowly. As Sabich establishes characters and relationships, his introspective Dostoyevsky-like monologues and recital of anecdotes that humanize the judicial system increasingly engage the reader. His images are bleak: his wife's moods are "black forests"; he himself is a "shipwrecked survivor holding fast to the debris," while his mistress is "a spider caught in her own web." Life, for Sabich, is a constant struggle with darkness, and images of darkness and shadows dominate the text—shadows that loom and envelop and threaten. Typical is Sabich's comment on life as snowflakes: "Every life, like every snowflake, seemed to me then unique in the shape of its miseries, and in the rarity and mildness of its pleasures. The lights go out, grow dim. And a soul can stand only so much darkness." Images of prison and confinement, both real and self-created recur. Turow says that Rusty's father had "played in the Olympics of confinement" [Nazi concentration camps] and could "survive a local jail," but he had "no knowledge of his real prison": his "hobbled soul" and "crippled spirit" (398). The ghetto projects he describes as a war zone, akin to what was described by the guys I knew who came back from Nam. It was a land where there was no future—a place where there was little real sense of cause and effect. Blood and fury. Hot and cold. Those were terms that had actual meaning. But you could not ask anybody to do anything that involved some purchase on what might happen next year, even next week . . . disconnected . . . hallucinating. (348)

He calls "having the jury out" the closest one comes to "suspended animation." Outside the courtrooms "there is a churning mass," like Sabich's "imaginings of the crushed poor in the steerage bowels of the old ocean-going vessels." Turow's instinct as a writer of prose is to resort to the tools of the past—metaphor, simile, analogy, imagery—to express the ineffable, the emotions and thoughts that truly define his characters.

Imagination

We may add to the above discussion Scott Turow's answer to what makes for quality in popular fiction, the intangible ingredient of imagination. His prime example is Stephen King, whom he sees as brilliant— "one of the smartest human beings I know"—determinedly unpretentious and working class—"He would much rather be beneath his readers than above them"—but with a staggering imagination—"the stuff just pours out of him." Turow sees plot and insight into character bound up in the imagination in important ways but finds it very hard to put a finger on exactly what it is that makes a work endure, just as it is very hard to determine exactly what makes certain books so readable. For example, *The DaVinci Code*, the book to read in 2004, is easy to dismiss in terms of its style and formal elements, which "are not well achieved"—"the mystery is unsolvable because the author doesn't tell readers enough to give them a fighting chance" (Macdonald interview, 2004). Nonetheless, says Turow, the themes and the materials are "fascinating." He asks why that book, "which in many ways is coarse," was the year's "the book" when just the year before (2003) the book to read was Alice Sebolt's *The Lovely Bones*, "which is a very artful novel." The books are so different that it is impossible to put them side by side and figure out what qualities they share that so attract readers. "Are the same people reading them?" asks Turow, who answers his own question: "I don't understand."

To achieve acceptance from the academic community and therefore to acquire a fresh, youthful readership and at least temporary endurance that comes with a new generation of readers probably is a matter of style as much as content. Turow says:

> That's probably true but then the academic establishment is reading for a living. When reading, they are doing their job, so they don't read the way other people do. Much as I like dealing with legal problems, I am also working when I do so. It's deep play. And so is reading a book. But I can't expect academics to tip their hats at books that are not fluently written. (Macdonald interview, 2004)

What most academics, critics, readers, and even many writers agree on is that writers are never the best judges of their own works. William Wordsworth the elder rewrote the poems of his youth, making them more conservative and stodgy and far less memorable. William Faulkner claims that he tried to write poems and couldn't so he wrote short stories, but then he couldn't write short stories so he wrote novels. The problem in Faulkner's case, says Turow, is that he just didn't know what he had in those short stories, like "A Rose for Emily." Turow says that he recently read Norman Mailer's *The Naked and the Dead*—"a wonderful novel and probably a better piece of work than all but one or two of the novels Mailer wrote subsequently"—and he was distressed by Mailer's introduction to the 50th anniversary edition, in which Mailer dismissed the book as amateur—"a ridiculous assertion because the fact of the matter is that he wrote little in the way of fiction that was any better" (Macdonald interview, 2004). Consequently, in talking about his early work, Turow says that he doesn't want to denounce those books as beneath him, although obviously he learned a lot more as he got older and more proficient as a writer.

Will Turow's works be read as literature in 2025 or 2040? As windows on the legal and civic culture of the late twentieth and early twenty-first centuries, they are unsurpassed, and their precision of theme and issue bode well for their survival. Just as we now see Graham Greene's novels being made into films half a century after they were written—*The End of the Affair, The Quiet American*—so, we think, Turow's works will speak to future generations, and not simply readers curious about death penalty issues, the aftermath of the 1960s, or the curious phenomenon of personal injury lawyers. Turow works within tried-and-true literary forms and means—the territory of social realism and a solid, accessible prose style—while indulging daring experiments in narrative chronology and in dialect, thus avoiding the "cutting edge" experiments that make some modern fiction unreadable to the average well-educated reader. He is a born raconteur, a storyteller whose first imperative is to engage his audience. Finally, he certainly has the imagination he praises in Stephen King, never repeating himself, pushing narrative to new limits, extending his tribe of Kindle County legal characters, and finding new ways to instruct and delight.

Glossary of Legal Terms

Acquittal
When a judge or jury declares a defendant not guilty, that defendant is acquitted of wrongdoing and released to resume his or her life.

Appellate Court
An appeals court that has the jurisdiction or legal right to review and change the decision made by a lower court, as does the court in *Reversible Errors*.

Attorney–client privilege
A client's right to expect information disclosed in consultation with a lawyer to remain confidential; a lawyer may not testify against a client; even a confession of guilt is privileged, or private, information, as Mack Malloy keeps reminding his lawyer, Brushy.

Autopsy
The examination of a dead body by a coroner or medical examiner to determine cause of death, a subject of contention in *Presumed Innocent*.

Award
In civil court, a sum granted by judicial decree as compensation for a loss or injury.

Bail
A cash or bond security paid to assure the future appearance of a released prisoner in court; if bail is denied, the prisoner must remain in the custody of the court.

Bar examination
The test one must pass before being admitted to practice law in a particular state; the bar examination is usually taken after graduation from law school and, if passed, permits one to legally practice law, a problem for Robbie Feaver in *Personal Injuries*. In *Pleading Guilty*, Mack Malloy fudges the bar exam results for his mentor.

Bench trial
A trial in which a judge, not a jury, hears and decides the case. Judge Sonia Klonsky agrees to conduct a bench trial in *The Laws of Our Fathers*.

Billable hour
A unit of time for which a client can be charged; it represents the amount of work an attorney invests in a case and is usually divided into tenths or quarters of an hour. The firm profits distributed in *Pleading Guilty* are based on billable hours.

Bribery
A bribe has been committed when one pays, solicits, or receives a private favor or a sum of money for personal use in exchange for performing a public action, the subject of investigation and the sting in *Personal Injuries*.

Brief
A compact and formal written statement setting out the legal arguments to be used in litigation.

Burden of proof
In a criminal trial, the prosecution has a duty to prove beyond a reasonable doubt that the accused is guilty; the burden of proof, thus, rests with the prosecution rather than with the defense; in civil litigation, the term refers to a party's duty to prove a disputed assertion in order for the legal proceeding to progress or the award to be made.

Capital case
A case whose end result could be capital punishment; that is, the defendant could be sentenced to death if found guilty, as was Rommy Gandolph in *Reversible Errors*.

Capital punishment
The death penalty; that is, death by execution.

Charge
The first official step in the move toward prosecution, a formal accusation of a crime: "The defendant is charged with the crime of. . . ."; Rusty Sabich in the second half of *Presumed Innocent* is formally charged with homicide.

Circumstantial evidence
Evidence based on inference rather than personal knowledge or observation; it does not involve eyewitnesses or scene-of-the-crime evidence, only questionable circumstances that might suggest involvement in a crime. Most of the case against Rusty Sabich is circumstantial.

Civil case
Litigation that is noncriminal, that is, not about a violation of the criminal code; its goal is to protect or preserve a civil or private right or matter. The case at the heart of *Pleading Guilty* is a civil case or action on the behalf of the victims of a TransNational airlines crash.

Class action
A lawsuit in which one person or a small group represents the interests of an entire class of people, as when a charge is brought against a tire company on behalf of all who were in accidents allegedly attributable to that company's tires. The case against TransNational airlines in *Pleading Guilty* is a class action suit.

Closing argument
The final statement that a lawyer makes to a judge and jury before the jury retires to deliberate on the case; the closing argument of each side sums up the key points of the case from the point of view represented (defense or prosecution) and urges that the court rule one way or the other based on the evidence and the law. The title of the last section of *Presumed Innocent* plays on this meaning.

Confession
A criminal's acknowledgment of guilt, either verbally or in writing, which provides sufficient details of the crime to convince the court of guilt.

Coroner's inquest
An official examination (held by the coroner with the assistance of a jury) into the causes and circumstances of any death by violence and any death under suspicious circumstances.

Coroner's report
In the case of a death, an official report made by the coroner to the court, detailing the findings of the scene-of-the-crime investigation and the autopsy results.

Criminal case

A case in which the defendant has been charged with committing one or more crimes, violations of the criminal code. The prosecuting attorney, acting for the government, initiates court action by filing a complaint against the individual, the defendant. If the court finds the defendant guilty of the criminal charge, the defendant will have to pay with a fine, court costs, prison time, or death.

Cross-examination

In a trial or legal proceeding, cross-examination is the formal questioning of a witness by the party opposed to the party that called the witness to testify.

Double jeopardy

A rule by which a defendant cannot be brought to trial a second time for a crime for which he or she has already been exonerated—as when there is insufficient evidence to prove murder and the defendant is pronounced "not guilty," that person cannot later be charged for the same offence; doing so would put that individual's life or freedom in danger twice.

Exoneration

A person exonerated of a crime has been proven not guilty of that crime.

Final determination

Synonymous with final judgment; once there is a final determination from the court, there is no longer any right of appeal.

Finding

The result of the deliberations of a jury or a court, their conclusions about the validity of the evidence in the case at hand.

Graft

Advantage or personal gain received as a result of the superior influence of someone in a position of trust or authority, such as a judge accepting bribes or a contractor taking kickbacks; in general, a lack of integrity in public officials associated with theft, corruption, fraud, swindles, and other forms of dishonesty.

Grand jury

A jury of inquiry, 12 to 23 citizens summoned by the sheriff or chief prosecutor to hear evidence and determine whether it is such that an indictment should be brought and a trial conducted. Grand jury proceedings are normally secret. District attorney Stan Sennett in *Personal Injuries* uses the grand jury to bring charges against corrupt court officials.

Guilt
In criminal law, the opposite of innocence; the motives or acts of a guilty person—their violation of the law—makes them punishable by law.

Hearing
In criminal law, the preliminary examination of a prisoner charged with a crime or misdemeanor and of relevant witnesses.

Homicide
The intentional killing of one person by another, with malice aforethought.

Hostile witness
A designation that permits the interlocuting lawyer to treat a person on the witness stand as if he or she is an opposition party witness.

Hypothesis
A theory set up as an explanation of the facts in evidence, possibly a claim of motive for the crime, a scenario of how the crime may have played out, or an inference of guilt or innocence.

Immaterial issue
A point not proper to decide the action; not relevant.

In camera
In the judge's chambers, in private, or with spectators excluded from the courtroom.

Incarceration
Imprisonment; confinement in a jail or penitentiary.

In evidence
Facts in evidence have already been proven.

Intent
By design or purpose; with a formulated plan or resolve.

Involuntary manslaughter
The unintentional killing of a person by someone engaged in an unlawful action (although not a felonious one).

Judgment
The official decision of a court of justice; the final determination or sentence pronounced by the court; the declaration of guilt or innocence and, if guilt, the fixing of punishment.

Jurisdiction
The power and authority constitutionally given to a court or judge to pronounce sentence and to award remedies or take action for or against persons brought before the court.

Juror
A member of a jury.

Jury
A number of citizens, selected according to law, invested with legal power, and under oath to declare the truth based on the evidence presented to them; called a petit or "small" jury in contrast to a grand ("large") jury used to decide indictments.

Lawsuit
A common term for a civil action or case brought by two or more contending citizens to a court of law.

Lawyer
An attorney, counsel, or solicitor licensed to practice law (lawyers must have passed the bar examination in the state in which they practice law).

Malice
Doing a wrongful deed intentionally without just cause or excuse.

Malice aforethought
A particular category of murder; the murderer intends to cause death or grievous bodily harm to the victim.

Mandate
A judicial command from a court or officer of the court directing an officer of the court to enforce a sentence or a court judgment.

Manslaughter
The unlawful killing of a human being without malice, deliberation, or intent.

Material
Relevant to a case or situation, as in material witness.

Motion
An application to the court by legal counsel (either verbally or in writing) in order to obtain some court ruling or order, as in a motion to suppress evidence.

Obstructing justice

Acting to impede or obstruct those who have the power to administer justice—for example, frightening witnesses into not appearing, tampering with the jury, manufacturing false evidence, or hiding pertinent evidence.

Opening Statement

The initial speech that a lawyer makes to a judge and jury to lay the groundwork for the legal argument which will follow. Therein, the lead lawyers for the defense and the prosecution establish an interpretation of the case that they hope to prove.

Opinion

An inference or conclusion drawn by a witness based on facts or assumptions.

Parties

Those who take part in, are directly interested in, or are actively concerned in the prosecution and defense of any legal proceeding.

Penalty

A sum of money charged to an individual for failing to carry out the conditions of a bond.

Pending

Begun but not completed, in process; a suit that is "pending" has not yet had a final judgment rendered by the court.

Perjury

Willfully lying under oath; knowingly providing false evidence to the court.

Personal injury

Harm or damage done to an individual that may be remedied by civil litigation if another party is found negligent; more broadly, hurt to some-one, such as to a reputation or to mental well-being, that can be addressed by a suit.

Plaintiff

A person/party that brings a legal action or institutes a suit in court.

Plea

At the beginning of a criminal court case, the judge will ask the accused for a plea, a criminal defendant's formal response of guilty, not guilty, or no contest (nolo contendere) to a criminal charge.

Presumption of innocence
The principle that a criminal defendant may not be convicted of a crime unless the government proves guilt beyond a reasonable doubt, without any burden on the accused to prove innocence.

Probative fact
A fact that serves as evidence and proves a point that needed to be proven.

Pro bono
For the public good; in a *pro bono* defense, the lawyer defends the accused without pay, as Arthur Raven does for Rommy Gandolph in *Reversible Errors*.

Proceedings
The actions of the court as it conducts judicial business; an orderly progress followed in the application of the law, such as charging the accused, selecting a jury, delivering an opening address, and so on.

Proof
The establishment of fact by evidence.

Prosecuting attorney
The public officer charged with conducting criminal prosecutions on behalf of the state and its citizens.

Quid pro quo
Giving one valuable thing for another, as in an exchange of information between defense and prosecution attorneys; the phrase also refers to a key definition of bribery.

Reasonable and probable cause
The evidence and circumstances are sufficiently strong to make a reasonable person believe that the charge is justified; a standard commonly used for police searches.

Reasonable doubt
The evidence is such that it would make a reasonable person believe that the accused is innocent of a crime, but there is not enough evidence to confirm innocence with absolute certainty.

Recognizance
A person charged with an offense or pursuing an appeal of a guilty judgment might be released on his or her own recognizance—that is, under a promise to remain in the area and to reappear in court when called upon to do so.

Reversible error
An error that warrants an appellate court to reverse the judgment of a lower court in a case brought before it; such an error is substantial enough to have prejudiced the judgment.

Search warrant
An order issued by a judge that authorizes police officers to conduct a search of a specific location, for instance, Rusty Sabich's home in *Presumed Innocent*, where they find carpet fibers that match the crime scene.

Seizure
When a person has been restrained of freedom in a manner in which a reasonable person would not have felt free to leave.

Sentence
After a jury finds a criminal defendant guilty, the judge formally pronounces the sentence—that is, the punishment doled out, whether it be a fine, imprisonment, execution, or some other form of repayment to individuals or to the community.

Sidebar
An informal, spontaneously called, and brief meeting of the judge and attorneys during a trial outside of the hearing of the jury and spectators; the parties gather at the "bar" along one side of the judge's bench to settle a minor point of law before proceeding.

Stay of execution
The execution of a prisoner condemned by the courts to die may be stopped by the governor of the state, especially if evidence suggesting innocence is uncovered; a stay of execution may occur up to the final moment of the execution.

Sting operation
An undercover operation conducted through the prosecutor's office or police to "sting" criminals; that is, officers of the court may set up seemingly criminal activity in order to catch criminals in the act as they take bribes or receive stolen goods and so forth from representatives of the court. *Personal Injuries* describes a major sting operation.

Subpoena
An official court order in written format requiring an individual to testify in court; the court may subpoena witnesses—that is, legally require witnesses to appear in court, even against their wishes.

Testimony
Evidence given by a competent witness under oath.

Tort
In a civil case, a deliberate or careless act causing harm or loss to another person or a person's property.

Venue
Where a trial takes place; that place is generally connected to the events that originally led to the lawsuit; a lawyer may ask for a change of venue if the accused might not receive a fair trial in the jurisdiction where the crime occurred.

Verdict
The finding or decision made by a jury on a particular issue in a criminal or civil lawsuit; a determination of responsibility and degree of responsibility that affects the sentencing.

Warrant
A court order issued by a judge directing law enforcement officers to search a particular location for evidence in an investigation, to seize documents possibly relevant to the case, or even to make an arrest (an arrest warrant as distinguished from a search warrant).

With prejudice
The dismissal of a case for just causes; therefore, the litigant cannot bring an action on the same claim again.

Witness
Witnesses give testimony under oath during a legal proceeding about what they have seen, experienced, know, or can confirm as true.

Writ of Habeas Corpus
An official document issued by the court charging the police authorities to bring an individual before the judge and the court.

Based in part on *Black's Law Dictionary*, St. Paul, MN: West Publishing Company, 1891.

Bibliography

WORKS BY SCOTT TUROW

Novels

The Burden of Proof. New York: Farrar, Straus and Giroux, 1990; Warner Books, 2000.
The Laws of Our Fathers. New York: Farrar, Straus and Giroux, 1996; Warner Books, 1997.
Personal Injuries. New York: Farrar, Straus and Giroux, 1999; Warner Vision, 2000.
Pleading Guilty. New York: Farrar, Straus and Giroux, 1993; Warner Books, 1994.
Presumed Innocent. New York: Farrar, Straus and Giroux, 1987; Warner Books, 2000.
Reversible Errors. New York: Farrar, Straus and Giroux, 2002.
The Way Things Are (first novel, unpublished).

Short Stories

"The Detective," *Playboy,* December 2002: 94–96, 190–92, 194.
"Loyalty," *Playboy,* 2003.
"The Secret Enchanted Dress." In *Great Writers and Kids Write Mystery Stories,* eds. Martin H. Greenberg, Jill M. Morgan, and Robert E. Weinberg. New York: Random House, 1996 (with Eve Turow).
"To Kill or Not to Kill," *New Yorker* 105 (2004); reprinted in *The Best American Crime Writing: 2004 Edition: The Year's Best True Crime Reporting* (audio version:

The Best American Mystery Stories 2004; read by Nelson DeMille), ed. Otto
   Prenzler. New York: Houghton Mifflin, 2004: 105–120.
"The Way Things Are," *Best American Short Stories,* Boston: Houghton Mifflin,
   1971/1972.

Play

"Minor Characters Step into the Light," produced in 1990s.

Other Works

Guilty as Charged: A Mystery Writers of America Anthology (editor). Thorndike, ME:
   Compass Press, 2001.
Guilty as Charged, Vol. 2. Audiocassette, 2003.
One L: The Turbulent True Story of a First Year at Harvard Law School. New York:
   Putnam, 1977; London: Penguin, 1978; Farrar, Straus and Giroux, 1988;
   Warner Books, 1996; as *What They Really Teach You at Harvard Law School.*
   London: Sceptre, 1988.
Ultimate Punishment: A Lawyer's Reflections on Dealing with the Death Penalty. New
   York: Farrar, Straus and Giroux, 2003.

Essays

"Bellow's Gift: A Nobel Laureate Meditates on Enduring Inexplicable Love," *Chi-
   cago Tribune,* 17 August 1997: 1.
"A Brand New Game or No Turning Back from the Dart the Court Has Thrown,"
   Washington Post, 17 December 2000.
"The Burden of Race," *Washington Post,* 15 September 1996.
"Can Whites Write about Blacks?" In *The Writing Life: Writers on How They Think
   and Work.* New York: Public Affairs, 2003: 105–110.
"The Chicago Rules: Essays on the City's Political Landscape," Revisiting the Sins
   of the Fathers Series, *Chicago Tribune,* 28 August 1996: 1A3.
"Clemency without Clarity," *New York Times,* 17 January 2003: A27.
"Cry No Tears for Martha Stewart," *New York Times,* 27 May 2004: A29.
"Doomed; Prosecution Failed to Convict Because It Defended Evidence," *Austin
   American-Statesman,* 5 October 1995.
"The End of the Affair," *Washington Post,* 4 August 1991: WBK1.
"1st Impressions Weigh Heavily on Outcome," *Chicago Sun Times,* 23 January 1995.
"Forever Marilyn (Monroe)," *Playboy,* June 2001: 85–90.
"Francie Brady: Ireland's Shrewd, Sad, Quintessential Bad Boy," *Chicago Tribune,*
   11 July 1993: 144.
"Grading the Independent Counsel," *New York Times Op-Ed,* 28 January 1998.

"Hey Cubs: Spend the Money! Baseball Teams with the Highest Payrolls Are the Ones in the World Series," *Chicago Tribune*, 30 March 1997: 11.

"The High Court's 20-year-old Mistake," *New York Times*, 12 October 1997: 15.

"Holding on to Good Life," *Chicago Sun Times*, 9 December 1999.

"If I Were President," *George*, November 1996.

"In Praise of Gov. Ryan," *Chicago Tribune*, 4 February 2001: 19.

"Law and Literature," Tenth Circuit Judicial Conference, 29 June–1 July 2000.

"Like Mozart, Jordan's an Incomparable Genius with Unbelievable Gifts," *Chicago Sun Times*, 27 April 1998.

"Lying to Get the Bad Guy," *New York Times*, 20 February 2000: 13.

"Memo to Voters: Remember the Cruz Case," *Chicago Tribune*, 6 October 2002: 11.

"Miranda's Value in the Trenches," *New York Times*, 28 June 2000: A27.

"An Odyssey that Started with *Ulysses*," *New York Times*, 22 November 1999: E1.

"On Intellectual Property," *Society*, November/December 1991: 73.

"Order in the Court," *New York Times Magazine*, 18 April 1999: 109.

"Over the Wall: Paradoxically, the Best Chance to Win the O.J. Simpson Case Might Have Come from Suppressing the Evidence Police Found at His Home while Supposedly Ensuring His Safety," *Tampa Tribune*, 8 October 1995.

"Partisanship a Factor in Nicarico Case" (with Lawrence C. Marshall, Counsel for Rolando Cruz; Scott Turow, Counsel for Alejandro Hernandez), *Chicago Tribune*, 25 March 1994: 122.

"Prosecutor and Judge," *New York Times*, 10 November 1998: A33.

"Real Life Isn't Like a Legal Thriller," *Wall Street Journal*, Eastern Edition, 24 July 2001: A16.

"Reducing the Risk of Executing the Innocent," *Congressional Testimony by Federal Document Clearing House*, 12 June 2002.

"Repeal or Repair," *Wall Street Journal*, Eastern Edition, 24 April 2002: A22.

"Review of Yonnondio: From the Thirties." In *The Critical Response to Tillie Olsen*, eds. Kay Hoyle Nelson and Nancy Huse. Westport, CT: Greenwood Press, 1994: 28–32.

"Scott Turow: Sometimes the Law Makes a Mistake," *People Weekly*, 15 September 2003: 126.

"A Secret Proceeding with No Secrets," *New York Times*, 2 August 1998: 15

"Simpson Prosecutors Pay for Their Blunders," *New York Times*, Op-Ed, 4 October 1995: A21.

"Something's Up," *Vanity Fair*, September 1999.

"Taping Interrogations a Much-needed Reform" (with Thomas P. Sullivan), *Chicago Tribune*, 6 May 2003: 23.

"To Kill or Not to Kill," *New Yorker*, 6 January 2003: 40–47.

"Trial by News Conference? No Justice in That," *Washington Post*, 13 June 2004: B01.

"20th Century Chicago," *Chicago Sun Times*, 1999.

Untitled, *Rolling Stone*, 16 August 2001.

"When a Writer's Rights Are Violated, so Are a Reader's," *Chicago Tribune*, 15 December 1993: 123.
"When I Was 25," *P.O.V. Magazine*, June/July 1997.
"Where Have All the Radicals Gone?" *Newsweek*, 2 September 1996: 47.
"You Think You Know Why the Diallo Cops Were Acquitted. Think Again," *Washington Post*, 5 March 2000.

Turow on Turow

"Even before Writing," *Writer*, March 2003: 11.
"Scott Turow," *Inc. Technology* 16 (1994): 42.
"Writers on Writing: An Odyssey that Started with *Ulysses*," *New York Times* on the Web, 22 November 1999: www.nytimes.com/library/books/112299 turow-writing.html.

Film

Chicago episode of the television program *Urban Heartlands*.

WORKS ABOUT SCOTT TUROW

Almanac of Famous People. Detroit, MI: Gale Press, 1998, updated 2003.
Amende, Coral, ed. *Legends in Their Own Time*. New York: Prentice-Hall General Reference, 1994.
Authors and Artists for Young Adults, Vol. 53. Detroit, MI: Gale Research, 2003.
www.authorsontheweb.com.
Bestsellers 90, Issue 3, Detroit, MI: Gale Press, 1991.
Biography Index. Vol. 11: September 1976–August 1979. New York: H. W. Wilson, 1980.
Biography Index. Vol. 15: September 1986–August 1988. New York: H. W. Wilson, 1986.
Biography Index. Vol. 16: September 1988–August 1990. New York: H. W. Wilson, 1990.
Colby, Vineta, ed. *World Authors 1985–1990*. New York: H. W. Wilson, 1995.
Colford, Paul D. "Daily News, New York, Publishing Column," *Knight Ridder Tribune Business News*, April 25, 2003: 1.
Contemporary Authors. Vols. 73–76. Detroit, MI: Gale Research, 1978.
Contemporary Authors, New Revision Series. Vol. 40. Detroit, MI: Gale Research, 1993.
Contemporary Authors, New Revision Series. Vol. 65. Detroit, MI: Gale Research, 1998.
Contemporary Authors, New Revision Series. Vol. 111. Detroit, MI: Gale Research, 2003.
Current Biography Yearbook, 1991. Vol. 52. New York: H. W. Wilson, 1991: 55–60.
"(L.) Scott Turow," *The Writers Directory*. Chicago: St. James Press, 1991, 1999, 2003.

Lundy, Derek. *Scott Turow: Meeting the Enemy*. Toronto, Ontario, Canada: ECW
    Press, 1995.
Macdonald, Gina. "Scott Turow: Overview." In *Contemporary Popular Writers*, ed.
    David Mote. Detroit, MI: St. James Press, 1997.
————. *St James Guide to Crime and Mystery Writers*, ed. Jay Pederson. Detroit:
    MI: St. James Press, 1996.
————. *Twentieth Century Crime and Mystery Writers*, ed. Lesley Henderson.
    Twentieth-century Writers Series. Chicago: St. James Press, 1991.
Macdonald, Gina, and Andrew Macdonald, "Scott Turow," *Encyclopedia of U.S.
    Popular Culture*. The Popular Press, 1995.
Marquis Who's Who. Wilmette, IL: Marquis Who's Who, 2004.
The Oxford Companion to Twentieth-century Literature in English, ed. Jenny Stringer.
    New York: Oxford University Press, 1996.
"Scott Turow," *The Authors*, www.twbookmark.com/authors/52/547/index.htm.
"Scott Turow." www.bookreporter.com, 2004.
Scott Turow Web site, www.scottturow.com, October 1, 2001.
Who's Who in America, 1986–1989. Wilmette, IL: Marquis Who's Who, 1988.
Who's Who in America, 1990–1991. Wilmette, IL: Marquis Who's Who, 1990.
Who's Who in the Midwest, 1992–1993. Wilmette, IL: Marquis Who's Who, 1992.
Who's Who in the Midwest, 1993–1994. Wilmette, IL: Marquis Who's Who, 1993.
Who's Who in the Midwest, 1996–1997. Wilmette, IL: Marquis Who's Who, 1996.
Who's Who in the Midwest, 1997–1998. Wilmette, IL: Marquis Who's Who, 1997.
Who's Who in the Midwest, 1998–1999. Wilmette, IL: Marquis Who's Who, 1998.
Wilson, Kathleen, ed. *Major Twentieth-century Writers*. Detroit, MI: Gale Research,
    1999.
Woods, Tim. *Who's Who of Twentieth-century Novelists*. London: Routledge, 2001.

INTERVIEWS WITH SCOTT TUROW

Bonetti, Kay. "An Interview with Scott Turow," *The Missouri Review* 13 (1990): 103–
    126.
———. "Scott Turow," in *Conversations with American Novelists: The Best Interviews
    from The Missouri Review and the American Audio Prose Library*, eds. Kay
    Bonetti, Greg Michalson, Speer Morgan, Jo Sapp, and Sam Stowers. Colum-
    bia: University of Missouri Press, 1997: 153–169.
"Book Club: Scott Turow." *USA Today*, www.usatoday.com, 7 November 2002.
Buckley, James, Jr., "Going Undercover in Life and Law: A Talk with Scott Turow."
    BookPage, www.bookpage.com, 1 October 2001.
Goldstein, William. "Scott Turow," *Publishers Weekly*, July 1987.
Grant, Karen. "Scott Turow," Celebrity Guest Interviews. www.karengrant
    show.com.
Interview, June 1990: 170.
Libman, Norma. "Scott Turow City Provides Inspiration for Two Careers," *Chicago*

Tribune, 2 May 1992: 8; reprinted as "Turow City Provides Inspiration for Two Careers," 2 May 1993: 108.

Macdonald, Andrew, and Gina Macdonald. Personal interview with Scott Turow, July 2004. Unpublished.

McCrum, Robert. "To Hell with Perry Mason," *The Observer,* online Guardian Unlimited. books.guardian.co.uk, 24 November 2002.

Mudge, Alden. "When Characters Slip from the Confines of Plot: A Talk with Scott Turow." www.bookpage.com.

Neill, Mike and Johnny Dodd. "Scott Turow: Sometimes the Law Makes a Mistake," *People,* 15 September 2002: 126.

Nolan, Tom. "Scott Turow," *Mystery Scene* 65 (1999): 68–71.

Pate, Nancy. "Interview with Scott Turow," *Knight Ridder/Tribune News Service,* 12 June 2000: K3405.

"A Practiced Eye: Scott Turow's Line to Success," *Reuters,* 7 August 2000.

Rezek, John, and Paul Engleman. "Twenty Questions: Scott Turow," *Playboy,* August 1993: 113–114, 132.

Slobogan, Katherine. "Pros and Cons: A Profile of Scott Turow," *Time,* 22 October 1999, www.cnn.com/books/dialogue/9910/Turow.

Taylor, Elizabeth. "Is the Serious Book in Deep Trouble," *Chicago Tribune,* 31 May 1998: 6.

Woelfe, Scott. "The Burden of Innocence: Scott Turow Interview," *Playboy* and *St. Petersburg Times,* 23 September 2003.

REVIEWS AND CRITICISM

One L

American Libraries, September 1990: 824.

Armchair Detective, Summer 1990: 374.

Blewitt, Justin. *Best Sellers,* November 1977.

Elkins, James R. "A Beginner's Guide to Legal Education: Scott Turow's *One L: First Year at Harvard Law School.*" www.wvu.edu.

Green, Mark. "Hypos and Lawspeak at Harvard: One-L," *Washington Post,* 2 October 1977: E6.

Haines, Carol, and Rose Moorachian. *School Library Journal,* October 1977: 132.

Herrick, Roxanna, and Mark Annichiarico. *Library Journal,* 15 November 1997: 91.

Love III, Edgar. *ABA Journal,* February 1978: 250.

Newsweek, 17 October 1977.

New York Times Book Review, 25 September 1977.

Nguyen, Lan N. *People Weekly,* 20 January 1997: 33.

Pumphrey, Mark. *Library Journal,* 15 June 1998: 121.

Reference and Research Book News, Fall 1989: 17.

Rinzler, Carol Reisen. "Romping through Law School," *Washington Post*, 1 September 1979: B2.

Stern, P. M. *New York Times*, 15 September 1977.

Stern, Seth. "'One-L'—A Survivor's Tale," *Christian Science Monitor*, 24 October 2000: 13.

Stuttaford, Genevieve, Maria Simson, and Jeff Zaleski, *Publisher's Weekly*, 4 May 1998: 36.

"Washington Best Sellers," *Washington Post*, 27 November 1977: E2.

Presumed Innocent

Amsen, D. "Justice Stands Trial," *Newsweek*, 30 July 1990: 56.

Armchair Detective, Spring 1988: 150; Summer 1988: 319; Fall 1989: 402; Summer 1992: 186.

Behrens, Leigh. "Presumed Engaging," *Chicago Tribune*, 25 May 1988.

"Best Sellers," *New York Times Book Review*, 12 August 1990: 26.

Book List, 1 May 1987: 1315.

Books, December 1987: 22; September 1987: 11, 130; November 1988: 14.

Book World, 21 June 1987: 3; 6 December 1987: 19; 10 April 1988: 16.

Blum, Bill. *Los Angeles Times*, 24 July 1987; 12 October 1989.

Brownjohn, Allan. *Encounter* (United Kingdom), April 1988: 58.

Chan, Mei-Mei. *USA Weekend*, 1 June 1990.

Chase, Anthony. "An Obscure Scandal of Consciousness," *Yale Journal of Law and the Humanities* 1 (1 December 1988): 105–128.

Chicago Tribune Books, 29 May 1987: 3; 7 June 1987: 1; 11 June 1987; 17 April 1988: 4.

Clemons, Walter. *Newsweek*, 29 June 1987: 70.

Coll, Steve. *Washington Post*, 30 August 1987.

Denby, D. "To the Courthouse," *New York*, 6 August 1990: 45.

Donahugh, Robert H. *Library Journal*, 1 June 1987: 130.

Fox, Bette-Lee, and Kay Sheldon. "*Presumed Innocent*," *Library Journal*, 9 August 1989: 178–179.

Gardiner, Hilliard. "Book Reviews," *American Business Law Journal (pre-1986)*, Winter 1979: 389–390.

Goldstein, William. "Scott Turow," *Publishers Weekly*, 19 July 1987: 52.

———. "Warner's *Presumed Innocent*: Assuring an Audience for a $3 Million Paperback," *Publishers Weekly*, 8 April 1988: 21.

Gray, Paul. "By Scott Turow," *Time*, 10 August 1987: 71.

———. "Who Killed Carolyn Polhemus?" *Time*, 20 July 1987: 71.

Higgins, George F. "Web of Lies: The Trials of a Prosecutor," *Chicago Tribune*, 7 June 1987: 1.

Jaynes, G., and B. Sacha. "The Alien among Us," *Life*, August 1990: 64.

Kauffman, Stanley. *The New Republic*, 10 September 1990: 34–35.

Kaye, Sheldon. "Audio Reviews: *Presumed Innocent,*" *Library Journal*, August 1989: 178.

Kehr, Dave. "Innocent Attraction Whodunit? Just Blame the Victim," *Chicago Tribune*, 27 July 1990: 5.

Kimberly, Nick. *New Statesman* (United Kingdom), 22 January 1988: 33.

Kirchhoff, H. J. *Globe and Mail* (Toronto, Ontario, Canada), 11 July 1987; 8 August 1987.

Kirkus Reviews, 15 May 1987: 752.

L., I. *New York Times Book Review*, 24 April 1988: 46.

Lazare, Lewis. "Presumed a Smash: Novel Catapults Lawyer to Big Time," *Crain's Chicago Business*, 18 May 1987: 1.

Listener, 26 November 1987: 29.

"Looking Back: Aspirations," *Publishers Weekly*, 6 January 1989: 46.

Macdonald, Andrew, and Gina Macdonald. "Scott Turow's *Presumed Innocent*: Novel and Film—Multifaceted Character Study versus Tailored Courtroom Drama." In *It's a Print: Detective Fiction from Page to Screen*, eds. William Reynolds and Beth Trembley. Bowling Green, OH: Popular Press, 1994: 175–193.

Meier, Robert H. "Getting away with Murder," *Armchair Detective: A Quarterly Journal Devoted to the Appreciation of Mystery, Detective and Suspense Fiction*, Spring 1988: 150–152.

Nation, 26 December 1987: 793.

"New in Paperback," *Washington Post*, 10 April 1988: x16.

New York Times, 8 February 1987; 15 June 1987: 19; 6 August 1987; 1 December 1987; 19 April 1988.

New York Times Magazine, 7 June 1988: 94.

New York Times Review of Books, 19 November 1987: 21.

New York Times Book Review, 28 June 1987: 1.

Observer, 4 October 1987: 27.

Osborne, Stephanie, "Presumed Innocent," *Twentieth-century American Bestsellers*, www3.isrl.uiuc.edu/~unsworth/courses/bestsellers.

"Paperback Best Sellers," *New York Times Book Review*, 12 August 1990: 28.

Phillips, Michael J. "Review 8," *American Business Law Journal (pre-1986)*, 1979: 386–390.

Postman, Andrew, and Tom Spain. "Audio Reviews," *Publishers Weekly*, 22 January 1988: 75.

Publishers Weekly, 10 July 1987; 8 January 1988: 43; 4 March 1988: 106; 15 September 1989.

Pym, John. *Sight and Sound*, Autumn 1990: 279.

Redinger, Paul. "Kiss Me Deadly," *ABA Journal*, August 1987: 140.

Rice, Anne. "She Knew Too Many, Too Well," *New York Times Book Review*, 28 June 1987: 1, 28–29.

Sanger, Carol. "Seasoned to the Use: *Presumed Innocent/The Good Mother,*" *Michigan Law Review,* May 1989: 1338.

Schickel, Richard. *Time,* 30 August 1990: 57.

"Scott Turow, Author in Court," *Washington Post Book World,* 30 August 1987: F01.

Seidenberg, R. "Presumed Innocent," *American Film,* August 1990: 50.

Sharkey, Betsy. "ABC Movies: Top of the Lyne," *Mediaweek* 8 (11 May 1998): 8.

Shear, Jeff. *New York Times Magazine,* 7 June 1987.

Siegel, Rochell. "Presumed Accurate When the Movies Have Their Day in Court," *Chicago Tribune,* 29 July 1990: 25.

Simpson, A.W.B. *Times Literary Supplement* (United Kingdom), 16 October 1987: 1136.

Siskel, Gene. " 'Presumed Innocent' Makes a Compelling Case," *Chicago Tribune,* 27 July 1990: C.

Sokolov, Raymond. "Bookshelf: Presumed Important," *Wall Street Journal,* Eastern Edition, 30 January 1987: 1; 30 June 1987: 28.

Spectator, 27 February 1988: 30.

Spitzer, Jane Stewart. *Christian Science Monitor,* 13 August 1987: 18.

Steinberg, Sybil. "Fiction—*Presumed Innocent,*" *Publishers Weekly,* 22 May 1987: 65.

Stevens, Mary. " 'Presumed Innocent' Leads List of Wild Ones," *Chicago Tribune,* 22 March 1991: 43.

Sweeting, Paul. "A View from Abridge," *Publishers Weekly,* 22 April 1988: 53.

Towers, Robert. "Inconclusive Evidence," *New York Times Review of Books,* 16 August 1990: 45; 19 November 1987: 21.

Travers, Robert. "Grace Street Blues," *New York Review of Books,* 19 November 1987: 21–22. *American Spectator,* December 1988: 18.

USA Today, 18 June 1987: 6D; 14 July 1987: 1D.

Van Gelder, Lawrence. " 'Innocent' Enthusiasm: Turow's Best-seller Fascinates Filmmaker Pakula," *Chicago Tribune,* 2 February 1989: 11D.

Vogue (1987).

Voice of Youth Advocates, December 1991: 300.

Will, George F., "The Last Word," *Newsweek,* 29 June 1987.

————. "Presumed Innocent," *Washington Post,* 9 August 1987: C07.

Yardley, Jonathan. "Finally, Best Sellers that Are Good Reads," *Washington Post,* 30 November 1987: B02.

————. "A Prosecutor on Trial," *Washington Post,* 21 June 1987: X03.

Burden of Proof

Armchair Detective, Winter 1991: 120.

Bauers, Sandy. "Top of the Charts Scott Turow Best Seller Is Better as a Full 'Burden,' " Knight Ridder Newspapers, *Chicago Tribune,* 17 January 1991: 10B.

"Best of Books," *Time,* 31 December 1990: 55–57.

"Best Sellers," *New York Times Book Review,* 1 June 1990: 20; 3 June 1990:1; 17 June

1990: 26; 1 July 1990: 20; 8 July 1990:26; 15 July 1990: 30; 29 July 1990: 30; 12 August 1990: 26; 19 August 1990: 26; 9 September 1990: 40; 26 May 1991: 20.

Blackburn, Doug. *Times Union,* 7 December 1997.

Blum, Bill. *Los Angeles Times,* 3 June 1990; 11 June 1990; 27 July 1990; 9 September 1990; 19 May 1991: 14.

Boon, Jo-Ellen Lipman. *Magill Book Reviews,* 1 November 1990.

Book List, 15 April 1990: 1586; 15 December 1990: 871.

Book World, 20 December 1990: 3; 3 June 1990: 3.

Cannon, Margaret. *Globe and Mail* (Toronto, Ontario, Canada), 6 June 1990.

"The Capital of Real Life," *Newsweek,* 9 September 1991: 47.

Chesnoff, R. Z. "Grievous Burden," *Time,* 10 February 1992: 76.

Connoisseur, July 1990: 13.

D'Evelyn, Tom. *Christian Science Monitor,* 22 June 1990: 13.

Donahugh, Robert H. "Fiction: *The Burden of Proof,*" *Library Journal,* 1 June 1990: 186.

Dorrier, Amanda. "*Burden of Proof,*" *Twentieth-century American Bestsellers,* www3 .isrl.uiuc.edu/~unsworth/courses/bestsellers.

Dorris, Michael. "Self-deceived Scott Turow Depicts a Desperately Driven Attorney," *Chicago Tribune,* 3 June 1990: 1, 141.

Drabelle, Dennis. "Telling Tales out of Court," *Washington Post,* 20 September 1992: X02.

Feeney, Joseph J. *America,* 13 October 1990: 250.

Feldman, Gayle. "FSG Signs Second Novel from Scott Turow," *Publishers Weekly,* 15 September 1989: 92.

The Financial Times (London), 1 July 1990.

Glenn, Joshua. "The Examined Life: Turow's *Burden of Proof,*" *The Boston Globe,* 5 October 2003: H3.

Goldberg, Stephanie. "A Thriller with Style, Grace, and Intelligence," *Chicago Tribune,* 10 April 1992: 3.

Gray, Paul. *Time,* 11 June 1990: 68–72.

Gross, K. and B. K. Mills. "Out with Another Presumed Blockbuster Novel," *People,* 11 June 1990: 57–58.

Harper's Bazaar, June 1990.

Illustrated London News, #7097 1990: 88.

Johnson, Steve. " Presumed Invincible Scott Turow's New Books Are Blockbusters in the Making," *Chicago Tribune Books,* 16 February 1990: 1, 51.

Kagan, Rick. "Mini-mystery ABC's Minor League, 4-hour 'Burden of Proof' Strikes out 'The Burden of Proof' 'Roc' 'Titmuss Regained,'" *Chicago Tribune,* 7 February 1992: 11.

Kaganoff, P. "Forecasts: Paperbacks," *Publishers Weekly,* 26 April 1999: 57.

Kirkus Reviews, April 1990: 465.

Koenig, R. "Mixed Message," *New York,* 4 June 1990: 78.

Kucherawy, Dennis. "Two-track Mind," *Maclean's*, 9 July 1990: 43.

Listener, 30 August 1990: 21.

London Review of Books, 13 September 1990: 18.

Maryles, Daisy. "Turow's Double Whammy," *Publishers Weekly*, 13 April 1992: 14.

Maryles, Daisy, and Diane Roback. "A Bonanza for Legal Eagles," *Publishers Weekly*, 16 November 1992: 14.

Mass, Peter. "And Scott Turow's New Mystery," *New York Times Book Review*, 3 June 1990: 1.

McCormick, John. "The Man with Two Brains," *Newsweek*, 4 June 1990: 78.

www.mysteryguide.com/bkTurowProof.html.

Newsweek, 21 October 1996.

New York Magazine, 11 June 1990: 34; 10 June 1991: 26.

New York Times, Late Edition, 31 May 1990: C19; 3 June 1990; 30 June 1990.

Observer, 21 July 1991: 54; 26 August 1990: 55.

"Paperback Best Sellers," *New York Times Book Review*, 12 August 1990: 28; 19 August 1990: 28; 9 September 1990: 42; 23 September 1990: 60.

Pollock, Ellen Joan. "Law," *Wall Street Journal* (Eastern edition), 17 September 1990: B1.

Prescott, Peter S. "Lust and the Middle-aged Lawyer," *Newsweek*, 4 June 1990: 78.

Punch, 7 September 1990: 46.

Queenan, Joe. "Nothing but Shuck and Jive," *Wall Street Journal*, Eastern Edition, 5 June 1990: A22.

Randle, Nancy. "Turow Already a Fan of 'Burden of Proof' Mini-series," *Chicago Tribune*, 4 February 1992: 7.

"Right and Wrong and Read All Over," *US Catholic*, November 1990: 48–50.

San Diego Union-Tribune, 3 June 1990.

Shales, Tom. "Burden of Proof: Split Verdict," *Washington Post*, 8 February 1992: D1.

Sheppard, R. Z. "Crimes of the Heart: *The Burden of Proof*," *Time*, 11 June 1990: 71.

Smith, Kristen L. "Audio Reviews: *The Burden of Proof*," *Library Journal*, 15 November 1990: 112.

Steinberg, Sybil. "Forecasts: Fiction: *The Burden of Proof*," *Publishers Weekly*, 20 April 1990: 57.

St. Louis Post-Dispatch, 17 June 1990.

St. Petersburg Times, 10 June 1990.

"Time: No Conflict," *Newsweek*, 18 June 1990: 20.

The Toronto Sun, 22 December 1996.

Towers, Robert. "Inconclusive Evidence," *New York Times Book Review*, 16 August 1990: 45–46.

USA Today, 1 June 1990.

Washington Post, 6 June 1990; 9 June 1990; 12 June 1990; 27 July 1990; 13 October 1996.

West Coast Review of Books, #5 1990: 19.

"What They're Reading on College Campuses," *Chronicle of Higher Education*, 25 August 1990: A2; 26 September 1990: A2; 2 October 1991: A38.

Wiehl, Lis. "Love and Death: *The Burden of Proof*," *ABA Journal*, June 1990: 84–85.

Yardley, Jonathan. *Washington Post Book World*, 3 June 1990; 2 December 1990: 2.

Zimmer, John. "Audio Reviews-Fiction: *The Burden of Proof*," *Publishers Weekly*, 7 September 1990: 56–57.

Pleading Guilty

Adams, Michael. *Magill's Literary Annual*, 1994.

"Also Worth Reading," *Chicago Tribune Books*, 17 July 1994: 8.

Ames, Katrine. "A Summer Book Bag—*Pleading Guilty*," *Newsweek*, 5 July 1993: 55.

Armchair Detective, Fall 1994: 401ff.; Winter 1994: 101.

Australian Book Review, August 1993: 49.

Bauers, Sandy. "Hot Properties Turow and Grisham, Attorneys at Fiction," *Chicago Tribune*, 19 August 1993: 11C.

"Best Sellers," *Maclean's*, 14 June 1993: 6.

Book World, 22 November 1992:15; 27 June 1993: 1ff.

Champlin, Charles. *Los Angeles Times Book Review*, 13 June 1993: 11.

"Clean Sweep," *Publishers Weekly*, 14 June 1993: 33.

Cox, Meg. "Booksellers Shelve Gloom, Expect Hits," *Wall Street Journal*, 28 May 1993: A5.

Gray, Paul. "A Lawyer on the Lam," *Time*, 31 May 1993: 66.

Guardian Weekly, 31 October 1993: 29.

Illustrated London News, Winter 1993: 82.

Jones, Jr., Malcolm, and Laura Shapiro. "A Summer Book Bag," *Newsweek*, 5 July 1993: 54.

Kaminsky, Stuart. "Corruption's Human Face Scott Turow Captures a Lawyer Who Is Searching for Self-respect," *Chicago Tribune Books*, 30 May 1993: 3, 143.

Kirkus Reviews, 1 April 1993: 408.

Kirshenbaum, Jerry, and Richard O'Brien. "Thriller with Bonilla," *Sports Illustrated*, 14 June 1993: 14.

Kliatt, September 1994: 13ff.

Klinkenborg, Verlyn. "Law's Labors Lost," *The New Republic*, 14 March 1994: 32–38.

Korelitz, Jean Hannff, "Defence by Dictaphone," *Times Literary Supplement*, 5 November 1993: 20.

Lambert, Pam. "Picks and Pans: Pages: "More than Ever, Enjoying His View," *People*, 7 June 1993: 30.

Maryles, Daisy. "Aimed at the Top," *Publishers Weekly*, 24 May 1993: 32.

Miller, Jeffrey. "A Detective Tale that's Rambling but Rewarding," *Chicago Tribune*, 31 January 1993: 3.

Mortimer, John. "The Lawyer Vanishes," *New York Times Book Review*, 6 June 1993: 7.

www.mysteryguide.com/bkTurowGuilty.html

Newsweek, 5 July 1993: 55.

New York, 7 June 1993: 27.

New Yorker Magazine, 23 August 1993: 165.

New York Times, Late Edition, 3 June 1993: C18.

New York Times Book Review, 5 December 1993: 56.

Nolan, Tom. "Bookshelf: Some New Smudges on the Police Blotter," *Wall Street Journal*, Eastern Edition, 9 June 1993: A10.

Observer (London), 3 October 1993: 18ff.

Podolsky, J. D. "Helping Hand," *People*, 13 September 1993: 113.

Realbooks.com.

Ross, Michele. *Christian Science Monitor*, 12 July 1993: 13.

Russell, Brandeis. "Pleading Guilty," *Twentieth-century American Bestsellers*, www3 .isrl.uiuc.edu/~unsworth/courses/bestsellers.

Smith, Candace. *Booklist*, 15 March 1994: 1385.

Steinberg, Sybil S. "Forecasts: Fiction, *Pleading Guilty*," *Publishers Weekly*, 19 April 1993: 47–48.

Stewart, Thomas A. "Secrets in the City—*Pleading Guilty*," *Fortune*, 9 August 1993: 99.

Thomas, Ross. "Summertime, and the Reading Is Thrilling: *Pleading Guilty*," *Washington Post Book World*, 27 June 1993: X1, 8.

Walls, Jeannette and Jan Gelman. "Turow Pitches Ball and Book," *New York*, 24 May 1993: 8.

Wexler, Joyce. *America*, 27 November 1993: 22.

Wilkens, Mary Frances. *Booklist*, 1 April 1993: 1387.

Will, George F. "The Tangle of Egos and Rules," *Newsweek*, 26 July 1993: 60.

Zinsser, John. "Audio Reviews: Fiction," *Publishers Weekly*, 2 August 1993: 30.

The Laws of Our Fathers

Annichiarico, Mark. *Library Journal*, 1 August 1996: 115; 15 February 1997: 115.

Arnold, Martin. "You Can't Judge Book Publishers by Their Covers," *Journal Record* (Oklahoma City, OK), 14 November 1997: 1.

"Audio Reviews: Fiction," *Publishers Weekly*, 5 January 1998: 28–29.

Basbanes, Nicholas A. "Scott Turow Confronts the '60s in *The Laws of Our Fathers*," *Telegram & Gazette* (Worcester, MA), 3 November 1996: C5.

"Best-sellers," *Maclean's*, 2 December 1996: 15.

"Best sellers," *New York Times Book Review*, 10 November 1996: 66.

"Best Selling Books," *Wall Street Journal* (Easter edition), 8 January 1997: B10.

"Briefly Noted," *New Yorker*, 14 October 1996: 100.

Brozan, Nadine. "Chronicle," *New York Times*, 26 February 1996: A14; 18 October 1996: B23.

Brown, Jeff. *People*, 14 October 1996: 39.

Carpenter, Teresa. "Disorder in the Court," *New York Times Book Review*, 13 October 1996: 10.

Clee, Nicholas. "In Kindle County Court," *Times Literary Supplement*, 29 November 2000: 23.

De Haven, Tom. *Entertainment Weekly*, 25 October 1996: 104–5.

Detroit News-Free Press, 1999.

Diggs, Terry K. "Through a Glass Darkly," *ABA Journal* (Chicago), October 1996: 72–75.

Giles, Jeff. "Turow's Latest Gets a Hung Jury," *Newsweek*, 21 October 1996: 89.

Gray, Paul. "Up against the Law," *Time*, 14 October 1996: 90.

"Hardcover Bestsellers," *Publishers Weekly*, 4 November 1996: 88; 10 November 1996: 66; 5 January 1997: 84.

Harr, Jonathan. "A Legal Ease: Scott Turow's Surpassing Legal Fiction, *Chicago Tribune*, 13 October 1996: 1, 141.

Herrick, Roxanna, and Mark Annichiarico. *Library Journal*, 15 November 1997: 91.

Kakutani, Michiko. "The Case of a Lawyer and His Judicial Sting," *New York Times Book Review*, 5 October 1999: 6.

————. "A Courtroom Haunted by the Turmoil of the '60s," *New York Times Book Review*, 8 October 1996: 4.

Keil, Beth Landman, and Deborah Mitchell. "Was Carpenter's Review Scott-free?" *New York*, 21 October 1996: 21.

Kenney, W. P. *Magill Book Reviews*, 1 April 1997.

Kirkus Reviews, 1 August 1996: 1090.

Kliatt, November 1996: 49.

Ladies' Home Journal, July 1996: 124.

Library Journal, August 1996: 115.

Maryles, Daisy, and Dick Donahue. "Behind the Bestsellers," *Publishers Weekly*, 18 August 1997: 16.

Nolan, Tom. "Bookshelf: Turow Puts the '60s on Trial," *Wall Street Journal*, Eastern Edition, 15 October 1996: A20.

"Paperback Bestsellers," *Publishers Weekly*, 1 September 1997: 114; 8 September 1997: 86.

"Paperback Best Sellers," *New York Times Book Review*, 31 August 1997: 20.

Plowden, Piers. *Resident Abroad* (London), December 1996: 82.

Publishers Weekly, 1 April 1996: 22; 22 July 1996: 225.

Reardon, Patrick. "More than a Thriller," *Chicago Tribune*, 14 August 1996: 1.

Scott, Whitney, *Booklist*, 1 June 1997: 1734.

"Scott Turow: *The Laws of Our Fathers*," www.mysteryguide.com/bkTurow Fathers.html.

Steinberg, Sybil S. "Forecasts: Fiction: *The Laws of Our Fathers*," *Publishers Weekly*, 22 July 1996: 225; "*The Laws of Our Fathers*," 4 November 1996: 38.

Wilkens, Mary Frances. "Upfront: Advance Reviews," *Booklist*, 1 September 1996: 31.

Personal Injuries

Baker, John F. "Hot Deals," *Publishers Weekly*, 1 December 1999: 20.

————. "A Turow for Fall," *Publishers Weekly*, 1 February 1999: 20.

"The Best Books of 1999," *Time*, 20 December 1999: 104.

"Best Sellers," *Maclean's*, 19 July 1993: 8.

Bethune, Brian. "Best-sellers," *Maclean's*, 28 June 1993: 8.

Books, Autumn 1999: 19.

Chicago Tribune Books, 28 February 1999: 5.

De Haven, Tom. "Brief Encounters: Scott Turow Presents the Best Book of His Career," *Entertainment Weekly*, 8 October 1999: 64–65.

"Double Threat," *Maclean's*, 19 July 1993: 33.

Drabelle, Dennis. "Legal Lies," *Washington Post Book World*, 3 October 1999: X5.

Esquire, October 1999: 84.

"Fall Preview," *Newsweek*, 30 August 1999: 58.

Giles, Jeff. "The Sting: Scott Turow Goes Undercover," *Newsweek*, 27 September 1999: 66.

Gitlin, Todd. "Disorder in the Court: Scott Turow's Latest Legal Thriller Is a Near Perfect Story," *Chicago Tribune*, 25 September 1999: 1.

Globe and Mail (Toronto, Ontario, Canada), 9 October 1999: D15; 27 November 1999: D50.

Gray, Paul. *Time*, 6 September 1999: 76; 20 December 1999: 104.

Groner, Jonathan. *Salon.com*, www.salon.com, 5 October 1999.

"Hardcover Bestsellers," *Publishers Weekly*, 11 October 1999: 88; 18 October 1999: 96; 25 October 1999): 92.

Hiett, John. *Library Journal*, 15 February 2000: 214–215.

"Hoffman to Direct Turow Thriller," *Chicago Tribune*, 12 June 2001: 2.

Kirkus Reviews, 1 July 1999: 997.

Krist, Gary. "When in Doubt, Lie," *New York Times Book Review*, 24 October 1999: 7.

Kubisz, Carolyn. "Upfront Fall Preview: Adult Fiction," *Booklist*, 1 July 1999: 1896.

Kulish, Nicholas, and Jason L. Riley. *Wall Street Journal*, 1 October 1999: W6.

Lambert, Pam, et al. "Picks and Pans: Pages," *People Weekly*, 18 October 1999: 55–56.

Library Journal, August 1999: 143.

Lippman, Laura. *Baltimore Sun*, 17 October 1999.

Los Angeles Times Book Review, 10 October 1999: 10.

Macdonald, Andrew. "Personal Injuries." *Beacham's Encyclopedia of Popular Fiction*, ed. Kirk H. Beetz. Biography Series. Osprey, FL: Beacham's Publishing, 1996.

Maryles, Daisy, and Dick Donahue. "Behind the Bestsellers," *Publishers Weekly*, 11 October 1999: 21.

McCay, Mary. "New Mystery Audiobooks," *Booklist*, 1 May 2000: 1627.

McNicol, Nancy. "Book Reviews: Fiction: *Personal Injuries*," *Library Journal*, 1 August 1999: 143.

Meager, L. D. "Latest from Turow Is Masterfully Written," CNN Headline News Online, 18 October 1999, www.cnn.com/HLN/.

Mortimer, John. *Boston Herald*, 1999.

O'Leary, Shannon. "Legal Letdown," *January*, www.januarymagazine.com, November 1999.

"People," *Maclean's*, 6 December 1999: 41.

Pritchard, William H. "Fiction Chronicle," *Hudson Review*, Spring 2000: 136.

PR Newswire, 4 October 1999: 8441.

Publishers Weekly, 1 November 1999: 47; 2 August 1999.

Riley, Jason L., and Nicholas Kulish. "Bookmarks," *Wall Street Journal*, Eastern Edition, 1 October 1999: W6.

Sheppard, R. Z. "Pay His Honor," *Time*, 18 October 1999: 114–15.

Steinberg, Sybil S. *Publishers Weekly*, 2 August 1999: 69.

"The Sting: Turow Goes Undercover," *Newsweek*, 27 September 1999.

Time, 6 September 1999: 76.

Warshaw, Justine. *Times Literary Supplement*, 5 November 1999: 24.

Guilty As Charged, Vols. I and II

Steinberg, Sybil. "Audio Reviews: Fiction: *Guilty as Charged*," *Publishers Weekly*, 5 January 1998: 28–29.

Reversible Errors

A., N. "USA Today Book Club," *USA Today*, 31 October 2002.

———. "The Year of the Book Clubs," *USA Today*, 19 December 2002.

Baker, John F. "Short Takes," *Publishers Weekly*, 21 January 2002: 16.

"Best-sellers," *Maclean's*, 16 December 2002: 63.

Blum, Bill. *Los Angeles Times Book Review*, 2002.

Blumenstock, Kathy. "Scott Turow Thriller Translated to TV," *Washington Post*, 23 May 2004: Y07.

"By-products of the Law," *Books in Canada*, July 2003: 32–33.

Byrne, Bridget. "Huffman Teams with Macy to Star in Turow's 'Errors'," *Chicago Tribune*, 20 May 2004: 2.

Clodfelter, Tim. "Legal Appeal Miniseries' Respect for the Justice System Drew

William H. Macy to Role as Lawyer," *The Times* (London), 4 January 2005: 23.

Dalton, Stephen. "Film Choice," *The Times* (London), 4 January 2005: 23.

Donahue, Dierdre. "Thrilling 'Emperor' Rules," *USA Today*, 4 June 2002.

————. "Turow Thrills with Timely 'Errors'," *USA Today*, 31 October 2002, www.usatoday.com.

————. "Turow's 'Errors': A Fight to the Death Penalty," *USA Today*, 7 November 2002.

Dunn, Adam. "New Novel Considers the Death Penalty," *Publishers Weekly*, 19 August 2002: 65.

Dwyer, Jim, and Jodi Wilgoren. "The System Dances with Death," *New York Times*, 21 April 2002: 4.

Fetts, Bruce. "Case Dismissed," *Entertainment Weekly*, 8 November 2002: 109ff.

G., M. "Guilty Pleasures," *New York*, 9 September 2002: 88.

Green, Jodi. "Opposing Executions, in Fiction and Real Life," *New York Times*, 30 November 2002: B9.

Grumman, Cornelia. "Reasonable Doubt," *Chicago Tribune*, 10 November 2002: 12.

Huntley, Kristine. *Booklist*, 1 September 2002: 8.

Hupp, Stephen L. "Reversible Errors," *Library Journal*, 15 September 2003: 106.

"Is that What a Killer Is Like," *Chicago Tribune*, 10 November 2002: 17.

Italiano, Laura. "Pages: *Reversible Errors*," *People*, 4 November 2002: 51–53.

Kakutani, Michiko. "Nerdy Workaholic Lawyer Infatuated with Justice," *New York Times*, 29 October 2002: E7.

Kellerman, Carol. *Kliatt*, March 2003: 63.

Kirkus Reviews, 1 August 2002: 1073.

Kloberdanz, Kristin. "The Angel of Death Row," *Book*, November–December 2002: 20.

Leithauser, Brad. "Matters of Life and Death," *Chicago Tribune*, 3 November 2002: 1.

Lesser, Wendy. "Presumed Guilty," *New York Times Book Review*, 3 November 2002: 8.

Mason, Dave. "This Detective Different from Selleck's Magnum," *Ventura County Star* (California), 24 May 2004: 3.

McCarthy, Terry. "Dead Men Walking Free: In His Art and in His Life, Scott Turow Takes on the Legal Nightmare of Wrongful Executions," *Time*, 28 October 2002: 56, 64.

McFadden, Kay. "Strong Actors Give Needed Boost to *Reversible Errors*," *The Seattle Times*, 24 May 2004: E1.

McNichol, Nancy. *Library Journal*, 15 September 2002: 94.

Mills, Steve. "Scott Turow's Books Rise far above the Courtroom-thriller Genre," *Chicago Tribune*, 26 October 2003: 22.

Minzesheimer, Bob. "Don't Close the Book yet on Big Best Sellers," *USA Today*, 17 December 2002.

————. "Timely Novelist Turow Tackles Politics of Law," *USA Today*, 14 November 2002.

"Miscellany," *Writer*, March 2003 10–11.

Nolan, Tom. "Old-fashioned Police Work, High-tech Noir," *Wall Street Journal*, Eastern Edition, 29 October 2002: D6.

O'Brien, Sean. *Times Literary Supplement*, 29 November 2002: 23.

Ogle, Connie. "Author Scott Turow Has Mixed Feelings about the Ultimate Punishment," *Knight Ridder/Tribune News Service*, 27 November 2002: K4743.

"Prepub. Alert: Audio," *Library Journal*, 15 May 2003: 20–22.

Rabinowitz, Dorothy. "Weekend Journal; Review/TV: Messenger from God," *Wall Street Journal*, Eastern Edition, 21 May 2004: W3.

Robinson, Bill. *Mostly Fiction*, www.mostlyfiction.com, 22 December 2002.

Rosenzweig, Sue. *Kliatt*, May 2003: 50.

Rubinoff, Joel. "Nothing Straightforward about *Reversible Errors*," *The Record* (Kitchener-Waterloo, Ontario), 22 May 2004: C4.

Shales, Tom. "Turow Mystery, Showtime 'Lion': When Networks Think Big," *Washington Post Book World*, 23 May 2004: N01.

Shiffman, Stuart. *Book Reporter*, 2004: bookreporter.com.

Smith, Andy. "*Reversible Errors* Makes Few Mistakes," *The Providence Journal* (Rhode Island), 23 May 2004: T-03.

Smith, Candace. *Booklist*, 1 February 2003: 1005.

Starr, William W. *Knight Ridder/Tribune News Service*, 13 November 2002: K4537.

Stern, Bezalel. "Ultimate Justice," *The Jerusalem Post*, 26 December 2003: 33.

Walker, Dave. "Love and Legal Limbo," *TV Focus*, 23 May 2004: 7.

Weber, Eugene. *Los Angeles Times Book Review*, 15 December 2002: 134.

Yardley, Jonathan. "The Author of *Presumed Innocent* Ponders Life and Death Quandaries in an All-too-human Legal System," *Washington Post Book World*, 27 October 2002: T02.

Zaleski, Jeff, and Adam Dunn. "*Reversible Errors*: New Novel Considers the Death Penalty," *Publishers Weekly*, 19 August 2002: 64–65.

Ultimate Punishment: A Lawyer's Reflections on Dealing with the Death Penalty

American Lawyer, September 2003: 82–90.

Appleyard, Bryan. "A Matter of Life and Death," *Sunday Times* (London), 25 January 2004: 41.

Bowness, Leah. "From Court to Bookstore," *Maclean's*, 2 August 2004: 87.

Campbell, Susan. "Off the Fence on the Death Penalty," *Hartford Courant* (Connecticut), 23 January 2005: H1.

"Catholic Tastes," *US Catholic*, January 2004: 6.

Charles, Harry. *Library Journal*, 15 August 2003: 107.

Daniels, Anthony. "Reflections on the Black Cap," *New Criterion*, March 2004: 27–33.

"Death Row Conversions," *Library Journal*, August 2003: 107.

DeFiglio, Pam. "Celebrities Give Us a Piece of Their (Unconscious) Minds," *Chicago Daily Herald*, 7 October 2003: SL1.

Doran, Leslie. "Nonfiction Arguments on the Death Penalty: Turow, Fuhrman," *The Denver Post*, 28 December 2003: F13.

Flynn, Gillian. *Entertainment Weekly*, 26 September 2003: 97.

Grieve, Tim. " The Ultimate Punishment: Scott Turow Tried—and Failed—to Build a Better Death Penalty. Now He Wants It Abolished," *Salon.com*, 17 October 2003.

Jones, Nora A. "A Death Penalty Topic of Book Review by Former DA," *Daily Record*, 15 2004: 1.

Kirkus Reviews, 1 August 2003: 1009.

Levine, Adina. "*One L*'s Turow Crusades against Death Penalty," *The Record*, 24 February 2005. www.hlrecord.org.

McLeese, Don. *Book*, November–December 2003: 84–85.

Moran, Greg. "Til Death Do Us Part," *The San Diego Union–Tribune*, 5 October 2003: Books-8.

Neill, Mike, and Johnny Dodd. "A Changed Man," *People*, 15 September 2003: 125–166.

Peterson, Thana. "Scott Turow's Death Row Turnarounds," *Business Week Online*, 16 September 2003: N.

Publishers Weekly, 3 November 2003: 30.

Rakove, Jack. "Ultimate Questions," *Chicago Tribune*, 5 October 2003: 1.

"Restoring Forgiveness," *US Catholic*, January 2004: 6.

Rotella, Mark, Sara Gold, Lynn Andriani, Michael Scharf, and Emily Chenowith. "Ultimate Punishment: A Lawyer's Reflections on Dealing with the Death Penalty," *Publishers Weekly*, 25 August 2003: 48.

Selwynn, Laurie and Ann Burne. "Ultimate Punishment: A Lawyer's Reflections on Dealing with the Death Penalty," *Library Journal*, 1 March 2004: 127.

Shuman, R. Baird. *Magill Book Reviews*, 1 February 2004, #12417229.

Stanley, Alessandra. "Looking for the Flaw that Can Save a Life," *New York Times*, 21 May 2004: E1.

Trollinger, William Vance. "No More Death Row," *Christian Century*, 10 February 2004: 34–35.

Wilkens, Mary Frances. "Ultimate Punishment," *Booklist*, 1 September 2003: 4.

Yardley, Jonathan. "Lives in the Balance," *Washington Post*, 16 October 2003: C04.

OTHER SECONDARY SOURCES

General Readings

Arnold, Martin. "You Can't Judge Book Publishers by Their Covers," *Journal Record*, 14 November 1997: 1.

"A Brand New Game: No Turning Back from the Dart the Court Has Thrown Scott Turow," *Washington Post,* 17 December 2000: B01.

Brozan, Nadine. "Chronicle," *New York Times,* 26 February 1996: A14.

Claiborne, William. "Illinois Order on Executions Lauded," *Washington Post,* 1 February 2000: A02.

Crawford, William B. "Attorney Panel Probes Lawyer, Author Turow," *Chicago Tribune,* 5 August 1987: 3.

Drell, Adrienne. "Murder, They Write," *ABA Journal* (Chicago), June 1994: 46–52.

Fields, H., and M. Reuter. "Ralph Oman and Scott Turow Voice Reservations of Fair-use Proposals," *Publishers Weekly,* 12 June 1991: 16.

"Fluent in Legalese, Scott Turow Proves Himself a Writer," *People,* 7 March 1994: 82.

Goldsborough, Bob. "Author Puts Wilmette Home up for Sale . . . Heading for Glencoe," *Chicago Tribune,* 1 April 2001: 3.

————. "Author Turow Pays $4.79m for Manse," *Chicago Tribune,* 19 April 2001: 3.

Grundmann, Roy, and Cynthia Lucia. "Between Ethics and Politics: An Interview with Tim Robbins," *Cineaste,* June 1996: 4–10.

Haskell, Stephane. "Getting into Character," *New York Times Magazine,* 29 October 1995: 46–52.

Howlett, Debbie. "Illinois Panel to Urge Revisions in Laws," *USA Today,* 29 March 2002.

James, Caryn. "Chicago, Tugging the Sleeve and Heart," *New York Times,* 16 July 1996: C13.

Jones, Malcolm, and Ray Sawhill. "Publish or Perish," *Newsweek,* 12 June 2000: 68–72.

Karp, Josh. "The Honorable Dustin Hoffman Presiding," *Book,* November–December 2001: 14.

Kaufman, Joanne. "Legions of Lawyers Turned Novelists," *Wall Street Journal,* Eastern Edition, 1 August 1991: A10.

Keil, Beth Landman, and Deborah Mitchell. "Was Carpenter's Review Scott-free?" *New York,* 21 October 1996: 12.

Kiley, M. "Turow Strikes a Chord," *Chicago Tribune,* 6 April 1997: 13.

Kopper, Edward A., Jr. "The Influence of *Heart of Darkness* on Scott Turow's *Pleading Guilty,*" *Notes on Contemporary Literature,* 25 September 1995: 8–9.

"Letters to the Editor: Seeking Justice in and out of the Courtroom," *Washington Post Book World,* 18 June 2004: A28.

Lundy, Derek. *Scott Turow: Meeting the Enemy: A Biography.* Toronto: ECW, 1995.

Mortimer, John. "The Lawyer Vanishes," *New York Times Book Review,* 6 June 1993: 7.

Nathan, Paul. "The Next Turow," *Publishers Weekly,* 1 April 1996: 22.

"No. 99's Last Stop: 3,000 Attend Gretzky's Hall of Fame Induction Ceremony," *Maclean's,* 6 December 1999: 41.

Pelton, Tom. "Turow Trying to Win New Trial for Hernandez in Nicarico Murder," *Chicago Tribune*, 4 January 1996: 2D1.

"Roger Straus," *Economist*, 5 June 2004: 81.

Romano, Lois. "On Trial in Illinois: The Death Penalty," *Washington Post*, 16 October 2002: A01.

Salamon, Julie. "Film: Harrison Ford, *Presumed Innocent*," *Wall Street Journal*, Eastern Edition, 6 July 1990: A1.

Sanger, Carol. "Less than Pornography: The Power of Popular Fiction," *Michigan Law Review*, 1989: 1338; reprinted in *Representing Women: Law, Literature, and Feminism*, eds. Susan Sage Heinzelman and Zipporah Batshaw Wiseman. Durham, NC: Duke University Press; 1994: 75–100.

————. "Seasoned to the Use—*Presumed Innocent* by Scott Turow/*The Good Mother* by Sue Miller," *Michigan Law Review*, May 1989: 1338.

Smith, Dinitia. "Novelists Get Back at Hollywood Mostly Gently," *New York Times*, 25 September 1999: 66.

Smith, Greg B. "New York Times Op-ed Piece Angers Martha Stewart's Lawyer," *Knight Ridder Tribune Business News*, 4 June 2004: 1.

"Spinners of Words Come up with Some Kind Ones for a Publisher," *New York Times*, 21 September 1996: 11.

Stangness, Sarah. "Meet Scott Turow, Just an Unassuming Lawyer," *Chicago Tribune*, 10 June 1987: 9.

Stevenson, Kathy. "Author Events Let You Learn from the Best," *Writer*, March 2001: 23–24.

Struzzi, Diane. "Doctor, War Hero David D. Turow, 80," *Chicago Tribune*, 29 December 1998: 9.

Szuberla, Guy. "Paretsky, Turow, and the Importance of Symbolic Ethnicity," *Midamerica: The Yearbook of the Society for the Study of Midwestern Literature*, 1991: 124–135.

Taylor, Ed. "Supreme Court Shuns Lawsuit by Hockey Player versus Arizona Comics Creator," *Knight Ridder Tribune Business News* (Washington, DC), January 13, 2004: 1.

"They Say," *Writer*, April 2000: 3.

Wechsler, Pat, and Roger D. Friedman. "Good-bye Foucault, Hello Scott Turow," *New York*, 24 October 1994: 11.

Will, George. "Reason and Death," *Washington Post*, 30 October 2003: A23.

Williams, Kevin. "Rocking Writers a Riot," *Chicago Tribune*, 2 November 2001: 2.

Wiltz, Teresa. "Turow's Guilty Pleasures," *Chicago Tribune*, 24 January 1997: 3.

Yardley, Jonathan. "Turow's Conduct Questioned," *Washington Post*, 2 December 1987: B11.

The Legal Procedural

Breen, Jon. L. *Novel Verdicts: A Critical Guide to Courtroom Fiction*. New York: Rowman & Littlefield, 1984; reprinted 1997.

Grisham, Johan. "The Rise of the Legal Thriller: Why Lawyers Are Throwing the Books at Us," *New York Times Book Review,* 18 October 1992: 33.

Orwell, George. "A Hanging." In *Insight: A Rhetoric Reader* ed. Emil Hurtik. New York: Lippincott, 1976: 14–17.

Pike, B. A. "Legal Procedural." In *The Oxford Companion to Crime and Mystery Writing* ed. Rosemary Herbert. Oxford: Oxford University Press, 1999: 261.

Stracher, Cameron. "Taste: The Case of the Legal Thriller—The Law Is Dull; So Why Are These Books Popular? A Cross-examination," *Wall Street Journal,* Eastern Edition, 17 March 2000: W13.

Literary Criticism

Abrahms, M. H. *A Glossary of Literary Terms.* New York: Heinle, 1998.

Bressler, Charles E. *Literary Criticism: An Introduction to Theory and Practice.* Upper Saddle River, NJ: Prentice-Hall, 2003.

Cuddon, J. A., and Claire Preston. *The Penguin Dictionary of Literary Terms and Literary Theory.* London: Penguin Books, 2000.

Culler, Jonathan. *Literary Theory: A Very Short Introduction.* Oxford: Oxford University Press, 2000.

Guerin, Wilfrid L. et al. *A Handbook of Critical Approaches to Literature.* Oxford: Oxford University Press, 1998.

MEDIA ADAPTATIONS

The Burden of Proof, a two-part television film, 1992. Screenplay by John Gay. Starring Hector Elizondo, Brian Dennehy, and Adrienne Barbeau.

One-L, an NBC television series, once scheduled for 1997.

Personal Injuries, a Disney Punch Production. Directed by and starring Dustin Hoffman. In planning.

Presumed Innocent, Warner Brothers, 1990. Screenplay by Frank Pierson and Alan J. Pakula. Directed by Alan Pakula. Starring Harrison Ford, Bonnie Bedelia, Raul Julia, and Brian Dennehy.

Reversible Errors, a CBS miniseries, May 23 and 25, 2004. Screenplay by John Gay. Starring William H. Macy, Felicity Huffman, and Tom Selleck.

Index

About the Authors

ANDREW F. MACDONALD holds a Ph.D. in English (Renaissance Studies) from The University of Texas in Austin and is a Professor at Loyola University New Orleans. Author of *Howard Fast,* he is also co-author of *Mastering Writing Essentials, Shapeshifting: The Native American in Recent Fiction, Shaman or Sherlock? The Native American Detective,* and *Jane Austen on Screen* (CUP). He has published numerous articles for books, journals, and encyclopedias on a wide range of topics including popular fiction, cross cultural concerns, English as a Second Language, and cultural literacy.

GINA MACDONALD holds a Ph.D. in English (Renaissance Studies) from The University of Texas in Austin and is an Associate Professor at Nicholls State University. Author of *James Clavell* and *Robert Ludlum,* editor of *British Mystery and Thriller Writers Since 1940, Dictionary of Literary Biography,* Volume 246, she is also co-author of *Mastering Writing Essentials, Shapeshifting: The Native American in Recent Fiction, Shaman or Sherlock? The Native American Detective,* and *Jane Austen on Screen* (CUP). She has published numerous articles and encyclopedia entries about popular fiction, Shakespeare, English as a Second Language, and Spanish, Polish, and Russian authors.

Critical Companions to Popular Contemporary Writers
First Series—*also available on CD-ROM*

V. C. Andrews *by E. D. Huntley*

Tom Clancy *by Helen S. Garson*

Mary Higgins Clark *by Linda C. Pelzer*

Arthur C. Clarke *by Robin Anne Reid*

James Clavell *by Gina Macdonald*

Pat Conroy *by Landon C. Burns*

Robin Cook *by Lorena Laura Stookey*

Michael Crichton *by Elizabeth A. Trembley*

Howard Fast *by Andrew Macdonald*

Ken Follett *by Richard C. Turner*

John Grisham *by Mary Beth Pringle*

James Herriot *by Michael J. Rossi*

Tony Hillerman *by John M. Reilly*

John Jakes *by Mary Ellen Jones*

Stephen King *by Sharon A. Russell*

Dean Koontz *by Joan G. Kotker*

Robert Ludlum *by Gina Macdonald*

Anne McCaffrey *by Robin Roberts*

Colleen McCullough *by Mary Jean DeMarr*

James A. Michener *by Marilyn S. Severson*

Anne Rice *by Jennifer Smith*

Tom Robbins *by Catherine E. Hoyser and Lorena Laura Stookey*

John Saul *by Paul Bail*

Erich Segal *by Linda C. Pelzer*

Gore Vidal *by Susan Baker and Curtis S. Gibson*